Light Shines in the Darkness

My Healing Journey Through
Sexual Abuse and Depression

Lucille F. Sider

Read the Spirit

For more information and further discussion, visit
LightShinesInTheDarknessBook.com

Cover design by Becky Hile
www.RadiantPunch.com

Published by
Read the Spirit Books, an imprint of
Front Edge Publishing, LLC
42015 Ford Road, Suite 234
Canton, Michigan

Front Edge Publishing specializes in speed and flexibility in adapting
and updating our books. We can include links to video and other online
media. We offer discounts on bulk purchases for special events, corporate
training, and small groups. We are able to customize bulk orders by adding
corporate or event logos on the cover and we can include additional pages
inside describing your event or corporation. For more information about
our flexible publishing or permission to use our materials, please contact
Front Edge Publishing at info@FrontEdgePublishing.com.

Dedicated to my dear son
Soren Dayton

"There is no greater agony than baring an untold story inside you."
Maya Angelou, *I Know Why The Caged Bird Sings*

"Nothing makes us so lonely as our secrets."
Paul Tournier

Contents

Dear readers,

I have changed the names in this account of my life, even though public records document many of the events I recount. I have done this to focus readers on the urgent issues of sexual abuse and mental illness in this true story. I am not writing this book as an effort to make personal attacks. I am writing to help the countless readers who have been suffering in silence as I did for so many years.

Lucille Sider

Praise for
Light Shines in the Darkness

Timely, compelling and courageous, this autobiography lays bare the trauma of both child and adolescent abuse. This book deserves to be read by any adult who, living in a culture where 80 percent of females have experienced some form of sexual abuse by the age of 18, are no longer content to keep their proverbial head in the sand.

Carol Schreck, Professor Emerita of Pastoral Care and Counseling, Palmer Theological Seminary. Licensed Marriage and Family Therapist, Kairos Counseling Services, Devon, PA.

Lucille's poignant and heartfelt account of mental illness, survival, and recovery, drew me in and reminded me that courage is born out of the struggles and hopes of ordinary folks, and healing comes through simple kindnesses and the love of those who stand by our side through it all. Lucille's story inspires. Whether we are living in a place of hurt and shame, or care for those who are, *Light Shines in the Darkness* inspires us all to live into hope.

Lisanne Finston, MDiv., MSW, Executive Director, Gould Farm.

From the first compelling sentences, Lucille invites the reader into the rooms of her soul. Each room has a different texture and fabric that adds depth in the process of healing. I walked into some areas of my own heart that had been closed and was restored. The book is arranged to also be a valuable tool in the hands of persons in the helping professions, such as clergy, social workers, psychologists. In this manner a story may be excerpted for a particular person with whom you are journeying toward a healing process. This writing is so powerful, yet gentle that people will be able to add their own words to combat the pain. Lucille's credentials enhance the power of the story. Truly a book for these days!

The Rev. Dr. Jo Anne Lyon, General Superintendent Emerita and Ambassador of The Wesleyan Church and author of *The Ultimate Blessing: My Journey to Discover God's Presence.*

Darkness permeates much of Lucille Sider's book, as she recounts her sexual abuse as a child and teen, her marriages and divorces, and her struggles with mental illness. But her honesty and insight help the reader to see these challenges with exceptional clarity, and her faith and resilience provide a guiding light to those in similar situations. At one point in *Light Shines in the Darkness*, she learns that the biblical word "blessed" can also mean "mature" or "ripe." Readers will be blessed by this story of adversity, faith, maturity and ripeness.

The Rev. Henry G. Brinton, Presbyterian pastor and author of *The Welcoming Congregation: Roots and Fruits of Christian Hospitality.*

In her memoir of heartache and hope, Lucille Sider invites us inside her journey from her Canadian Anabaptist farm roots to experiences of abuse, divorce and depression, and finally, with support from a loving son, siblings and friends, to forgiveness and peace. By so doing she gifts us with a more empathic understanding of the realities of suffering and grace.

Dr. David Myer, professor of psychology at Hope College.

Lucille Sider doesn't just *tell* us the story of her life; she invites us to journey through it with her. She writes with warmth and candor in the present tense, giving readers the feeling they are reading a personal journal—a record of life's many changes and challenges in the very way the author is experiencing them at the time. *Light Shines in the Darkness* exposes the emotional damage that results from sexual abuse and the dark shadow such abuse can cast over future years, including the severe depression Lucille Sider experienced at various times. But it's also a book about healing, resilience, friendship, family relationships, love and loss, hope and faith.

Letha Dawson Scanzoni, Coauthor of *All We're Meant to Be: Biblical Feminism for Today.*

Foreword

"Your Shorts Are Too Short and Your Touches Are Too Long."

That was the title of a workshop I was required to attend in seminary, teaching us about appropriate pastoral boundaries. The men were attending a different workshop, reminding them to keep their office door open during one-on-one meetings to protect themselves from allegations of misconduct. Meanwhile, the women were taught to blame themselves if a man makes sexual advances.

That has been the narrative in our churches for a long, long time. We are taught this story at a very young age. Often, our teachers use selected passages from the Bible to undergird this story—making it all the more indelible. The lesson in these stories, as they are told over and over again, is: Women are dangerously sexual. Men must protect themselves from this temptation.

If that weren't bad enough, there is an even darker message underlying these oft-told tales: Women are the property of men—objects that can be owned and controlled. Look carefully at any of the case studies emerging in headlines these days. Statistically, perpetrators usually know their victims. They aren't the stereotypical strangers who lurk in shadowy corners, waiting to pounce. They are men who have a hint of power, or wish they did, who understand women as objects to be taken—objects to be stolen.

When such a predatory sexual assault happens to anyone, the injustice and trauma becomes a legacy that lasts a lifetime. When it happens to children, the tragedy is even more profound.

Light Shines in the Darkness reveals the hidden and secret depths of sexual abuse through Lucille Sider's multifaceted lens of religion, psychology, sociology and justice. Her keen intellect and compassionate heart make this a fascinating and moving story. Her memoir is an immersive journey through the courage and suffering of one who has experienced childhood sexual abuse.

Lucille Sider's honest and thoughtful memoir draws this trauma out of the impersonal realm of "issues" and into an intimate lived experience. Chronicling her encounters with sexual predators, Sider portrays how each experience destroys not only her personal life but how it also unravels her family ties.

Theft of another person's body uproots us all, divides us, breaks the bonds of community.

Quite simply, Lucille Sider was stolen from her childhood. She was stolen from her faith community. She was stolen from her own body.

Compounding that injustice, the church too often has been complicit in sheltering such predators. Simply read the headlines from Catholic dioceses around the world these days. So far, Protestant churches may not have attracted quite as much media scrutiny—but our collective history of protecting predators has been just as devastating. This problem crosses all religious boundaries.

Most heartbreaking is the realization that our faith should shape safe communities that are the very opposite of this dark cycle. At our best in our religious communities—love grounds us, roots us, nourishes us. That's why we, as the church, should be getting this right. We belong to the family of God in Jesus Christ and have the love of Christ to root us and ground us. We must not allow lives to be uprooted, within the church or anywhere in our community. We must not defend, or hide, or applaud those who steal the bodies of others.

Rooted and grounded in love, we must seek justice for those who have been stolen. We must pray for the victims and the perpetrators of these thefts. And we must transform our community and our society with the love, justice, and mercy of Jesus Christ to protect the vulnerable from predators.

This is no small assignment. But Christ is the one who calls and equips us for this work. We must undertake this calling. We certainly can. In this new book, you will be inspired as Lucille Sider proclaims the hard truths we need to unearth—and calls for responses that can root and ground us, once again, in a truly loving community.

Ultimately, this book is not a story of victimization. It is a story about the triumph of faith and hope. The thread of faith, from Sider's conservative Christian upbringing, through ordination in a mainline Protestant denomination, runs through the narrative. Also running through the narrative is her rootedness in a contemplative lifestyle where daily meditation is at the bedrock of her spirituality. The communities of faith and faithful people who surround and support Sider through her trials offer a counterpoint—to those people and communities of faith who fail her as she suffers trauma and injustice.

Sider's enduring faith in a loving God shines through even the darkest times in her life, bringing healing and hope. I know this book will inspire and give courage and comfort to others who share Sider's experience of sexual abuse.

This is an essential story for our time—and for all time—reminding us to hear and believe victims of sexual abuse so that we can provide the healing and justice they need.

The Rev. Amy Morgan is the pastor of First United Presbyterian Church in Loveland, Colorado. A teacher and writer, she is co-author of Friendship & Faith: The WISDOM of Women Creating Alliances for Peace and The Girlfriends' Clergy Companion: Surviving and Thriving in Ministry.

Preface

Light Shines in the Darkness is a powerful, moving, timely book. It makes an excellent contribution to our understanding of the trauma that results from sexual abuse, the agony of mental illness and their complex interconnections. We have walked with Lucille through the many agonizing years described in this book and rejoice in the healing she describes. Our prayer and belief is that her story will encourage and strengthen countless others suffering similar trauma.

As Lucille's brother, I, Ron, have tried (with varying degrees of failure and success) to be a caring, supportive older brother. Thank God for the time (a couple decades ago, as I was waiting for a plane in Chicago O'Hare Airport) when on an impulse I called Lucille and discovered she had dangerously overdosed on sleeping pills and was in great danger. Thank God I was able to reach her son who quickly rushed assistance to her.

As I walked with Lucille over the years, I slowly (much too slowly) came to understand a little more about the lifelong damage inflicted by sexual abuse and the devastating impact of mental illness. As I traveled the journey with my sister, she taught me so much. And now I believe this book will similarly enlighten and encourage untold numbers as they read her exceedingly powerful yet ultimately hopeful story.

As Lucille's sister-in-law, I, Arbutus Lichti Sider, was so deeply moved when I first read the manuscript she sent us, that I immediately wrote to her: "This is a book that needs to be published. It will be an encouragement to those who are just beginning their journey through the darkness of abuse, in search of that light in the cracks. It is also a book for the rest of us who, by God's grace, have a much easier path. It opens our eyes to the hidden trauma in a neighbor's eyes or the puzzling words of a questioning friend. Your story, Lucille, could become a lifeline that we can offer to the neighbor or friend, helping them find the courage needed to begin their journey toward healing."

Lucille's journey was long and heavy. Our hearts were often heavy as we journeyed with her. But, finally, Lucille persevered to a point where she was able to put her story into words. We rejoice in a one sentence summary she has written: "This is my journey through sexual abuse and mental illness to a place of forgiveness and freedom."

For a long time we wondered if God would indeed grace her with "forgiveness and freedom."

Here you have her ringing answer. Read on!

Ronald J. Sider *is the Founder and President-emeritus of Evangelicals for Social Action and a Distinguished Professor of Theology, Holistic Ministry and Public Policy at Palmer Seminary at Eastern University. He is the brother of author Lucille Sider. His wife,* **Arbutus Lichti Sider** *is a retired Marriage and Family Therapist.*

I

Drenched With Guilt

Drenched with guilt, I race to the altar, desperately in need of relief for my sins. The children's song, *Come Into My Heart Lord Jesus*, has opened the floodgates of my heart. I'm sobbing, shaking with guilt, with tears dripping onto my light-blue dress. I'm 6 years old.

It's summer camp meeting, where families gather for a week of Bible Study and soul searching. Camp meeting is mostly fun, with lots of good food and plenty of time to play with cousins.

We children have our own special tent for services. Our chairs are small—just right for us. The altar up front is a row of wooden benches, perfect for kneeling in prayer. The Bossert sisters, nice spinster ladies in proper gray dresses, tell Bible stories we've heard a million times. But somehow, with their bright, flannel cutouts, we feel like we're hearing them for the first time. We love the story of the flood—with elephants, giraffes and turtles marching up the ramp to Noah's ark, to be saved from the flood that otherwise is going to destroy the whole earth. The bad people all drown in the flood, but God saves Noah, his family and the animals. While we love the story, it is a little scary, too, because we just hope we'd be one of Noah's family, saved in the ark.

Then the Bossert sisters give the altar call, inviting children to come forward: to repent for being bad, for disobeying parents or for fighting with brothers or sisters. We must give our hearts to Jesus to be spared of hell. Kneeling at the altar, I sob and sob, shaking with guilt. I don't know what I'm crying about. All I know is that I need to cry and that at the altar, my burdens are lifted—at least for now. My cousin, Cherry, age 4, is close behind me. We do everything together, so of course, she follows me. But she doesn't cry very hard at all.

It will be 50 years before I understand why I'm crying and why I rush to the altar time and time again. It's from guilt, shame and fear—for already I am being sexually abused by the hired man, Jim, on our farm. Jim is a very tall man with big, thick shoulders. His hair is light brown. His eyes are dark and mean and he has a heavy Dutch accent. He somehow gets me to the living room when the door to the kitchen is halfway closed. With only one light bulb hanging from the ceiling, the room is quite dark. Jim forces me to stand by him. He puts his gigantic hand under my skirt and inside my panties, with the newspaper held behind my back to hide what he is doing. He shoves me away at the slightest sound. Sometimes it even feels good for a second or two. But then it feels dirty and sinful. Bad, tainted, shameful.

One day I'm in the barn, where Jim is cleaning the stables. He suddenly gets angry with me. I don't know why. I haven't been bad. He takes a huge shovel of wet cow manure and throws it all over me, leaving it dripping down my face and over my dress. It's so heavy that it almost knocks me down. The smell of it almost smothers me. Racing into the house, I cry for mother. Her eyes are shocked at first, but then they become soft. She quickly takes off my dress and rushes to the bathroom, filling the tub with warm, soapy water. She scrubs and scrubs, ever so gently. She wraps me in a big, white towel, sprinkles her special powder over me and takes me to the kitchen to be near her while she cooks.

I'm very scared and very confused, because I thought the hired man liked me. My mother, though quiet, is very angry. I've never before seen her like this. When my father comes in the house, she begs him to fire the hired man—but he will not. It's spring, and he needs Jim to get through the haying. But come fall, my father fires him for forking a cow in the stomach when the cow tries to run away. I secretly hate my father after this, for not protecting me. But hating is a big sin. And so I repeatedly race to the altar, confessing my guilt and unburdening my shame. And again and again I feel Jesus coming into my heart. My heart feels warm, full of love. Yet the feeling doesn't last long.

But then I have my grandpa, my mother's father. He thinks I'm pure and perfect and he loves to be with me. Grandpa and grandma live in a little Canadian town, 3 miles from our farm and not too far from Niagara Falls. Grandpa loves to take me fishing down at the creek near his house. I carry my 8-foot pole with the sharp hook and the red-and-white bobber fastened to the end of the line. Grandpa shows me how to put a worm on the hook. It wiggles and squirms, but I do it just right. Grandpa gives me a big grin, patting my back. We catch three little bluegills, and I'm beaming inside as he strings them on the line before we head to his house.

On our way home we stop by the high school, for he's janitor there and the big lawn is peppered with huge dandelions. Grandpa won't have those dandelions spoiling his lawn. He asks me to help, so I race around, pulling the big, yellow dandelion heads off their stems. The sun is hot and we're both sweating. Grandpa pulls out his red hanky and wipes the sweat off of my face, then his own. He gives me that big grandpa smile from his soft, round face, saying, "Time to quit, Susie girl. You did such a good job." And then he pulls out a brand-new nickel from his pocket, saying, "This is for you, Susie girl."

Then comes the best part of all. When we get to his house, he sits down in his big, brown, cushy rocking chair. Reaching out his arms to me, I climb onto his lap. He starts singing quietly. It's our special song, the one that he made up just for me. *Sweet little Susie girl. Sweet little Susie girl. Sweet little Susie girl, sweet little Susie girl. You're my sweet little Susie girl.* I drift off to sleep, safe and warm inside and out, just knowing that I'm the best little girl in the whole wide world.

It is almost 50 years before I truly understand the role my grandpa played in my life. He somehow conveyed to me not only that I was very, very special, but that I was very, very good. As a child, I was bearing the shame of sexual abuse and the guilt for enjoying it for just a second. This led me into a dark fear of hell. I believed that just one sin could damn me to an eternity of a flaming hell. One sin could render me forever abandoned. And it is this fear of abandonment that was the primary foundation for severe mental illness, which developed later in life.

Back on my farm, I get scared sometimes. I try not to think of the hired man, Jim, because he is gone—but sometimes I do think of him. I get very upset that my father didn't fire him when he threw manure on me. I also remember how my mother pleaded with him. I love her for that. She's so gentle. Plus, she hardly ever scolds.

Even though I sometimes get scared on the farm, we have lots of fun. Our family loves sports and often, after a hard day of work, we play baseball. I play catcher for my brother, Peter, who is eight years older than me. He throws those fastballs that sometimes almost knock me over. But I do not fall. I can tell he is very proud of me. I adore Peter. He gets all A's at school. I want to be like him and I want to marry a man just like him. My father doesn't play with us, but mother does. She races around the bases with her skirt flying in the air. Mother is small, almost petite, and that seems to make her even faster. She's just so much fun to watch.

I love Sunday nights at our house. After church we sometimes gather around the piano, with mother playing and all of us singing. I'm hoping to sing alto like my mother, but my voice is too high for that now. I will begin piano lessons soon, and I can hardly wait.

We all have our chores on the farm. I hate weeding the garden but I love feeding the chickens and gathering the eggs. But there is a problem. The chicken coop is in the middle of a field where the pigs graze, and I'm deathly afraid of the pigs. My sister, Ruth, hates chickens but is not afraid of the pigs. Ruth is four years older than me and is plenty big enough to protect me. So it is her job to walk with me through the field of pigs to the chicken coup. She is supposed to wait for me there and walk me back. But sometimes a mean streak comes out in her, and she leaves me trapped in the chicken coop with all of those gigantic pigs rooting around in the field. Ruth has a big smirk on her face. Terrified, I scream for mother, and soon she comes and scolds Ruth. But that doesn't keep Ruth from doing it again the next day.

Being 6 years old, it's time for school. I love it from the very first day. As Canadians, we start the day by proudly singing *O Canada* or *God Save the Queen*. The classes are fun—spelling most of all. And before we know it, it's recess, when we race around playing tag or swinging on those extremely tall swings.

Soon I meet my first boyfriend, Desmond. He does not go to my church, but my parents don't seem to mind. He gives me an engagement ring, which is a ring from a ballpoint pen. While my church does not believe in wearing jewelry, my parents don't mind that, either. Ruth teases me about my boyfriend, and sometimes she finds and hides the ring. I'm a little scared of her at times. While she's not big for her age, four years older seems big to me. Otherwise, we look quite alike. Brown, straight, thin hair. But her face is a little rounder than mine, a bit more like my father's.

My other sister, Rachel, looks quite different. She is 11 years older than me, has thick hair and, often, a soft smile. Yet she usually has sadness in her eyes, too. But I can always count on Rachel to come to my rescue. Rachel teases Ruth that my boyfriend must be hers, and that somehow makes Ruth give me back my ring. I love her for always helping me out.

Rachel is from the shelter and she is a foster sister. I later realize that not really belonging in our family is the reason for the sadness in her eyes. One happy day, my parents gather Peter, Ruth and me for a very serious meeting. They ask if we would like to adopt Rachel. Without giving it a thought, we all say, "Yes, we'd love that!" And soon after the meeting, my parents go to the shelter and fill out some papers—and, officially, she is our sister. Her last name is now Sider. Her eyes become twinkly, and they are no longer sad.

It is around this time that my baby brother, Benny, is born, and things are hard for a while. He is the sweetest baby in the whole world, but he is born with a hair lip and cleft palate. He needs special surgeries and a feeding dropper. My mother gets very sad because she cannot stay with him at the hospital. It is not allowed. She worries that somehow, she is the cause of his problems. When he gets back from the hospital, she is too upset to learn how to use the dropper to feed him. Mother seems to withdraw from all of us for a while. But Rachel steps right in and learns how to feed Benny. He is such a sweet baby.

I later come to realize that my mother suffers from depressive episodes. Usually she manages them by praying to God for help. But this time, at Benny's birth, she had an actual breakdown and could not function. Later in life, I also hear that my grandfather suffered from some depression, although I do not know if this is true.

While I love my new baby brother, life is confusing at times. I have night terrors. I sleepwalk, racing through the house with a fear of being chased by some bad man. My parents do not ask me about this. They mention that my father was also a sleepwalker, but they say no more. I am left alone to handle this. I just try to forget it until it happens again.

Something else that happens in the night is that I wet my bed. I'm ashamed, but my mother is not at all upset with me. Mother just puts a rubber mat on my bed and hangs the sheet out to dry on the line. Ruth knows about my bedwetting, but does not tease me. I like her for that. Much later in life, I learn that bedwetting and sleepwalking are common symptoms of children who have been sexually abused.

Something else I get confused about is how my father acts. Sometimes he is very kind and gentle to me—like the time I drive into the silo with the tractor. I expect a hard spanking, but he just scolds me lightly. Or the time our barn burns. It was stuck by lightning, and we all huddle together as it goes up in flames. We are all crying, including my father. Also, he is soft at church, where he now preaches every fourth Sunday. When he tells the story of Jesus inviting the little children to come to him, it's almost as if my father is inviting me to sit on his lap—something he never does.

But other times, I'm scared of my father and I don't quite trust him. His temper flares when someone misplaces something, like the keys. And I never quite forget about the hired man, Jim, whom my father would not fire when he threw manure on me.

All of this gets harder when my grandpa dies. I am 9 years old. He is found dead from a heart attack in his Model T Ford. As I see him in his casket, I cannot believe he is dead. I weep quietly to myself. It is only—*only*—when around him that I feel safe and good and perfect. As I see him there in the casket, his song keeps singing: *Sweet little Susie girl. Sweet little Susie girl. You're my sweet little Susie girl.*

I worry constantly about my sins, and I go to the altar time and time again to wash them away. Also, I confess my sins at home. It's a nightly ritual. It happens when all of the family is in bed, settling down for the night. We are all upstairs in our house, where Peter and Rachel have their own rooms and Ruth and I share a bedroom. We have been taught that Jesus may return at any time and will take only those people without sin. So we clear the slate of sin every night by calling to each other: "Ruth, forgive me for anything. Peter, forgive me for anything. Rachel, forgive me for anything." Then, with a clear conscience, we can go to sleep.

Only much later in life do I come to understand my church. It is a small denomination called Brethren in Christ. It has revival meetings, like many Evangelical and Holiness churches do. We also bear similarities to the Mennonites, or even the Amish. We believe that war is always wrong; we're pacifists.

Like the Mennonites and Amish, we are taught that we must be separate from the world. This includes such things as wearing plain clothes. For girls and women, plain clothes means that dresses are simple: no frills, solid colors or tiny patterns. The dresses often have capes—a second layer of material over the breasts. I believe that the purpose of this is to hide the breasts because men are so excited by women's breasts. And women have to do what is necessary to keep the men from being aroused.

Also, girls and women must have long hair. Saint Paul teaches that women's hair is a glory that is to be left long to show submission to men. The hair is pulled back and twisted around to form a bun. Neatly placed over this bun is a round, white, mesh hat that is called a "covering." When I first join the church, I like the plain dresses, the long hair and the covering, but it is not long before I start to change.

There are two parts to actually joining the church. The first is baptism, and it is baptism by immersion—not by sprinkling, as the liberal churches do. The baptism takes place at the Niagara River. This is, at first, scary. The river is freezing cold and flowing fast, and we fear we'll be caught in its vicious current and flung over Niagara Falls, which is about 10 miles away. But Rev. Charles takes the hand of each of the converts and slowly guides us into the water until it reaches our waist. He gently but firmly dunks us under the water: three times forward, in the name of the Father, the Son and the Holy Ghost. Shivering, we are led from the water, and an older lady quickly dries us off with a big, white towel. Then friends, family and everybody who has gathered join in singing *Shall We Gather at the River*. Our souls seem to lift up to the heavens and angels themselves seem to join us.

The other part of joining the church involves taking vows to follow Jesus. This happens on a different Sunday. All of the converts are lined up in the front of the church; Cherry is by my side. Now, Cherry and I are prone to getting the giggles just when we're not supposed to, and here—in front of everybody, when taking our solemn vows—we get the giggles. We try desperately to stop, but the harder we try, the more we giggle. We don't wet our pants, but that can happen at times like this. Our parents do not punish us for giggling, but they sure have good reason to.

The next week is our first Communion. Again, we're lined up in front of the church with many others. The bread is passed, and we solemnly take a piece and eat it, the way we're supposed to. But when it's time for the wine—the grape juice—I get an idea. I love grape juice, and I'd like more than one sip. I whisper to Cherry, "I'm going to take two sips." While shaking her head from side to side, she has a sparkle in her eyes, telling me to go ahead. With a wild, rebellious feeling inside of me, I take two sips. No one seems to notice. Sometimes, it's just so much fun being naughty. Only later do I realize that underneath these small acts of rebellion was a person who was destined to break free from her family in a myriad of ways.

Soon after joining the church, our family moves to a farming community about two hours away. My father, by this time, has become one of the laypersons who takes his turn preaching. He surprises himself by how much he loves preaching and how good he is at it. He takes correspondence courses on the Bible, which he loves. So we sell the farm and my father is called to be a full-time pastor at Rosebank Brethren in Christ Church near Kitchener, Ontario. His sermons are mostly filled with love and compassion. My favorite sermons are about the good shepherd who protects his sheep. My father often recites from memory Psalm 23 (1-4): *The Lord is my Shepherd, I shall not want. He makes me lie down in green pastures. He leads me beside still waters. He restores my soul. Even though I walk through the valley of the shadow of death, I fear no evil for you are with me.* When my father preaches about the good shepherd, I almost feel like he is the good shepherd, protecting me. But I'm not sure about that because he did not protect me from the hired man who threw manure on me.

There is still some harshness in my father, but it is not as strong as when we were on the farm. In his new ministry, my mother joins him full-heartedly and the two of them are quick to step in and help anyone in need. Often, my father helps a church family on their farm, and it is not unusual for me to see my mother bring a needy woman to our home and help her wash her hair. I later realize how devoted they are to their ministry and how unstintingly loving they are to their parishioners. Without my realizing it, they have instilled in me a deep commitment to serve others.

While at Rosebank, the church where my father is pastor, I get to spend more time with my mother than I did when we lived on the farm. We are not so busy. I love to help her with her garden, and together, we savor the gladiolas and peonies as they come into bloom. Mother teachers me to sew using our beautiful, pedaled Singer sewing machine. But one day I have a mishap. By this time, I'm 11 years old. I'm making a light-green doll dress for my beautiful, blonde-haired, blue-eyed doll. Somehow, my finger gets under the needle and I sew right through my finger and fingernail. Mother is so sweet and comforting, and in a few days—after my finger heals—she lets me keep sewing my doll dress.

Most of the time I like being "a preacher's kid," and I'm a model child: learning my Bible verses, helping clean the church and singing in the children's choir. If I do sin, I go forward at a revival meeting, confess, and am thus ready to go to heaven should the Lord return. One can never be too careful about escaping the eternal fires of hell.

But there is one big exception to my goodness, and that is around the issue of wearing long pants. Part of being plainly dressed and showing submission to men is that a woman is not to wear pants like a man. However, if playing in sports—where her skirt would fly up—it is only modest to wear pants under the skirt. The rule that both pants *and* a skirt must be worn is my problem. When my mother buys me a beautiful pair of pants with little red-and-black checkers, I love those pants and want to wear them without my skirt. I struggle and struggle over taking my skirt off during gym class at school. Finally, I do it. I'm thrilled. I feel like a regular little girl, and not an outsider who has to always look different. I wear those pants day after day. Although I feel very guilty, I never confess my disobedience to my mother. And I never confess it privately to God. Only later in life will I understand what a big step this is.

After two years, it is time for me to go to high school. Like my brothers and sisters, I do not go to the local high school: it is secular, and we need to remain separate from that world. Instead, we go to our church's high school, which is near our former farm in Stevensville—not far from my grandfather's house. I'm a year younger than most 9th graders because I skipped a grade, but that doesn't seem to be a problem. I love high school immediately. I know at least half of the students, who are cousins or friends from the Brethren in Christ Church. My extended family is big and the Siders have a good reputation.

I love sports and immediately take to basketball. I get aggressive and sometimes foul out in games, but no one seems to notice. My school has a great music department, and by my second year, I have joined the choir and am singing in a ladies' trio and a mixed quartet. I love to carry the low alto part, like my mother. With the mixed quartet, I sing with one other girl and two boys, and I'm always on the lookout for a nice boy. All during grade school I had boyfriends, and it is no different now. My family teases me about this, but it doesn't stop me from finding a new one whenever the old one gets sour.

I love the drama program, and especially the costumes we get to wear. When performing a Shakespeare play we wear long, Victorian gowns with wide skirts and frilly collars. It is so different from the plain clothes we usually wear. Memorizing the lines of the Shakespeare plays can be hard; understanding what Shakespeare is saying is sometimes confusing. But there are two lines in *The Merchant of Venice* that become implanted in my mind, and I will repeat them for the rest of life: *The quality of mercy is not strained. It droppeth as a gentle rain from heaven. It is twice blest. It blesseth him who givest and him who receiveth.*

Later in life, I come to understand the topic of mercy—and that is why I am drawn to these lines. With Shakespeare, mercy is so generous and gentle—dropping as gentle rain from heaven. In my own religious experience, mercy is much more scarce and is dependent on good behavior.

But there is one bad thing about high school, and that is that I still wet my bed. It happens during my whole first year of high school. I try and try to wake up in the middle of the night to go to the bathroom, but it doesn't work. Lucky for me, though, my roommate is Ruth, and she is so kind about this. She helps me change my wet sheets and hang them over the dresser to dry. Then she helps me make my bed as soon as the sheets are dry. We keep this a secret, and even our friends next door never know. I just love Ruth for being so good to me. I forget the times she used to tease me on the farm. She becomes one of my best friends.

By this time, Ruth has a serious boyfriend, Edmond Galter. He is from a big and prominent family from our church. Ruth has been dating him since she was 14 and she is totally in love. Edmond is four years older than she is, but our parents don't seem to mind. He does not go to high school with us, so Ruth takes every chance she can get to go home on weekends to see him. Like all of the Galters, he's a hard worker and we know he's saving his money to get married. He holds hands with Ruth at every possible chance. I sometimes see him pressed up against her when the two of them sit on the sofa.

At the end of my freshman year, which is Ruth's last year, Edmond proposes to Ruth—and she, of course, accepts. She plans a wedding for the summer after graduation, and I help her whenever I can. The best part of it is that she asks me to be her maid of honor. I'm thrilled. I love the material she chooses for the bridesmaid dresses: a light mauve that looks embroidered, although it is not. It seems so luxurious. By this time, we no longer wear dresses with capes, but our clothing is still plain and simple. This bridesmaid's dress is the prettiest dress I have ever worn, apart from the costumes for the plays at high school.

Ruth and Edmond's wedding is beautiful—especially Ruth's long, bustled gown. But most of all, I am proud of being the maid of honor. I have just turned 15, and this is the most grown-up thing I have ever done. I just love Ruth for asking me and it makes me feel closer to her than ever. All of this makes me want to help Ruth in the new house that Edmond has bought for her. We're so impressed with him, and while the house needs some fixing up, we'll gladly help with that. Our family always helps out with these kinds of things.

After the wedding and the summer, I go back to high school in the fall, and it is wonderful even without Ruth. The sports, the plays, the singing, the boys; the classes are great, too. I get top grades. On weekends I come home and help Ruth and Edmond with their house. And now it is even more fun, because they are expecting a baby. We must have the house in tip-top shape for that baby! But this is when a very, very bad thing happens.

I am at their house for two days during spring break. The baby is due in just one month. There is lots of painting to do, but we work hard and are happy with our progress. We work after supper and well into the evening. It's time for bed, and I go upstairs to a bedroom there. There is no door to the bedroom, but rather just a curtain that covers the entrance to the room. I don't give it a thought. I just pull the curtain closed, fall into bed and am soon fast asleep.

At about 2 a.m., I am awakened by a presence in the room. I know it is Edmond. He is a big man with thick, square shoulders. I feel him touching me with his hands. Gigantic, strong hands. He is touching my breasts. First one, then the other. At the same time, leaning over me, he whispers, "I love you." At first I lay there, limp with fear—but then I try to stop him. I do not holler, but I fight him off. I swat at him. I'm terrified; desperate. And soon, he quietly leaves. I lay there, frozen in my bed, for the rest of the night. The next morning I act as if nothing happened. Edmond acts the same. Yet I secretly despise him. Ruth and I go about our day, painting and getting ready for that new baby, and I try not to think about what happened last night. The day passes rather quickly.

The real problem comes when it's time to go to bed. I go to my room and still there is no door. What can I do? I look around the room and find some straight pins. Perhaps Edmond will stay away if I can somehow pin the curtain into the cracks of the molding around the door. I work and work to get both sides of the curtain fastened. Finally, I stop. I go to bed, but I cannot sleep. I listen for his steps on the stairway. But they do not come. I have been spared.

I get up the next morning and again act as if all is normal. Ruth and I finish our painting, and by mid-afternoon, it is time for me to go home. I must tell my parents. My father picks me up after inspecting our work and compliments us on a job well done. I can't wait to get home. I can't wait to tell my parents. I know they will listen and I know they will help.

When we arrive, I tell mother and father that something bad happened. My father says we should sit down and talk. He motions us to the kitchen table, which is in front of a window. Before we are seated, I am already shaking. Then I blurt it all out in one long sentence. "Edmond came into my room, he was touching my breasts, he said he loved me, I fought him off, I didn't tell Ruth." By this time I am crying—quietly crying, still trembling. My parents listen quietly. My father is a big man and he looks so strong. My mother is petite, but her eyes look fiery and resilient. I just know they will help. But they are quiet at first. I think they are very upset with Edmond, but they don't say it. Then my father says, "We need to pray about this." And so we bow our head and my father prays. I do not really hear his words. I am too upset. After the prayer my parents say nothing, although I do see extreme distress on their faces. I wait for them to say something, but they say nothing. In fact, they say nothing all day—and nothing the next day, either. I keep waiting for them to say more. Or even to pray more. But there is only silence. In fact, they never say anything about it again—never.

Time and time again I imagine my parents talking about this. I imagine my mother pleading with my father to do something about it. To talk to Edmond ... to tell Ruth ... to tell me I will never have to stay at their house again. But they say nothing. My mother and father will go to their graves saying nothing more about it. I am left to handle this secret on my own. Abandoned. And this only adds to my fear of being abandoned by God.

2

Racing Up the Court

I return to high school and throw myself into it. By now I'm a very serious basketball player. Racing up the middle of the court and dunking a basket—well, this is heaven. Furthermore, I fall in love. My boyfriend is Mike, the son of a minister of a liberal church, the United Church of Christ. To have a boyfriend outside of my denomination is a small act of rebellion. Though thrilling, the fear of hell always lurks in the background. Mike and I catch a kiss and a very tight hug whenever and wherever we can; the back hallway of the girls' dorm is our favorite spot. He is generous with gifts, giving me pretty figurines and small dishes. By the end of my senior year, Mike makes it clear that he hopes we will get married. But I am not ready. I sadly return the gifts, and he is heartbroken. It just doesn't feel right to build a life with Mike. My parents do not really approve of him, and that counts for something; but more important is the fact that Mike is not headed to college, like I am. He is not like my brother, Peter—the brilliant student who has not only finished college but is now in seminary at the prestigious Yale Divinity School.

Ninety-nine percent of the time I forget about Edmond—about that dreadful night he came into my bedroom, fondling my breasts and telling me he loved me. But when I'm home from boarding school and see his shifty eyes, I find myself hating—hating in a dark, desperate way. I see

Edmond at all our family gatherings. I see him at church. I realize later in life that there was no real safe place for me.

Then, back at high school, a miracle happens—at least, that's how it feels: I discover psychology. I find books by Sigmund Freud and Carl Jung in the high school library. First I read Freud, the father of modern psychology. I'm totally fascinated by Freud's ideas about the power of the unconscious mind; with his belief that most of what we do and say is rooted in the unconscious mind, with all its wily secrets. But I'm also deeply troubled by Freud, for he declared religion an expression of psychological neuroses. Carl Jung, on the other hand, integrated religion and psychology. Furthermore, I am fascinated by Jung's analysis of personality types: extroverts and introverts. For I know immediately that I'm an extrovert and that I've found a friend in Jung!

I'm also intrigued by Jung's analysis of dreams. As a person with persistent frightening dreams, Jung teaches me that dreams are to be welcomed and analyzed. Dreams teach lessons we need to learn and they provide clues to our psychological wounds—especially those that have been held in secret. Although I don't grasp everything he says, I already know that I need it. I do not tell anyone about my own dreams or about Jung's understanding of dreams. This is way too personal and sensitive.

What I do share is Jung's understanding of different personality types—of extroverts and introverts. Here, I find liberation—and with this, I give my first feminist declaration of liberation. The occasion for sharing is graduation, for which I am asked to give the salutatorian address. This is the address given by the student who is second in the class in regards to grades. It hurts a bit that I am not first—for I have been secretly aiming for that spot, even though it's not totally acceptable for girls to outshine boys. But Henry is the top student in the class. As such, he will be giving the valedictorian address. I am giving the salutatorian address.

In Canada, the addresses given by students at graduation are often research reports, and this is what I want to do. In fact, as soon as I am asked to give the salutatorian address, I know my topic: introverts and extroverts as understood by Carl Jung. I'm excited as I prepare it. On graduation day, I proudly stand before the audience and explain that God created some of us as introverts and some of us as extroverts. All are equally good. I carefully explain: "Extroverts receive their energy by being with people, and introverts receive their energy by being alone." I end my address by proclaiming, in a very preacherly voice: "And God loves us all." I like my preacherly voice.

I later realize why this is so important to me. I had felt squeezed into molds that often did not fit. I had been made to behave in ways that did not really work for me—whether it be that of wearing plain clothes or in believing that women are to be submissive to men. In Jung, I found space for me to be the extroverted person that I truly am.

Upon graduation, I return to live with my parents for an additional year at the local secular high school. This is for grade 13, which is a pre-college year in Canada. In the U.S. it is considered to be the freshman year of college. When I return home, I am very, very careful around Edmond. I do not sit by him at the dinner table. I hate to be hugged by him, although I cannot totally avoid it. Edmond and Ruth's baby is now born, but I spend little time with them.

At the end of summer I become agitated. As I anticipate my year at a secular school, I do not want to go into that setting with long hair; I want to look like the other students. I want to cut my hair. I feel pressure from the inside and agonize for days, but in trepidation, I decide that I must cut my hair—even though it is against my parents' rules and my church's standard. But my church is beginning to change.

Furthermore, I am carefully watching my brother, Peter, and his wife, Eunice, as they are changing. Eunice has cut her hair and she looks stunning in her red, thick, pageboy hairstyle. I want the same. So when Peter and Eunice are visiting, I ask Eunice: "Will you cut my hair, please? I want a pageboy, just like yours." She hesitates at first, but then agrees.

We do it at my house when my parents are away. Eunice carefully cuts a few inches at a time. My plan is to leave my hair just long enough so that the length can be hidden at church. I've seen others do this with their hair, carefully pinning it around a mesh roller at the back of the neck. But something happens and Eunice cuts it too short.

I'm extremely frightened as my parents arrive home and walk through the front door. My father's reaction is worse than I even imagined. He almost falls to the floor, shouting at me for disobeying. "How could you disgrace me and our family? How could you?" Then my father's anger turns into weeping. Loud weeping. My mother, who has watched silently, begins to weep also.

I feel very, very sad that I have disappointed my mother, but not sad enough to change my mind. It is finished. And this is my first big—even gigantic—step away from my parents.

When I look back on the whole issue of my hair-cutting, I will, in time, be stunned. My cutting my hair was considered a huge disgrace. Edmond's abuse of me was never pronounced a disgrace. It was never even mentioned! And my parents never defending me was not considered a disgrace! Perhaps, in fact, that was the greatest disgrace of all. No wonder I later developed serious mental illness problems!

Something else was happening in my church at this time. An older, married deacon was having an affair with a younger, married women. Not only was this causing disgrace and havoc in the church, but it was considered a sin that required public confession before the entire congregation. It meant also that the deacon was deposed of his position. Again, only later would I understand the absolute incongruity of my own situation in comparison to theirs. My abuse by Edmond was totally shoved under the rug. The affair between two consenting adults required public confession and a consequence of disbarment for the deacon. Again, I later would come to understand that I did not have a safe church. My church was fraught with danger.

Grade 13 goes by quickly. It is a little harder, academically, than I had imagined, yet my grades are well above what is needed for college. But where to go to college becomes another sticky problem. I assume I will follow my brother, Peter, and go to Waterloo Lutheran University, which is close to our home. But while there, he was influenced by an atheist professor and seriously questioned his faith. My parents were devastated and prayed fervently that he would find a professor to help him regain his faith. The next year, a Christian professor began teaching at the college, and his faith was restored.

My parents beg me to not attend that college. They beg me to attend our church college—Messiah College, in Pennsylvania, which is eight hours away. In fact, they offer to give me money to attend, even with their limited resources. I accept their offer, although a part of me wants to go where Peter went.

My parents assume that at Messiah College I will be influenced only in the tradition of the Brethren in Christ Church. But what they don't realize is that Messiah College is now a place where differences of opinion are valued. You might be a pacifist refusing to go to war, or you might be sporting your army fatigues, just back from Vietnam. You might have long hair rolled in a bun with a prayer covering, or you might have short hair—and it may even be permed or dyed blonde. You might be an atheist.

As I drive onto the college campus, I feel like I can breathe. I am immediately drawn to the chapel, which stands at the center of campus and has a colonial look with its tall, white pillars. The women's dorm, in contrast, is a rather plain, brown, brick building with nothing that draws me to it. But it soon gains luster as I get to know my roommate, Paula. Paula, like me, is a Canadian, but unlike me, she dresses stylishly. Her family has not insisted on plain clothes, even though she is from my denomination. Seeing her in a bright-red, scooped-neck, somewhat tightly fitting sweater gives me confidence in my own ability to dress in styles so different from my Amish-girl look. At the fall formal banquet, I wear a pink, skimpy dress with spaghetti shoulder straps. I am both thrilled and filled with guilt. My parents would be appalled if they saw me. Messiah College, unlike my home, does not strangle me.

At college, I first major in psychology, hoping to learn more about dream interpretation. But I soon learn that the psychology program is more interested in training social workers than in assisting my pursuit of an esoteric understanding of dreams. Since I'm not interested in social work, I turn to the religion department. Maybe there I can satisfy my other interest: trying to understand my faith and putting my childhood dogma and guilt to rest. I know that I do not want to give up on my faith. I know there is much good in it. My early experiences of Jesus's love are still with me, and my parents' example of lovingly serving people in need never leaves me. Yet the guilt and rigidity of my childhood religion is also still raging in me. I know I must sort all of this out. And then I have the good fortune of discovering Dr. Schneider.

Dr. Schneider is a distant cousin, a Rhodes Scholar from Oxford University. I study Greek, the language in which the New Testament was written, and I learn that the Bible I have been taught is just one translation. I learn that there are many translations and many ways of understanding

Scripture. On the issue of hair length, Dr. Schneider firmly declares, "Of course such practices do not apply to all people at all times. Having long hair was simply a first-century fashion." I can breathe. A brilliant authority figure is not condemning me.

Here at college, I'm sporting my pageboy with no prayer covering. Yet there is one big exception to this: the chapel, where I feel compelled to wear my prayer covering. I keep the covering in my purse and discretely take it out and slip it on my head during worship, thereby still following some of my father's rules. Only much later will I understand that his rules are indelibly fixed in my psyche, and to truly break away from them will require years of heartache and therapy.

But at the present time, it is Dr. Schneider whom I turn to. Most attractive about Dr. Schneider is his whistling. On quiet mornings, he whistles his way across the tree-lined campus in pure tenor tones. It might be Beethoven's *Symphony No. 5* or *Amazing Grace*. It all ascends to the heavens from his heart of deep joy. There is a glow in his face, a gentleness in his spirit and a lightness in his step that I have never before encountered. It's almost as if he glides a foot above the ground as he whistles his way across campus.

Furthermore, Dr. Schneider is married to Charity, an impeccably kind and gentle soul. She is also a perfectly coiffed woman in her soft, blue dress and broad-rim, matching hat—a hat that might be worn by Queen Elizabeth herself. Again, this is in such contrast to my upbringing, in which women's clothes were drab and hung loosely. The Schneiders adopt me, in a way, and ask me to be godmother to their son. While I don't know what this means, I relish it, for I am embracing a Christianity different from my own. I'm part of a family for which fear is essentially absent; disgrace is not even a word they seem to know.

At times, the Schneiders take me with them to their new church—it is Episcopalian—and I experience its flowing liturgy, melodious chanting and weekly Communion at the altar. In my childhood, I repeatedly raced to the altar to repent of my sins; here, I go to the altar to receive the bread and wine—the heart of God's unending love and nurture. I dare at times to ask myself: "Will I, like them, someday reject my conservative religious heritage?"

The one part of college that is not satisfying is that of romance. I cannot find a relationship in which the romantic spark gets ignited and is mutual. Tim repeatedly asks me out, but I simply do not find him physically attractive. Ted, on the other hand, I find very attractive. He is good-looking, with his thick, brown hair and dark-brown eyes. He is very smart, and he is from a well-known church family. His parents live nearby, and he invites me to his family's home for Sunday dinner. It goes very well except for the fact that, in cutting a cherry tomato, I splash juice on my white blouse. Ted doesn't seem to notice, though, and it all gives me hope that he is serious. Thanksgiving is around the corner, and I assume I'll be invited again. I wait and wait for the invitation, but is does not come. I'm crushed. For Thanksgiving, I'm destined to the college cafeteria with all of the other students who were not invited anywhere. Ted later remarks that he went hunting over Thanksgiving break, but this only tells me where I am on his priority list—and that is low. We simply drift apart after this, and I'm very lonely. I do not meet any other attractive men in my remaining year at college.

By the last term of my senior year, I turn to the next step in my life— but that is problematic. Majoring in religion leads nowhere for a Brethren in Christ girl. Yet my appetite for understanding religion is not satiated. I joke that I want to be a bishop, knowing it is far beyond my grasp as a woman. I talk to Peter about my dilemma, and he suggests I attend Yale Divinity School, following in his footsteps. I apply and am accepted. I buy a large, black trunk, fill it with my favorite (somewhat fashionable) outfits and my prized theology books, and hop on a train to New Haven, Connecticut. I'm both excited and scared. I take comfort in the fact that my brother—now completing a Ph.D.—is nearby, as is his wife, Eunice.

Yale Divinity School is the first real step out of my Brethren in Christ world. College was, after all, my church college. At Yale Divinity School (shortened to YDS), I find Methodists, Presbyterians, Lutherans, Episcopalians, Catholics, Congregationalists and even agnostics—all people I was taught are heretics. My first chapel service, however, is full of fear. It is my first worship service without my prayer covering, and my father's anger is pounding in one ear while the call to break away is ringing sweetly in the other. My feeling of guilt surprises me, and I realize I have not left my father as far behind as I had hoped.

Soon I find a best friend, Lauh, who is a Presbyterian from Korea. Like me, she sings in the choir, and we start singing duets in our dorm rooms. While her English is sometimes hard to decipher when she speaks, it seems perfectly clear when she sings. With her high, pure soprano voice and my low, resonant alto, we are like angels, lifting our hearts to God. We discover that our grandmothers, though from different continents, have taught us the same gospel favorites—*Amazing Grace* and *How Great Thou Art*. Lauh teaches me an unfamiliar hymn, and immediately it lodges deep into the cave of my heart and into my soul. We sing it night after night: *God of our life through all the circling years we trust in Thee. In all the past, through all our hopes and fears, Thy hand we see. With each new day, as morning lifts the veil, we own Thy mercies, Lord, which never fail* (words by Hugh T. Kerr, 1871-1950, and music by Charles Henry Purday, 1799-1885).

Lauh's hymn soothes me in my uncertainty about pursuing a life apart from my parents. It is a reminder of what I know on a very deep level: that God has been, and always will be, with me. I realize that despite a fear of hell and the rigidity of my childhood religion, I have a kernel of deep faith. I feel loved and protected by God. What I do not realize is that this hymn will soothe and comfort me for the rest of my life, especially when I walk on unfamiliar and dangerous paths.

In my first term at YDS, I discover Martin Luther. He is the Catholic priest who rebelled against Catholicism and became the founder of Protestantism. Luther rejected the idea that acts of penance are the key to heaven. He preached grace—unmerited favor from God. Luther takes the pressure off of me for always striving to be perfect. In his famous Latin phrase, *Simul Justus et Peccator*, he proclaimed that we are always being justified though always sinning. Luther proclaimed that God's grace and love flows endlessly and freely, covering our constant sinning. What a relief!

Then I fall in love with Joel. It is October of my second year. In my first year I dated a bit, but there was no real spark. This was quite painful, because a part of me gets desperate without a boyfriend. But then I meet Joel. He has just come back from studying abroad in Israel. He is a friend of my brother, Peter. What better recommendation could I have?

In our first meeting, at the library of YDS, I find in Joel a man who both intrigues and attracts me. Joel is a big man with beautiful, dark-brown eyes and brown hair. His hair is slightly thinning, so he combs it over to cover the slightly emerging bald spot. I find it attractive, even professorial. He has a gentleness about him. He is brilliant: a relentless student who skims three or four books a day. Joel is clearly the man I've been waiting for. Furthermore, he is from the Wesleyan Methodist tradition, which has some things in common with my own. This makes him acceptable to my family. By Thanksgiving, we're engaged and planning a June wedding.

Upon engagement, my father writes me a letter about sexual purity. I have a flashback to age 15 when my father did not defend me. I toss the letter into the garbage basket. Joel is a man I wish to travel with for the rest of my life. In so doing, I am not going to allow my father to intrude. What we do is our business. Joel is a gentle man, yet strong and brilliant. He has the intelligence and kindness that I found in my beloved professor at college. I am not going to let my father's rules impede our relationship in any way.

At Christmastime, I visit Joel's family in Kentucky. His mother is a librarian and a college professor. His father is a seminary professor. I realize that this is a family I could fit into, and his parents immediately take to me.

On June 9, 1969 at 11 a.m., Joel and I graduate, processing through the grand, tree-lined campus of Yale University. We have both graduated from small colleges, so to participate in a large-scale ceremony at a prestigious university thrills both us and our families.

On the day of our graduation, at 5 p.m., we are married in the chapel of Yale Divinity School. The chapel is graced with tall, white pillars and high ceilings. From its loft, the choir sings *The Gift of Love*. By my side is Lauh, in her apricot Korean dress and short, matching mantilla. She carries a single white rose. I'm wearing a gown I sewed in my dorm room—a full-length, ivory chiffon dress with three-quarter-length sleeves. I wear a long, French lace mantilla and carry a single red rose. The men are in tuxedos, but the best man's ankles are showing. The rental shop had failed to note that he was 6-foot-3. We chuckle.

Officiating at the ceremony is my beloved college professor, Dr. Schneider, with his very Episcopalian voice. My father says a prayer, dressed in his black suit with its standup collar. Also assisting is Joel's father, who is wearing a plain black suit and tie. My female relatives are wearing their prayer coverings, and our liberal friends are sporting their wide-brim hats (or no hats at all). After the ceremony, we have a reception with simple hors d'oeuvres and a two-tiered wedding cake. There is no dancing. Dancing is not part of the traditions of either Joel or I. In fact, I do not even know how to dance.

By this time, Joel and I have been admitted to master's level programs at the University of Kentucky: Joel in library science, and I in college student personnel. Joel also has been hired as a librarian at Asbury Theological Seminary in Kentucky. So the day after our wedding, we rent a trailer, pack it with 2,000 books—mainly Joel's—and begin our journey to our new home. On the way, we stop in New York City and in Pennsylvania, thrilled with each other and excited about the journey we are embarking on.

Our apartment is small but sweet. We purchase bricks and boards for making some of the bookshelves. For additional shelves, I paint the orange crates we had packed our books in and we stack them on their sides, filling them with the books. The orange, brown and green crates, filled with a variety of books, are as delightful to us as a plate of perfectly prepared food would be to a gourmet chef.

Our life in Kentucky is good. We both finish our degrees, and I work at the University of Kentucky in residence hall administration and informal counseling. But we both know that Kentucky is not where we want to stay long-term. After three years, we decide to move to Chicago, where Joel will begin a Ph.D. in church history at the University of Chicago. He also will be the librarian at North Park Theological Seminary and will teach church history. So again we pack up our books, which by this time have mysteriously grown in number to 3,000.

I do not have a job when we move to Chicago, which is quite distressing. Without clear goals and purpose, I get very restless. I also surprise myself, for I find that I'm moving toward deep melancholy and verging on depression. Fortunately, I am hired as assistant director at the Urban Life Center within three months. The center brings students from small colleges to the city for an urban term. We introduce our students to the despair of a drug-infused neighborhood; to Saul Alinsky's community organizing; to the standing ovations at Symphony Hall; to Bob Dylan concerts; and to lectures by feminist Gloria Steinem. All are experiences that are not available to our students at their small colleges. And although I'm a staff member, these experiences are mainly new to me. They point me to a bigger world than what I have known—and I want to know more.

The feminist lectures by Gloria Steinem are the ones that most deeply capture me. Steinem proclaims that "any woman who chooses to behave like a full human being should be warned that ... she will need her sisterhood ..." (humoropedia.com/Gloria-Steinem-Quotes). This evokes in me a deep longing. It also invokes in me an anger—albeit an anger that is mainly below the surface. At the surface is a low-level sense of depression. I try to talk myself out of this: I have Joel, and I have a job. But I need more. I need a sense of "sisterhood." So I decide to gather several female friends, and we take turns leading a study about women. Without noticing at the time, I later realize that this staved off the depression I was beginning to feel.

We meet in my basement. I have made a room in the unfinished basement by stacking walls made of crates of books. I tack posters to the unfinished ceiling and place brightly colored rugs on the bare cement floor. It's a perfectly cozy space.

We meet weekly, and a tight bond forms quickly. We are clearly budding feminists. We are painfully aware that most feminists are declaring both the church and the Bible key oppressors of women. We sisters are not convinced. We search Scripture and history and are surprised by both: we find many women who had dared to break the silence of oppression. We are exhilarated. My depression is lifted for several years.

In Scripture, we discover female leaders, evangelists and prophetesses. At Pentecost, the Holy Spirit was poured out on daughters as well as sons—on women as well as men—and all were expected to prophesy and preach (Acts 2:17). Perhaps most impressive of all is Mary Magdalene, who was at the cross with Jesus and at his tomb—and, after the Resurrection, was the first person to whom he appeared. Jesus instructed her to go and tell the other disciples about his resurrection. As such, she is "the apostle to the apostles." We women are thrilled!

We are also delighted by what we find in our long-lost church history. We find Anna Howard Shaw, who felt the call to become a preacher and, as a little girl in the woods in Michigan, stood on a stump and preached to the trees. In 1875, she entered the Boston University School of Theology.

Three years later, she was the second woman to graduate from that school. While there, however, she was denied privileges—cheap food and lodging, to name two—simply because she was a woman. Her family and friends were, for the most part, opposed to her becoming a minister, but she wrote, "Men have no right to define for us our limitations. Who shall interpret to a woman, the divine element in her being?" (*Wisdom of The Daughters*, edited by Reta Halteman Finger and Kari Sandhaas, Innisfree Press, Inc. 2001, p.238.) In 1880, she became the first woman ordained in the Methodist Protestant Church. Later, she left the pastorate to work for women's suffrage with Susan B. Anthony. She died knowing that the 19th Amendment was in the process of being ratified.

As we uncover long-lost history, we find evangelist Phoebe Palmer from our own conservative ranks, brilliantly defending her podium in her book, *Promise of the Father*. (Boston: Henry V. Degen, 1859.) Born in 1807, she was one of the most influential leaders in the Holiness tradition, which my childhood denomination embraced. In the later part of the 19th century, at a time when most evangelists were men, Phoebe Palmer claimed 25,000 converts in the U.S., Canada, Great Britain and Europe.

One of the women influenced by Phoebe Palmer was Frances Willard, who is well known for her work in the Woman's Christian Temperance Union. Willard was also prominent in the movement for woman's suffrage. She describes her call from God to work for woman's suffrage as follows: "While alone on my knees one Sabbath, in the capital of the Crusade state, as I lifted my heart to God crying, 'What wouldst thou have me to do?' There was borne in my mind, as I believe from loftier regions, this declaration, 'You are to speak for woman's ballot as a weapon for protection for her home.' Then for the first and only time in my life, there flashed through my brain a complete line of arguments and illustrations." (Ray Strachey, *Frances Willard, Her Life and Work*, New York: Fleming H. Revell, 1913, p. 208.)

And then we find Catherine Booth, from England. We love the story of her engagement to William Booth: of how she argued that a woman is equal to a man on every level, and that if he disagreed, she would break off their engagement. The two of them had sharp arguments about the differences between men and women, but gradually, William began to acquiesce, and they were married. She soon began to give public lectures about religion and, after one of these, she wrote to her father, "Indeed, I felt quite at home on the platform, far more so than I do in the kitchen!" (Note: References to Catherine Booth are found in *Wisdom Of The Daughters*, edited by Reta Finger and Karen Sandhaas, Innisfree Press, Inc. 2001, pp. 249-253.)

In their early years of ministry, Catherine and William worked together, but she later decided to strike out on her own, "thereby doubling the power for good." She was a more gifted speaker than William and drew huge crowds of people. At Hastings, England, 2,500 people attended nightly, and in Portsmouth, 1,000 people came for 17 consecutive weeks. Later, Catherine and William founded The Salvation Army—which, from inception, appointed women to all ranks.

Catherine and William had eight children. She instilled in their daughters a pride for their family name, and when they married, they retained it and hyphenated it, thus becoming Booth-Tucker, Booth-Clibborn and so on.

I find that I just love Catherine Booth. Of all the women we have discovered, she's my favorite. She feels like a mother to me. So strong and assertive, confronting her husband. She is so unlike my own mother, who was submissive to my father. I still have flashbacks to my childhood, when my mother pleaded with my father to fire the hired man on our farm after he threw manure at me. But my father refused. I just know that in a confrontation like this with her husband, Catherine Booth would have prevailed.

I find a portrait of Catherine Booth. I see strength and determination in her eyes. I see independence. I hang the print in my apartment. That print will hang in my apartments and houses for the next 40 years!

In addition to my feminist sisters, my husband, Joel, is a partner in this historical research. Part of his study in church history leads him to discover women in conservative denominations. The two of us team up and we start to lecture at evangelical colleges. In the next several years we visit 12 colleges, and we enjoy a fine reputation in doing so. We very much enjoy our time together on these visits, too. We are equal partners. My depression symptoms are now mostly gone.

Then another wonderful thing happens. We sisters get an idea. We are now eight in number, and we are bursting to share the discoveries we have made about women in history and in Scripture. We decide to publish a newsletter, and we name it *Daughters of Sarah*, after Sarah of the Bible. Sarah, the wife of Abraham in the Old Testament, was a strong woman and, like Abraham, was called by God to go to the Promised Land. Historically, women have always been referred to as "sons of Abraham"; we, as feminists, declare ourselves to be "daughters of Sarah," thereby giving both Sarah and ourselves the status that is rightfully ours. We, like men, are co-heirs of God's grace and life.

We then search our address books for names of people who might be interested in our newsletter. We find 200 names. We charge $2 per year for a bi-monthly subscription. In two years, we have 1,100 subscriptions. As we staple, fold and stamp our precious newsletter, we sometimes giggle like little girls; sometimes strut our newfound Queendom; but always we remain steadfast in our determination to free both ourselves and our sisters from a second-rate status in our churches and homes. On the front page of *Daughters of Sarah*, we declare, "We are Christians. We are also feminists. Some say we cannot be both, but for us, Christianity and feminism are inseparable." Our newsletter grows steadily into a magazine that will live for the next 20 years.

I later realize what *Daughters of Sarah* birthed in me: the confidence that I could make real change not only in my own life, but in the lives of others, too. When teamed up with sisters, we were unstoppable. This works for several years.

While delighting in my *Daughters of Sarah* sisters, I find another sister. Her name is Gloria, and she lives on the first floor of my building. Joel and I live on the second floor, and the *Daughters of Sarah* group meets in the basement.

Gloria and I are different in many ways. She's black, and she grew up in Pittsburg and New York City. She grew up in the world of jazz, knowing Duke Ellington and she, herself, being the niece of a leading jazz musician. Growing up on a farm in Canada, I have no idea about what life in Pittsburg might have been like. Gloria is sometimes boisterous and always witty as she pokes fun at those "silly white boys." She gives me a glimpse of life and energy that is simply not present in my white sisters or in my childhood farm life. Gloria is truly beautiful in perfect makeup, high-heeled shoes and fashionable dresses from Michigan Avenue. I have never owned a tube of lipstick. In recent years, I have adopted the hippie look of wire-rim glasses, baggy pants and brown capes purchased from thrift stores.

But Gloria is very frightened. She needs a job, and she needs one fast. Her husband, a college professor, has recently divorced her for one of his students, and Gloria is raising her 3-year-old daughter. She applies for a job at a nearby university; we wait and wait. She does not hear. Then, one day, I hear her bounding up the stairs, squealing, "I got it, girl. I got it!" I meet her in the entryway, shouting, hugging and high-fiving. "I knew you could do it, girl! I knew it."

While thrilled about her new job, she is sometimes sullen about her divorce. I console her—and soon, she will console me in my own. Gloria and I begin to share stories from our childhood. She tells me, in tears, of her family's trauma and of racism in her school. Gloria shares with me a fear of driving that sometimes paralyzes her. And so I ride beside her as she drives to parts of the city well beyond her comfort zone. All the way, I'm whispering, "You can do it, girl. You can do it." And she does.

What I do not know is that Gloria will be a lifelong friend. As I have been her stability during bouts of anxiety, she will be mine during my bouts of depression. She will literally rescue me when I overdose, 38 years later—and I will literally rescue her when she has heart failure. We indeed are sisters, on the deepest level.

With Gloria as my sister in my building and *Daughters of Sarah* being published in my basement, I am perfectly content for five years. Then things start to shift.

3

Awakening Very Tired

At first I simply awaken very tired, even though I've slept for a full eight hours. I try to solve the fatigue by sleeping longer—but it does not go away. And now, added to the fatigue is a vague sense of despair. I try to talk myself out of it, for my life is very good: I have my dear friend, Gloria, living in the apartment below me; I have my feminist sisters; our newsletter, *Daughters of Sarah*, is thriving, and I am its editor; Joel and I are not only lecturing at colleges and seminaries, but also managing to squeeze out money for travel in Europe. My work as assistant director of the Urban Life Center is OK, although it is not as engaging as when I started three years ago.

I talk to my boss about my fatigue and despair, and with compassionate eyes, she suggests I seek counseling. She knows a good therapist, whom she is actually seeing herself: Jeff Allanson. This sounds like a good idea, so I begin. But this turns out to be a very, very bad referral.

The type of therapy that Jeff does is body therapy. The theory behind it is that trauma of the psyche is locked into the body, and so the therapy includes a form of massage. This goes well for three months. Some of my concern about my future career path is addressed. I have worked with college students in two settings, but it doesn't seem quite right to continue. Some of the fear of punishment and hell from my early upbringing is released. But I do not talk about the sexual abuse. If fact, it is only during the visits to my family in Canada—when I see Edmond—that I remember it. I stay well away from him on these visits. I realize later that by this time, I have tucked many of these memories way back into my unconscious mind.

But three months into the counseling, in a session that seems normal at first, I am shocked: in the massage, Jeff touches my breasts in a very seductive manner. I see that he has unzipped his trousers and is prepared for some sexual encounter. I do not say a word to him; I simply rush from his office and never return. I do not say a word to anyone about this abuse. I carry the secret alone. This now is the third sexual abuse secret—the first one by the hired man on the farm when I was 6, the second one by Edmond at age 15, and now this one.

I later realize some of the effects of carrying these secrets alone—one of which is feelings of intense loneliness, which I solve, at least somewhat, by reaching out to other people. I go out for coffee with a friend; I talk to my sister, Rachel, on the phone; I find a project to do. A great deal of the time, however, I unconsciously "forget" about the abuse. But repression always works its havoc on the psyche, and sometimes, it can even lead to destructive behaviors.

Of course, this horrible therapy experience adds to my despair. Yet it has one good outcome: it has reawakened my love of psychology, which began way back in high school. Now I wonder how to combine that psychology with the spirituality and theology I studied in college and seminary. This curiosity seems to grow and, over a period of several months, it seems to replace some of the despair.

I am filled with all kinds of questions. What part of dreams reveals a healthy spirituality? What part is neurotic? What part of the psyche gets stuck in a neurotic grasping for God; in living in fear of being abandoned by God? How does a healthy ego intersect with an oppressive church? How does psychotherapy actually work? I need a place to pursue these questions and a million more. I also need a place that will train me to be a therapist, because I have learned in my work with college students that I am a natural at informal counseling. With training, I believe I could be very good at it on a professional level.

I discuss all of this with Joel. While he does not understand my passion for psychology, he does know that I need a change in my life. He suggests

I do a Ph.D. in psychology and religion. At first I hesitate, fearing that I could not handle the rigor of a Ph.D., but he is convinced I can. With a little research, I find that Northwestern University has a Ph.D. program that perfectly fits my interests. Northwestern is located in Evanston, the first suburb north of Chicago, and is easily accessible to me. It offers a Ph.D. in conjunction with Garrett-Evangelical Theology Seminary, thus uniquely combining psychology and religion. It also provides the training necessary to become both a pastoral counselor and a clinical psychologist. I'm very excited. My plan is to end my work with the Urban Life Center, continue with *Daughters of Sarah*, and pursue my doctorate.

I apply for the program. The application has two parts to it: a written portion and a personal interview. The written portion goes well, and with Joel's help, I craft it in such a way that my interest in psychology and religion and counseling weave themselves together beautifully.

It is the interview with Dr. Leland, the chairman of the department, that gets complicated. It first starts out pleasant, with me making my case for my fitness in the program. But then it turns to my personal life. "Do you have any children?" Dr. Leland asks. Of course, my answer is "no." "Are you planning to have children?" he presses. I curtly respond, "I don't know if I ever want children, but if I do, I will not have them until after I finish my Ph.D." I am shocked at his questions. I do not ask him if he questions the male applicants about children. I do not tell anyone that he has asked—not even Joel. I carry this sexist inquisition on my own. I think I have settled the issue: I go to the doctor and have my IUD checked— this is the birth control device that is supposedly foolproof—and all is well. I am 29 years old, and there is plenty of time to have children, should I want them.

There is yet one more requirement for full acceptance into the program: the commitment to receive individual counseling. The purpose of this is to understand inner conflicts and early wounds so they can be managed and not interfere with the counseling one provides. I agree that this is an excellent requirement, and I immediately begin counseling with a reputable woman recommended by Dr. Leland.

My counseling is quite disturbing. Dreams of men chasing me—the same dreams I had in my childhood—begin to surface. Fear of failure and judgment haunt me. A fear of being alone surfaces. Anger, at times, seems to come out of nowhere. With help from my counselor, I come to understand the origin of these, and I express the pain that has been held for so long. I only hope that they are now resolved; I soon learn that they are not. Also, once again, I do not discuss the sexual abuse.

My courses start in September of 1975, and I am 30 years old. I love the courses. While demanding, they are not overwhelming. I know this is where I belong, and I am deeply grateful to be part of the program. But in late October, I start to get sick. At first, I think it's the flu. I become very nauseous—nauseous in a way that is unlike anything I've experienced in the past. Could it be? Yes, it is. It is morning sickness. I share this with Joel, but we tell no one. I'm not ready. Yet, I find that I'm already in love with my baby. I do not consider an abortion—not even for a moment.

One week after I learn I am pregnant, I make an appointment with Dr. Leland. I'm very worried that I may lose my place in the program. After all, I had promised to not get pregnant. As I enter his office, I feel myself tearing up. I feel like a little girl confessing to an angry father. So after I tell him about my pregnancy, I say, "I'm sorry Dr. Leland, I'm sorry." But Dr. Leland is kind. With a gentle hand on my shoulder, he assures me that I will keep my place in the program. He gives me the choice of going part-time, of staying full-time or of dropping out for a while.

I decide to stay in the program full-time while I'm pregnant, then go part-time when my baby is born. Though I love my courses, I love the baby growing in my womb even more. I find myself often chatting with him, assuring him of my love. By this time I know my baby is a boy. Six months into my pregnancy, I realize we haven't chatted in a while. So I run the bath water, crawl into the tub, rub my big tummy and whisper to him, "Do you look like me? Like your daddy?" He seems to answer, "I look like both my mommy and my daddy." By this time, we have decided on a name for our baby boy: Nathan. It sounds just right. The kind of right you can feel in your stomach. The last three months of the pregnancy go quickly and smoothly, and before we know it, Nathan is born.

It is nothing short of sheer ecstasy to see him take his first breath and enter the big world beyond the womb. He has that red, shriveled baby skin, which to me is pure and beautiful. The love that I felt for him when I first learned of my pregnancy is now magnified into infinity, and Nathan's birth is an experience that takes me into a spiritual realm in a way that I have never felt before. It is a place where I am joined with the divine in some mystical and fundamental way. I feel it at the core of my being.

Breastfeeding has somewhat the same effect on me. It feels like a miracle, and it nurtures me as much as it nurtures Nathan. I surprise myself at the utter joy and delight of it all. My maternal hormones are running rampant. I surprise my feminist friends, although they in no way criticize me. They are totally supportive of me, as is Joel. I, however, now stop my work as editor of *Daughters of Sarah*, though I continue as a member. I realize that to be editor is far too much to juggle.

I rock and rock Nathan. I sing to him for hours. At least, that's how it feels to me. My mother has given me her rocking chair, which perfectly fits my small body. I sing the song my grandfather had sung to me 25 years ago, changing only the name: *Sweet little Nathan boy, sweet little Nathan boy. Sweet little Nathan boy, sweet little Nathan boy. You're my sweet little Nathan boy.* Nathan loves the rocking and the nursing, and soon he begins to sleep through the night. He is a baby who is easily satisfied, and I am deeply fortunate and grateful. I later realize how quickly the memories of my grandfather returned to me. I will, over the years, rock many children and sing to them the song my grandfather sang to me. And each time, there is that little child in me who is being loved. I bow my head in gratitude for my grandfather.

Come autumn, I set out for classes. I pack Nathan in a red-and-white-checkered sling fitted tightly over my heart and stomach. I place it in such a way that he can hear my heartbeat and can be soothed by it, safe in his cradle. My books are packed in a black bag slung over my shoulder. Nathan seems to enjoy my class on psychoanalytic theory as much as I do. The course on the psychology of religious experience speaks to me through my experience in mothering. The male professors do not sense this, but my mothering bones continue to tap into a power and presence much greater than ordinary reality. And so my interests begin to broaden.

Now that I'm a mother, I need to know about the psychology of mothering and about the role of breastfeeding in the development of an infant. I just must know more. I cannot find courses on these subjects at Northwestern's Evanston campus, but I read that a female professor—Niles Newton, in the downtown campus—is conducting research on maternal emotions. I sign up for her class. I start reading about her research even before class begins. She reports that the hormone oxytocin is present in lovemaking, at birth and at lactation. In her book on maternal emotions, she calls oxytocin the hormone of love. This resonates deep within me.

So I again wrap Nathan in his sling, and we hop on the train for the downtown campus. The train lulls him into a deep sleep. When we arrive in our classroom, however, he's hungry and starting to cry. I panic for a moment, but my professor motions to me, indicating that I can breastfeed him right in class. With some fear, I nurse him while taking notes on the side. My classmates approve, judging by the smiles on the faces, and all of this is deeply satisfying. I am grateful for the way in which I have been able to meld my mothering and my coursework.

In three years, my coursework is finished and it's time for exams: four written exams and one oral exam. I manage the written ones just fine, but am terrified of the upcoming oral exam. When I walk into the room where the exam will occur, my fear only intensifies. The examiners are three male professors. When I'm asked the first question, my mind goes absolutely blank. There is a long silence. I am frozen in fear. But Dr. Leland leans over to me, quietly saying, "Lucille, we know you understand the answer to this question. Let me help you get started." His prompting is all I need, and I proceed with the oral exam without another hitch. Dr. Leland, who had originally questioned me about having children, is now clearly an ally.

I then turn my attention to a requirement in my Ph.D. that I have put on hold (or essentially ignored): clergy status. The program prepares one to become both a clinical psychologist and pastoral counselor, but becoming a pastoral counselor requires ministerial standing in one's denomination. I'm stuck. I still belong to my childhood church, Brethren in Christ, but it does not license and ordain women. I agonize. What can I do? Do I jump through hoops and try to find a different denomination that does ordain women? Or do I turn to my own, even though I disagree with much of its theology? I take the easy route, although I do not feel totally comfortable about it.

I contact my church headquarters and am granted an interview. I will need to travel to Nappanee, Indiana for this, where I will go before an examining board of eight men. I am frightened, but I also feel feisty and confident. I make my case before the examining board. "I have a seminary education. I am receiving clinical training. I wish to become a certified pastoral counselor, but for this I need a ministerial license. Would you kindly grant me this?" The eight men are quiet. The room is still. They ask me to leave the room as they talk. In 20 minutes, they bring me back, and Rev. Royer speaks: "We will give you a license with the understanding that you will not be ordained and will not become a pastor. This license is solely for the purpose of you meeting the requirement of becoming a pastoral counselor." He adds: "We know you are qualified and capable of being a pastor, but women are not allowed in our pulpits."

"I understand," I respond. "I will not seek that status." On the one hand, I am relieved. I now have the credential required to become a pastoral counselor. But on the other hand, I'm enraged. My feminist bones are clamoring to fight for more, but I do not have the energy. Raising my son and completing my doctorate is all I can handle.

When getting a ministerial license in the Brethren in Christ, the clear expectation is that you attend a local congregation. Since there are no such congregations in the Chicago area, though, that is not feasible. However, since I have moved away from the conservative beliefs of this denomination, this is just as well for me. Joel and I are, in fact, very lax about attending any church on a regular basis. It's a low priority in our busy lives. He, like me, is more theologically liberal than is the denomination in which he was raised, and to seek out a congregation that better fits us— well, we just seem to never get around to it.

Furthermore, it's time for me to think about a dissertation—which, in some ways, is the most demanding part of my Ph.D. This is where my energy is. But at first, I cannot find a project that intrigues me. My professors suggest a wide range of topics in psychology and religion; nothing sparks my interest. By this time, I'm fretting about Nathan and my own mothering. When he throws temper tantrums, I agonize over whether or not I'm doing something wrong. Is he verbalizing enough? I torment myself with questions and insecurities. I'm consoled somewhat by Donald Winnicott, who reassures mothers that they should never try to be perfect and that "good enough" is plenty enough. I find some rest in Sheila Quirke: "Breathe it in, breathe it out. Let it wrap around you and soothe your tired, worried, guilty soul." Easy to say, but hard to do.

I need more assurance. "Good enough" has never been accepted by my family or by me; "perfection" is the requirement. So I propose a dissertation on mothering: "The relationship between the ego strength of the mother and the social, emotional and cognitive development of the child." The proposal is accepted. I set up a design in which my assistant and I interview 40 mothers who have children between the ages of 6 and 18 months. We go to their homes and observe them as they care for their children, the children stacking blocks or blowing bubbles and the mothers keeping their children from touching the hot stove or falling down the stairs. Then we have the mothers fill out tests on ego strength as we care for the children.

I carefully analyze the results of the data with the help of Dr. Leland. Again, Dr. Leland is my ally. The statistics are clear enough to establish a relationship between the ego strength of the mother and the positive development of the child. I breathe a gigantic sigh of relief. I have satisfied the requirements for my Ph.D. dissertation. But more important for me, personally, is that I have assured myself I'm a "good enough" mother for my darling son Nathan. I take great comfort in Nathan's clear and firm social, emotional and cognitive development, and I feel that my own ego strength is foundational for him. I feel particularly responsible for him, as most of his care falls to me. Joel is now finishing his Ph.D. at the University of Chicago as well as working as head librarian and seminary professor at North Park Theological Seminary.

When I stop to catch my breath at the end of my doctorate, I become aware of a very sobering fact: Joel and I have grown far apart. I have been immersed in my doctorate and in caring for Nathan. Joel has been immersed in his work and his doctorate. While he originally supported me, it soon became clear that he has very little understanding or interest in psychology.

I'm aware of so much that Joel has given me. When we were first married, he gave me that spark for adventure that led me to start *Daughters of Sarah*—something I desperately needed to stave off depression and discover sisterhood for the first time. Joel joined in the historical research on women, and together, we enjoyed lecturing at many colleges. We were a great team. Joel encouraged me to start a Ph.D., even helping me with the application. Then, when I got pregnant, he was as happy about the baby as I was. He loved baby Nathan. He gladly worked and made a living for us while finishing his own Ph.D.

But now home life has become very tense. I snap at Joel for spending our money on books; he snaps at me for spending our money on counseling. I blame him for not doing the dishes; he blames me for who knows what. He withdraws. He keeps his face in his collection of books, which has now grown in number to 8,000.

I start to get confused, and I lose my compass. Depressive symptoms return. Lack of energy and little spark for life sets in. At this low point I become aware of the fact that one of my professors, Dr. Hunter, is showing special interest in me. It's not intellectual; it's sexual. I wonder if he has preyed on other women in the department, but I do not know. At any rate, he approaches me. I later realize how slick and crafty he truly is. I succumb. It happens quickly, and it gives me attention I'm not getting from Joel. It lifts my spirits temporarily and is quite a "high." I later realize this is part of the "manic" in manic depression, which I will battle for years to come.

My relationship with Dr. Hunter soon leaves me feeling isolated, and I realize I cannot hold this secret alone. Holding secrets alone is an utterly lonely place. I must tell someone. I choose my friend Christa, who is a totally safe person. Christa is doing her doctorate in psychology, and we met when completing our clinical training. When I tell Christa, she is in no way judgmental of me, which is a huge load off my back. She is just very, very concerned. Soon after this, Dr. Hunter approaches her. She does not succumb.

At a much later time, Christa tells me that she believes Dr. Hunter is a predator and has preyed on many women over the years. Later in life, I will not only deeply regret my relationship with Dr. Hunter, but will be absolutely stunned that none of us reported him. As far as I know, he went to his grave with his reputation intact and his teaching and writing praised. For me, this is now the fourth sexual predator in my life. Only over time will I truly come to understand the depth of the devastation this has taken on my psyche.

After my relationship with Dr. Hunter ends, I become involved with another man. But where are the feminist muscles I thought I had so carefully developed? Those muscles seem to have atrophied. The fear of being alone that developed during childhood has not subsided, even with all the feminist thinking, individual counseling and marital commitment.

Joel and I seek counseling—or, more precisely, I badger him into counseling. I call him obsessive-compulsive. I call him a bookaholic. The brilliant man I had fallen in love with 12 years ago has become my enemy. A part of me wants him back; another part of me does not. I want to forge ahead and find a new life on my own. A month into the counseling, I know we've grown too far apart to ever recover the friendship and intimacy we once enjoyed. I build a case against him to my friends and family. Of course, I do not tell them of my own dark side, and so, they take my side. I file for divorce. When Joel is out of the country, I have the books appraised. They are only worth $11,000. When Joel returns, he is enraged that I have done this. Our marriage is essentially over.

My heart aches for my own loss, but it aches even more for Nathan. I hate to take him away from his father, for although I have been mainly responsible for him, he and Joel have a strong bond. Joel at times romps with him, builds tall buildings with Legos and reads Star Wars books to him. Seeing his father every other weekend will clearly damage that relationship.

I'm also very frightened. Am I able to survive on my own? I have never before had my own apartment. Will loneliness overwhelm me? I've lived in dorms or apartments with roommates, but can I live alone? Can I raise a child and make a living? I must—and I press on.

Before I find my apartment, I feel a great urgency to tell my parents about the divorce. I agonize. What will they say? Will they be silent? Will they quote Scripture? I'm very frightened of their disapproval. No one in our entire family has ever divorced. While I have left the family nest in so many ways, I want them there to support me when I falter. And they do.

When my parents are visiting, I sit down with them and tell them my version of the story. I see tears in their eyes, but—these are tears of love. Not one word of judgment comes from their lips. Not one word about disgrace. Only gentle hugs. They provide only loving help in caring for Nathan, and I realize that some of their rigidity of beliefs have loosened. I learn that there are many changes that have occurred in the Brethren in Christ Church. My father has softened, and thus my anger with him also softens.

Then, when it's time for graduation, my parents are there again. My mother is glowing. Ten years ago, she had quietly advised: "You go on with your education. I didn't have the chance." And now, again, she quietly relays: "I'm so proud of you, daughter."

For my graduation picture, Nathan—now 4 years old and dressed in a cute brown dress shirt and pants—poses with me. He takes my blue mortarboard and puts it on his head. It is true—he should receive some of the glory. He should be part of the celebration, for he has, indeed, been with me all the way. He was conceived within the first month of my program, and he was the inspiration for my dissertation. His presence gave me the courage to press on when life with Joel had become so difficult.

When my parents visit me in Chicago, our time together is sweet and tension is absent. But when I visit my family in Canada, my fear of Edmond resurfaces. When I see his shifty eyes, I feel revulsion. I stay away from him, never sitting by him at a meal. When I have to stay at his and Ruth's home, I shudder when I go to bed. I lie awake very angry and very frightened. Will he try again to come into my bedroom? But I keep all of this to myself, and I carry this secret alone. When I return to Chicago, the pain from it essentially recedes as I delve into my work and raise Nathan. I later realize how well my unconscious mind has spared me from the deepest hate I actually have for Edmond. It will be many years until all of this fully surfaces.

Upon graduation and armed with my Ph.D., I pursue a career as a pastoral counselor and clinical psychologist. Finding a job is easy—I'm hired by the Pastoral Psychology Institute in Park Ridge, where I did my clinical training. Wishing to expand their services, they ask me to open an office in Logan Square, on the north side of Chicago. My office is at St. Luke's Lutheran Church of Logan Square.

I rent a small apartment for Nathan and me, across from the church. I love the apartment: there is lots of light shining through its many windows, and I love the classic, dark, wood trim and brand-new kitchen. I'm happy with the two bedrooms—they are both small, but are sufficient for our needs. While living alone is a little frightening, it is not nearly as hard as I had imagined. Having the church nearby is comforting. Being a single mom is demanding, but I have chosen to work only two-thirds time. This leaves me with considerable time for Nathan. I soon find a preschool for Nathan where the teachers clearly adore the children and love to teach them their letters and numbers. I feel Nathan is in good and safe hands while I'm at my office. I struggle some when I am home alone, without Nathan, but I manage. I date some, and that helps.

I love my work. In my casual gray suit and red scoop-neck sweater, I visit neighborhood clergy and tell them about my counseling. Clients soon become plentiful—too plentiful for me alone. So I hire my friend, Christa—the special friend in whom I had confided that I had a relationship with my professor. She is totally trustworthy.

Soon after she begins work with me at St. Luke's Church, she moves into my apartment building. It's such a comfort to have her nearby. She adores Nathan and vice versa, so the stress of being a single mom is again alleviated. Christa is one of those people whose very presence is soothing and whose demeanor is invariably kind. She gently asks how you're doing and she listens intently. There is no harshness or judgment in her. I feel very blessed to have her in my life in such an intimate way.

A month after Christa joins me, a new pastor comes to St. Luke's Lutheran Church. The pastor is Luke Shannon. He is about our age, and is clearly a bachelor. I quickly realize that he shares many of Christa's qualities—he is kind, nonjudgmental and soothing in his very presence. Luke also brings with him a practice of silence and meditation. While an avid reader and brilliant individual, he does not have the compulsiveness for mastering knowledge and climbing professional ladders that has been so much a part of my being and approach to life. Luke filters his intellectual pursuits through silence and solitude. This brings him to a place of softness, a place of less intensity than what I have ever known.

In Luke and Christa, I sense an opportunity to create a very deep friendship—to be like a family for each other, and though not a marital or biological family, one that is deeply loving, committed, supportive and spiritual. I ask them if they are interested in meeting together on a regular basis. They are. As single people, they, too, need a family: Christa's family lives in Louisiana, and Luke's lives in Pennsylvania. We begin to weave our lives together.

We meet on Sunday afternoons at my house, and it soon becomes routine. We begin our time together by playing with Nathan—whatever he wants to play. Sometimes, it's kickball; at other times, it's simple football. While Luke is not athletic, he lets loose for Nathan. Often, we stay inside and piece together an animal puzzle or build a Sears tower with wooden blocks. Then it's time to eat. Again, we work around Nathan's favorites—spaghetti, meatloaf and pizza. One of us reads a story to him, and then Nathan is off to bed.

With Nathan asleep, we have time for each other. Luke does a short reading—often from Thomas Merton, a Catholic monk. Merton's contemplative words helps us settle into opening our hearts to God and to our own inner wisdom. After the reading we dim the lights, light a candle and sit in silence. A deep stillness comes into the room and into our hearts. After 15 minutes of silence, we share what is on our hearts. Sometimes, a comforting word or insight has grown out of the reading. We share our joys as well as our pain. The sadness about my divorce surfaces, and sometimes the anger breaks out. Sometimes contentment arises, simply because I know I've done the right thing. But what I do not share with Luke and Christa is the pain of my childhood sex abuse or the abuse from my therapist.

After sharing our joys and our pain, we pray. Holding hands, we ask God for wisdom and strength. We pray that I will have wisdom in parenting Nathan and in counseling clients. We pray that Christa will have wisdom in counseling and in finishing her doctorate. We pray that Luke will have strength in preaching Sunday after Sunday, in mediating some fierce conflicts in his church and in visiting the sick. We thank God for one another and for this family, where harshness is absent; conformity is not demanded; and achievements are not required. We feel deeply sustained by one another and by God. What we do not realize is that this family will sustain us for years to come.

With Luke and Christa, I have my first experience of sitting in silent meditation. I have taken to it quickly, and I know I need more of it. For my entire life, I have rushed from one achievement to another, never sitting still. I have never truly reflected on the experiences I've had or on the one I'm headed for. I later come to realize the compulsiveness in this—in the panic I feel if I am not productive.

But I want more silence. Sitting with Christa and Luke once a week is not enough. I need more. I tell my friends: "I've had too many words in my life. Too many words in church." So I decide to visit the Quakers. I know that they sit silently for worship, but I have not known anyone who is a Quaker. Yet I believe I need that experience for myself. So I pack Nathan in my orange Volkswagen Beetle and we head for the Quaker Meeting in Hyde Park, on the south side of Chicago.

When we arrive, we find a small group of people—about 30 adults and 10 children. We are warmly invited to join them. The children go off to their own class, while the adults sit in silence for one hour. The meeting room is small—about 30 feet by 50 feet. There are no crosses or other religious symbols in the room. The walls are beautifully paneled in dark walnut, and light comes in through the large windows at both the front and back of the room. Chairs are arranged in rows so that the worshipers at one end of the room are facing those at the other end.

At first, sitting in silence for an hour is hard. My inner chatter seems endless. But after 10 minutes or so, I settle. A deep peace seems to move through me. Sometimes a hymn comes to mind, and I find myself singing it silently. Often, the hymn that I learned in seminary surfaces: *God of my life, through all the circling years, I trust in thee.* Or, *Spirit of the living God, fall afresh on me.*

Sitting in silence in a large group of people is a different experience than sitting with just a few or sitting alone. It seems that the energy released in opening one's heart to God is magnified. It is a powerful and holy energy and presence. It is a place where one's own inner wisdom, and the wisdom of God, is so accessible.

A central Quaker belief is that of "the light within." God's light is in everyone. Everyone can experience it, and sitting silently together is a superb way to feel and know it. Most Quakers, then, do not have clergy, as do other denominations. All people are bearers of God's light.

It's not that Quakers have no spoken words in worship—they do—but these words can come from any worshipper who feels led by God to share. Most of the time, however, there is silence for the full hour of worship. When, on occasion, someone does share, the message is always short and is followed by more silence.

The children join the worship for the last 10 minutes. They, too, sit in silence, though they often squirm and need parents to remind them to be still. But it amazes me the way the children sense the spirit of silence, and I am proud of Nathan, now age 5, who naturally joins in.

At the end of the worship, there is time for audibly sharing joys and concerns. The Quakers express this: "Is there anyone you would like to 'hold in the light?'" I am so touched by that expression, "hold in the light." Perhaps it is really no different than saying "I'd like to pray for this person," but "holding them in the light" feels so much warmer.

It is for a full year that I worship with the Quakers. This, combined with the serenity I experience with Luke and Christa, leaves me more settled and peaceful than I have ever felt in my life. I am now beginning to comprehend, on a deep level, what Thomas Merton means about meditation: that it is a gift of awakening to God's spirit that is within us. (Paraphrased from *New Seeds of Contemplation*, page 3.) It is an awakening also to the inner wisdom that is within us. I often leave Quaker worship with a new wisdom about something I am wrestling with or new strength to carry on in my daily life. What I do not realize at the time is that meditation will become the bedrock of my spiritual life. Over the years, I will find countless ways to meditate and return to that bedrock. Yes, I will become part of congregations in several denominations. I will be fed— at least somewhat—by those congregations, and I will find many good friends in those settings. But it is the inner wisdom that I receive in silent meditation that will speak most deeply to my spiritual longings; that will nurture me through the most painful times.

Yet there are times when the peace from meditation does not carry through into my everyday life. Sometimes a mild depression hovers over me. Just a bad case of the blues; a bad case of loneliness. I can usually solve it by becoming productive—in my work, in my apartment or in doing something special with Nathan, Krista or Luke.

What I do not realize until much later in life is that within me, there is a low-grade depression that I am always keeping at bay. The reality is that it is not all that easy living without a partner. I am, after all, an extrovert, and I get my energy from being with others.

So, I look for men to date. I find one who may be a good candidate; I find another who, from the beginning, does not feel right. I also briefly date a man I meet at a spiritual retreat. But no one really fits. And then I meet Louie.

4

Nothing Short
of Endearing

He's a fascinating-looking man. Louie looks Mediterranean and I soon learn that his mother's family is from Iran and his father's family is from Germany. Louie is bald—very bald—and when he starts talking in his animated, warm voice, his baldness becomes nothing short of endearing. When I arrive at his apartment, the candles are lit, the wine is chilled and the steak is marinated. The evening is a total success, and we begin to date.

Louie, like Joel, is a scholar and a seminary professor. He's also an ordained Methodist minister, an archaeologist and a well-published expert in Holy Land pottery—and he leads expeditions in the Holy Land regularly. Louie teaches at Garrett-Evangelical Theological Seminary—where I did part of my Ph.D. work—but I have never previously met him. I've only heard about his captivating lectures and sermons.

Louie has now been divorced for three years and, like me, wants to settle. He is 44 years old and I am 36. He is as charming with Nathan as he is with me. What more can a mother want? I meet his son, Jimmy, age 13, and his daughter Carolyn, age 8. I like the idea of being a step-mom, and I find ways to engage his children—even though they are a bit distant at first. I invite them over for pizza and games. Very quickly, "Pig-mania"—a dice game in which the dice are tiny pigs that, when thrown, land in different positions—becomes our favorite game. Each position scores different points, and so Louie and I and the children shout, clap

and bicker around my kitchen table, thereby bonding with one another
and forming a new family.

Louie joins me on Sunday evenings with Christa and Luke. He helps
cook dinner, and when Nathan is settled, he sits with us in silence. He
freely shares his joys and sorrows, and in our prayers, he fervently seeks
God's wisdom and strength. He has a very tender side, and often, tears fall
gently from his eyes. I sense that he is a man of deep faith, and he appears
to have it well integrated with his sharp intellect. The only oddity about
Louie is that in the midst of it all, he steps out for a smoke—Marlboros,
with the filter twisted off. And then, after Christa and Luke leave, he has
a few bourbons before heading home. I'm not fond of this, but I ignore it,
reminding myself that he's from a family in which smoking and drinking
are—unlike in my family—quite normal.

Louie introduces me to his mother, his aunt and his uncle. They have
that Mediterranean warmth that attracts me to Louie. At Christmas, they
invite Nathan and me to join them, showering me with silk scarves and
Nathan with gigantic Star Wars figures.

In six months, Louie and I decide to get married. He takes me to a
high-end jeweler in downtown Chicago and we choose a dark, red ruby
for my engagement ring. I have never before had any ring other than my
perfectly plain wedding band, and I'm excited because I know I am entering a world quite different than what I've known.

We are married four months later, at St. Luke's Lutheran Church. One
of Louie's clergy friends performs the ceremony, Luke plays the organ and
Christa stands beside me. I wear a turquoise, street-length silk dress and
matching shoes. Louie wears a three-piece, navy-blue suit. Our boys wear
navy-blue suits and his daughter wears a blue-and-white dress. We blend
together very nicely.

My family comes to the wedding, relieved that I have found such a nice,
Christian man. The fact that he is a seminary professor, a Methodist minister and a well-published archaeologist are all in his favor. They in no way
seem to object to the fact that he is not a conservative evangelical Christian. They do not know about his smoking and drinking.

In the wedding service, the congregation sings Louie's favorite hymn: *I
love to tell the story of Jesus and his love.* Louie was raised in a home in which
his German father was often distant and sometimes cruel. He found love

and acceptance in a nearby Methodist church, where the minister was like
a father to him—who saw in Louie a jewel that needed polishing and a
mind that needed encouragement. Louie loves to tell the story of the love
he found in that home and the love that he found in Jesus. And so, in our
wedding, we sing about Jesus and his love.

The wedding is in April. Come June, we head to Lake Webster, in
northeast Indiana, to visit friends. We fall in love with Lake Webster, and
the next weekend, we return: we buy a sweet little green cottage just a
block off the lake. A month later, we buy a brand-new motorboat that
is big enough to seat six people. We buy two sets of water skis, life jack-
ets, wetsuits—all the paraphernalia for weekends at the lake. We have a
marvelous time. This is the first of our spending sprees—but, we have two
good salaries, and we can afford it.

Water skiing is a dream I've always had but never fulfilled. I take to
it immediately. Soon I am speeding across the water. By midsummer
I'm jumping the waves or skiing in pairs. Though our cottage is tiny, our
friends and family pour in. Louie grills hot dogs and steaks; I toss a salad
and then dip the ice cream. I've never been happier. Louie stays up late
for a couple drinks and a few more smokes, and I head for bed, happily
exhausted.

Back home, a complication arises in my professional life. My church,
the Brethren in Christ Church, disapproves of my marriage. I am called
to meet with the ministerial board. They say that marrying after divorce
is a sin—a form of adultery. Divorce itself is not a sin, but remarriage
is—and thus the requirement is celibacy. The result is that my ministerial
license is revoked—a license I had so carefully pursued, since it is required
for becoming a pastoral counselor. I'm angry, but my life with Louie is so
good that I do not let it consume me.

Furthermore, Louie soon finds a solution to my problem. He talks to a
friend of his—Les Chase, who is pastor of First Congregational Church of
Evanston. Les says that his congregation can ordain me. As it is independent and not part of a large denomination, the congregation itself ordains
its clergy. In four months, I meet with the church ministerial committee and am ordained. It is a relief on at least two levels: it gives me the
requirement I need for maintaining my status as a pastoral counselor, and
it situates me in a church that is consistent with my own spirituality and

theological understanding. I am no longer an evangelical in my thinking or in my way of living; I am a mainline liberal protestant, and have been since I studied at Yale Divinity School. Back in college, I had wondered if I would ever leave my family denomination. I now have my answer.

There is so much that I like about mainline Protestants. I like that they, in interpreting Scripture, do not attempt a literal interpretation; rather, they pay much more attention to historical context. I like the fact that becoming a Christian is understood to be a gradual awakening to God's love, rather than a sudden conversion. I like the fact that God's grace and love far outweigh God's judgment. I like the fact that all people are welcomed—black, white, gay, straight, divorced or remarried. For me, becoming a congregational minister is also about finding a church home where I fit.

Yet, I have not left all of my childhood spirituality behind. Some of this is sweet; some is harsh. In part of my psyche, there remains beautiful sentiments of the love of Jesus. At times, the children's song still sings to me: *Jesus loves me, this I know, for the Bible tells me so.* At the same time, however, deep feelings of guilt and fear are stowed away in my psyche. Sometimes, when Louie is not where I expect him to be, I fear for a second that the Lord has returned and I am left behind. Abandoned. This is the same fear I had as a child, when my mother was not where I expected her to be. I am dismayed at the depth of such fears. Even with all of the therapy I have been through, these fears sometimes catch me off guard and stubbornly remain within me.

When Louie and I are at home in Evanston, we are at church. But often, we are at our cottage in Indiana, delighting in the lake or just sitting on the porch with friends. I teach Nathan to fish, as my grandpa had taught me: capturing the worms, stringing them on the hook, attaching a sinker and casting the line. Nathan and I have fancy fishing rods, but I sometimes miss the long, bamboo poles that grandpa had. Still, it's great fun and we often land little bluegills, just like the ones I caught with grandpa. I fry them in flour and butter and serve them with fresh lemon. Grandpa would be proud, and I love fishing with Nathan as much as I loved it with him. In our blended family, I cherish these special times with Nathan. On occasion, Louie makes a disparaging remark about this, and I think he feels a little left out—so I'm careful to invite him to join us.

In the fall, I become acquainted with Louie in still different ways. There is the hunting and the guns. This is all new to me, and I'm fascinated. So I buy all the hunting gear—the orange vest and fatigues—and sometimes I go with him to hunt deer. While I am never with him when he kills a deer, the intensity of sitting silently and waiting for one provides a thrill of adventure that I've never had before. It also, is some subtle way, seems to be a type of meditation, sitting silently and expectantly in nature. Perhaps the analogy ends there, but there is something very grounding about it all.

In addition to hunting, I experience Louie's love for football. Back in college, at Illinois Wesleyan University, he had played tight end. Louie is not a large man—just medium-size— but he is strong and fast. He had been accepted at the University of Chicago but declined because they did not have football. He tells me: "I wanted a college where I could play football and become a preacher." Football is new to me, and I often sit with him as he watches—or, rather, as he shouts when his team scores and curses when they lose. He carefully explains the intricacies of the plays and scoring, but I do not get it. So, by midseason, I'm off cooking or cleaning. With a beer in hand, Louie seems fine. He watches every football game from beginning to end, all season long.

What I also experience that fall is Louie's quick and fierce temper. It seems to come out of nowhere, and I am stunned. He is sometimes very demeaning, as he shouts, "You can't sort shit from apple butter!" He frightens me. But I do not challenge him, just as my mother did not challenge my father in his angry outbursts. And as quick as Louie's temper flares up, it disappears—and he moves into his loving and charming self. I later realize how the pattern of repressing abuse, whether sexual or emotional, was set in me from early childhood. I will realize that reversing the pattern is as hard as removing superglue from paper.

Come summer, we're back at the cottage, palling around with friends. We compete in water skiing and cold-water dipping. For water dipping, the challenge is about enduring the cold water. Who can ski earliest in the spring and latest in the fall? Of course, I'm always up for competition. That first year I lose the competition, but in a few more years, I will win it in the fall. It is October 1. The water is cold but the sun is hot. Louie says, "Come on, we'll win! I'll take you skiing—you can be last in the water." I cannot resist. We take the boat out and I jump into the water, which is now freezing cold. He starts to pull me up, but the motor sputters and I drop back down. Eight seconds later, when the motor picks up, I pop out of the water—now twisting my back very sharply. I stay up on my skis and win the completion, but my back is injured—badly. I go for physical therapy, massage and acupuncture. I take pain pills. Nothing helps. What I do not realize is that this back injury will cause severe pain for the rest of my life, even though it will be slightly alleviated with surgery 15 years later. But I will always have the satisfaction of remembering that I won the competition!

The next summer, Nathan, Louie and I are off to Israel for one of Louie's archaeological expeditions. The site is Sepphoris, a city three kilometers from Nazareth. Nazareth is the town where Jesus lived; Sepphoris is a city Jesus most certainly would have frequented. The whole archaeological experience is exhilarating. We begin the day at 5:30 a.m. with a light breakfast at a hotel in Nazareth, where we stay. Then we take a bus to the site. The archaeologists have carefully laid out small squares, and we are assigned to one. We are given small tools for digging for small pieces of pottery and large picks for digging through layers of dirt.

Come 8:30, it's time for a break and a "second breakfast:" hard-boiled eggs, cheese, bread, hummus, plenty of fruit and ice water. The day's labor ends at noon, and we pile back on the bus to return to the hotel for showers and a nap. After naps, it's time for "pottery reading," when the archaeologists sit behind a long table and carefully examine each piece while explaining what it is. It's magical to those of us watching and listening. How do they know that this 5-inch piece of pottery was once part of a cooking pot? They explain why: it may be the texture—smooth, not rough; or it may be the shape—only slightly rounded; or it may be the color—medium brown, rather than light. It is truly thrilling to hear the explanations. The whole archaeological experience is one of great adventure, and we feel like true explorers. It is almost as much fun as founding a feminist magazine 13 years earlier. Back then, we women discovered long-lost women in our church history. In Israel, we are part of an expedition that helps piece together the early history of the Christian world.

In addition to the thrill of discovery is my great pride in being married to a man as distinguished as Louie. He is even more distinguished than my first husband. What I am not aware of, though, is the extent to which being related to a powerful and distinguished man is central to my identity and my sense of self. My feminist ideology is absolutely contrary to this, but my childhood experience of being the daughter of a beloved minister runs deeper in my psyche than does my feminism.

It is also a point of great pride to watch Nathan at the dig. Although only 9 years old, he keeps pace with the adults. I love to work side-by-side with him, and together, we discover a piece of pottery in the hard soil. It's like finding a diamond. His energy seems endless in the search, and he is just such a joy to be with. I feel truly blessed.

Back home, my professional life is humming along nicely. I am invited to become director of a pastoral counseling center in Evanston: The Samaritan Pastoral Counseling Center. This center is a member of the Samaritan Institute, in Denver, which oversees 50 other such centers across the country. The Evanston center is small, with only one other staff member, and my job is to develop it into a multi-staff center. I am to be executive director as well as a part-time therapist, and for me, this is the perfect combination. While I did this in Chicago, I will now be doing it on a larger scale.

Working in Evanston among upper-middle-class people is a challenge. I am well accustomed to the academic world, but functioning in upper-middle-class society—with lawyers and CEOs—is quite different. Establishing offices in churches, developing brochures and building budgets is sometimes a stretch. Fundraising is the biggest challenge of all—most especially the gala fundraisers, where dancing is the culmination of the evening. I am very awkward, and I find myself barely able to keep in step. Louie understands, and he gently guides me across the dance floor. I manage to avoid dancing with anyone else. With all my agility in sports, it amazes me that I can barely keep in step on the dance floor. But then I realize that my early upbringing is still with me, and on some unconscious level, I partly believe dancing is a sin.

While I like being an administrator, my love for clients never wanes. At the depth of my being, I am never more at peace than when sitting with clients. I leave my own agenda at the door and enter their world, providing that loving presence which enables them to grow. I believe that insight is necessary, of course, but without love it is empty. I tell my staff: "If you sense in the initial evaluation that you will not be able to grow to love this client, you must refer him or her at the outset. Without love, no one can heal, no one can grow."

For me, the challenge of love comes with a client named Carrie. Carrie is withdrawn and fearful, having been abused by both her father and husband. Carrie's very soul seems to be dark and full of shame. Her ego is paper-thin, and I quickly know that only long-term therapy will help her. I know that this will take special care and much love.

The care comes in many ways. It comes in terms of setting firm boundaries and consistent structures. I carefully keep the sessions to 50 minutes—no more, no less. I carefully show warmth toward her, but am in no way effusive—for she is overwhelmed easily. I am careful in telling her well in advance when I need to be absent, as sudden changes would feel like abuse.

Over time, Carrie begins to trust me. She shares her night dreams, which are full of abuse and terror; she shares her daytime feelings, which are filled with shame and doubt. Together, we gently uncover destructive patterns: her attraction to abusive men and her shame at the slightest hint of disapproval. Over a period of three years, Carrie develops a strong sense of self—an ego that will not be deflated at the hint of disapproval. She gradually finds inner peace. I know that my warm presence and love has been lifesaving for her. I am grateful that I knew, when we first met, that Carrie would be a client I could grow to love. I am grateful that I have been able to be consistent with her, even when things in my own life were shaky. Over time, she goes to graduate school and becomes a therapist. She provides love and stability for her clients, just as I provided these for her.

The clients I see are all individuals; I do not see couples or families. I have not been trained in marriage and family therapy and I am careful to not try to provide what I do not know. My divorce from Joel also erodes any confidence that I might otherwise have in helping others with marriage problems. While I had, in fact, initiated the divorce, I still feel a deep sense of failure. I sometimes feel regret that I had not tried harder. In some ways, I feel deep guilt. Only later do I come to understand how this guilt, combined with the shame and guilt from my childhood, plummets me into the dark hole of depression.

But life with Louie is good—at least most of the time. We love to entertain friends and family, both old and new. Louie's strong presence, filled with warmth and humor, provides fun for all. My friend Gloria—now a friend of 12 years—is usually around our holiday table. Her warmth and enthusiasm, matched with Louie's, makes it a party for all.

Christa and Luke are still in our lives, and we now join them monthly, along with four new friends. We share spiritual writings and we meditate together, sitting in warm silence. During these times of meditation, I experience an inner wisdom and peace that I know comes from God. I often emerge from the silence knowing an answer to a problem that had been weighing on my mind. The meditation is a very sweet time. I am also always touched by the depth of Louie's participation, which serves as a window to that part of his soul and psyche where love and peace reside; where the untamed and destructive parts of him are well under wraps.

Louie, Nathan and I make frequent trips to Canada. Louie comfortably joins in family gatherings, whether it is sitting around a table for a feast, playing a game of Monopoly or singing around the piano. I keep a safe distance from Edmond, but the deep pain of the abuse has receded, at least for a while. But I do not say a word about this to Louie. I do not tell him about any of the abuse of my past.

Three years into our marriage, we buy a house in Evanston and two more small boats at the lake. We're never happier than when we're shopping. Coming down from shopping highs, though, I sometimes dip into depression—not severe, but depression nonetheless. It's the kind of depression that makes it hard to get out of bed in the morning, and if I don't have something planned, I am at a loss for what to do. There is only a dark emptiness inside my stomach, or sometimes a low-grade anger at Louie for drinking too much or cursing for no apparent reason. This depression does not last long, and when I get to work or find a new project at home, I'm mostly functional. This is the same pattern that I had in my early years of marriage to Joel, and this is the pattern that will continue for years to come. This will continue until I face squarely both the depressive side of my psyche and the manic. I come to understand much later that my life with Louie was full of manic behaviors—especially shopping sprees. There is nothing like shopping to fill that dark empty feeling and drive away depression. But the cure is only temporary!

Six years into the marriage, we buy a new cottage—a beautiful cottage right on the lake. With its big deck and three bedrooms, we're set up for guests. They pour in—relatives from Canada and friends from Chicago, all so happy that Lucille has married a "family man." Louie's charm is flowing when they visit; his foul temper, smoking and drinking are safely stowed away.

Back home, our blended family is working well. Louie's son, Jimmy, moves in with us for high school. We go to his pole-vaulting contests and we listen to his band. Nathan, by this time, is playing chess. Joel taught him at age 6, though I did not pay much attention to his chess playing at first. Then, in middle school, he stays after hours to play. In high school, he goes to the Jewish Cultural Center and plays with the Russian-Jewish men. The fact that Nathan does not know Russian—and they do not know English—adds to the fun. It is at this time that I realize that Nathan is truly brilliant. He starts winning local and state competitions. This culminates in his last year of high school, when he takes first place in chess for the entire state of Illinois. This, of course, hits the local papers, and he becomes somewhat of an Evanston celebrity in the fall parade. I am one proud mama.

I, myself, have a good reputation in Evanston. The Samaritan Center has grown steadily over the past eight years. We have six therapists besides myself, which means that we're seeing more than 100 clients every week. Our center is known for providing top-notch care. On a broader scale, my professional work is moving ahead nicely: I have become a member of the advisory board of the Samaritan Institute in Denver, the umbrella organization of my center; I have published several articles in pastoral counseling journals; I have been licensed as a clinical psychologist; and I have been hired by the Illinois School of Professional Psychology to work one day per week.

Then something happens at my center: one of the counselors, Bart, becomes sexually involved with a female client. After the relationship ends, Bart tells me what has happened. He also confesses that he paid her $1,000 to cover up the affair. I fire him immediately and he moves away from Evanston, never to be heard of again. Yet, I later realize that in allowing him to just slink away, I helped in the cover-up and I kept the secret. I realize I never followed up with his victim; I never offered her support and care. I'm later very, very appalled at myself for repeating the whole pattern of secrecy that I had been victim to. I am stunned that, with all of my education and feminism, I did not truly defend this victim and I did not bring legal charges against Bart. I did nothing to prevent the likelihood of his abusing another client in a different setting. This will be a regret and a scar that I will carry for years to come. Only well into the future will I be able to forgive myself for all of this.

It is soon after this that I take a trip to Canada. I go by myself specifically to tell my sister Rachel about the sexual abuse by Edmond, about the response from my parents and about the abuse by the hired man at age 6. Rachel believes all of this without question. Rachel is always, always a person I can trust.

Later, I realize that the trip to Canada fades in and out of my memory. I remember it 8 years later, which is the time I go and stay with my sisters when I am so deeply depressed. At that time, I tell Rachel that I am afraid to stay at Ruth and Edmond's house overnight. She understands and she makes sure that I stay with her and Don every night.

But after that, it seems that I have forgotten about that trip. It is, in fact, 26 years later that Rachel tells me about the trip. I will later try to analyze this. Why did I not remember it? Was the whole secret of the abuse so painful that I did not even remember telling the secret? Now that is pain—pain at a dark, deep unconscious level.

It is now 10 years into my marriage; I am 47 and Louie is 55. We are sometimes in serious conflict, and in his angry outbursts, Louie calls me "a careerist"—meaning that I am too focused on my career and not on him. I respond by spending more time with him, watching TV together or cooking his favorite meals. I do not directly confront him about his accusations because I am afraid of his temper—not physically, but emotionally. In addition, I do not share with anyone the stress of keeping all of the family and professional balls in the air.

Louie also accuses me of being a "depressive." Again, I do not engage him in this, but I do begin individual counseling. The demons of depression that I address are those related to my strict religious upbringing. I come to understand, at a deeper level than in my previous counseling, all of the guilt and fear that I carry. I remember my early fear of burning in hell—even for a sin as small as getting angry at my sister. Yet even with all of this new understanding gained through counseling, I continue to live with fear. At the core of my being, I fear punishment—and Louie's deprecating accusations feed into that fear.

At this time I also see a psychiatrist. I ask him if he thinks an antidepressant would help, and his answer is "yes." So I try Zoloft. It helps a little, but not much. I do not realize that this begins a lifetime of taking antidepressants, with me always unsure of whether or not they're helping. But I still take them, just in case.

With our marriage on the verge of collapse, I insist on marriage counseling. The counseling works for a while: I come to understand some of Louie's volatility, and he comes to understand some of my depression. We give each other space and we both begin to change. I confront more demons of my depression, but I still do not address the sexual abuse, the anger related to it and the deep shame that lies repressed within me. I do not address the fact that my identity is rooted firmly in my relationship to a powerful male and in my academic and professional accomplishments.

In the marriage counseling, Louie confronts some of the roots of his own inner violence—some of the ways he was abused by his father and ignored by his mother. Louie does not, however, address his drinking—and surprisingly, our marriage counselor does not, either. But I begin to address it. I start to attend Al-Anon, the companion program of Alcoholics Anonymous that is for families and friends of alcoholics. Here I learn that I have expended tremendous amounts of energy trying, in subtle ways, to either keep Louie from drinking or cover up his drinking. I have denied the severity of it to myself and to others. I see how I have stayed loyal to him even when he is verbally abusive to me. I see how I have tried desperately to keep his love. All of this insight from Al-Anon is helpful, at least for a while.

Despite the problems, there is so much that I like about Louie and our marriage. I like his warmth, affection and humor in our good times. I like a "center stage man," especially one with such a strong intellect and wide range of experiences. I like his faith that shines through, despite his meanness and drunkenness. I like the shopping sprees and all the "stuff" we've accumulated. It is so different from my first marriage, where there were plenty of books, but not much else.

The "stuff" from a shopping spree, whether it be a fur coat or a new car, leaves me on a "high." I later realize that this is not all that different from the "high" I got when having an affair with my professor. All are part of the mania of manic depression—the diagnosis that still awaits me.

Furthermore, I simply cannot tolerate the idea of another divorce. One was tolerable, but to be doubly divorced would show that there is something defective in my character: something I have feared since a child, when I was not able to live up to the standards of perfection in my church. I also know, on some level, that a second divorce would resurface the deep shame that has been, for the most part, repressed since my sexual abuse. I am not ready to address this.

So we limp along for a few more years. Louie focuses some of his unhappiness on his career. He criticizes his colleagues and he begins to pursue a position at his alma mater, Illinois Wesleyan University in Bloomington, Indiana. I buy into the idea that he needs a change professionally, and that a move to Indiana would be good for us. He applies for and is accepted to a position as chaplain and professor. We then start to search for a house—and here, we come into conflict. He wants a modest house in town; I want a big house in the country. I am willing to sell our cottage for the big house, and I am willing to commute back and forth to Evanston to keep my big salary and pay for the house. I win this conflict, and we buy the big house.

While preparing for our move, I notice that Louie is spending a great deal of time with Debbie, one of his young Ph.D. students. I notice, but I don't notice. I don't want to know. Instead, I focus on our move, our big house and his establishing himself in a new setting. It is the summer of 1996, and I am 50 years old. Louie goes on an archaeological dig in the summer and I stay home and pack. When I pick him up at the airport, he is glum, quiet and clearly not happy to see me. I try to ask about the dig, but he says very little. We proceed with our plans, and we move in early September. I am enthralled with our new house. I take three weeks off of work to settle us in.

But Louie continues to be glum, to drink heavily and to be generally enraged with me. One day, he drinks until 2 a.m., falling down in the hallway; he is scheduled to preach at 10 a.m. the next morning. At 8, I wake him up with a strong cup of coffee in hand and bacon and eggs on the table. At 10, he is in the chapel preaching like an angel, with God's love shining into every broken heart in the room. I am proud of him. I do not remember that in Al-Anon, this behavior of mine is called "enabling"—big-time enabling.

Six weeks after the move, Louie tells me he does not love me and that he wants a divorce. I am shocked, crushed and heartbroken. At first, I do not believe what I am hearing. I think this must be a temporary fit of rage, which now is common. So I deny what he is saying. Yet with a week of his persistence, I realize he is serious. I start to collapse, emotionally. I cry nonstop. Shame overcomes me. Darkness overcomes me. I feel I must be defective if my husband wants to leave me. Somehow, I feel "left behind"—as if the Lord had returned and I am left. Abandoned once again! I call my older brother, Peter, and ask him to talk with Louie. Louie declares to Peter that the marriage is over and that he wants me to move out as soon as possible. I still do not totally believe him. I think he might change his mind.

Then a friend tells me that Louie is having an affair with Debbie, and that the two of them had spent the summer together on his archaeological dig. As my friend said, "They were an 'item' and everybody knew it." Louie then tells me about his affair and about his plan to marry Debbie as soon as we are divorced. I now realize that he is completely serious.

I continue to collapse. I cannot sleep. Sleeping pills help a little, though very little. I cannot eat and I quickly lose weight—eight pounds in two weeks. I begin to miss days of work. I fall behind on administration, and when I am with clients, I barely stay awake. I feel great guilt for my low level of functioning. I cry into my pillow. Where is the woman who built a great career—who has a Ph.D.? Where is the woman who loved to entertain friends, and who sped across the lake on skis?

I am shocked at my level of dysfunction, but I blame it all on Louie. He has cast away the wife who loves, cares for and defends him. I realize later that I do not allow into my consciousness the depth of my depression, with all of its shame, fear and anger. I do not allow into my consciousness my own history of abuse that most certainly contributes to my depression.

Due to my condition, I realize that I need to take a leave of absence from work. I talk with my relatives in Canada, and they ask me to come and recuperate with them. As soon as they ask, I know that this is the right thing to do. I call Nathan, and he totally agrees. He is now 20 years old and a student at the University of Chicago. He is amazingly compassionate and wise. I realize later that I had already become very dependent on him.

The plan is that I will go to Canada just before Thanksgiving and return after Christmas. Nathan will stay in Chicago for Thanksgiving, but will join me for Christmas. The thought of being away from Nathan at Thanksgiving is heartbreaking, but I console myself by knowing I will see him at Christmas.

Before I leave for Canada, I tell my board of directors a little about what is happening in my life—that I have some marital problems due to my move, and that I need to discern how to do it all. They do not ask questions, and it's as if they really do not want to know. I have been a competent director and they seem to trust my judgment. I am grateful for their trust. I do not realize that this is the beginning of the loss of my career as I have known it, as the impact of it all will not really unfold for another year.

In Canada, my grief over Louie subsides a little. My sisters, Rachel and Ruth, are constantly at my side, listening, consoling and praying. I am barely aware of the presence of Edmond, and he stays far away from me. My parents are now living in a retirement community. They are supportive and kind and do not judge me in any way for the failure of this marriage—now my second failed marriage.

I do a great deal of walking, especially with my niece, Joy, who is Edmond and Ruth's daughter. Joy tells me that she suffers from depression, too. We talk a little about Edmond, and I tell her to never let him be alone with her daughter, who is now 3 years old. I do not tell Joy about the sex abuse by her father; Joy does not tell me about her sexual abuse by him. It will be 15 years before we divulge those secrets. In the meantime, we enjoy a special bond, even though we don't really understand it.

After three weeks, Nathan arrives. It is such a comfort to be with him, for we have never been separated on holidays. Nathan and I cry together, knowing we are losing Louie; we hope that we are not also losing his children, Jimmy and Caroline. We are comforted by our Canadian relatives and know that they will not leave us. They make it clear that we will always have a place with them.

After Christmas, Nathan and I return to Chicago. I feel strong enough to return to work on a part-time basis: I will resume my counseling work, but will stop my work as director. The board of directors again accepts this without question. My staff is quietly caring, but we do not discuss my personal problems. We have always maintained professional boundaries.

My female friends surround me with warmth and love. On one hand, they are shocked by Louie's sudden insistence on divorce and on his affair with his young student. On the other hand, they have watched his increasing outbursts of rage as well as his constant drinking. My oldest and dearest friend, Gloria, is always by my side. As a person who struggles with her own form of mental illness—severe anxiety—she understands the tenacity of grief and depression that have overtaken me. Christa, now a friend of 15 years, calls me daily. Luke is now living in Pennsylvania, but I feel his love across the miles.

In addition to Gloria, Christa and Luke, I have a new friend: Tina. Tina was the realtor Louie and I used when we bought our house in Evanston, and she is both very bubbly and very strong. Tina has stayed in our lives, and now—after Louie's departure— she has become increasingly dear to me.

My friends talk with each other and with me. We all know that I will not be able to return to Bloomington and that I am too fragile to get an apartment and live alone. This is a very big problem. Tina then tells me that she has a solution. She invites me to her house, sits close to me on her sofa and says, "Lucille, I love you and I want you to come and live with me. I have a big house, with only one child, Mitch, living with me. We would gladly share it with you. Please, please, consider it. We do not want you living by yourself." I am immediately relieved, but I question: "Are you sure? Will it be okay with Mitch?" Tina persists in her invitation, and so I accept. A huge burden rolls off my back.

Tina and I then talk back and forth about living arrangements. I will have a large, beautiful bedroom. We will share the kitchen and the living room. We will invite Nathan, and Louie's children, Jimmy and Caroline, to come and visit as often as they wish. Tina assures me: "This is their home, too." I talk with the children, and they are relieved that they will have a home to come to. There will be a table full of food whenever they want it. We do not talk very much about the collapse of the marriage, and I worry about the children: after all, this is the second time they have experienced divorce. But we are all too fragile to talk about it yet.

What I focus on is the fact that Tina will provide a warm, safe home for me and a comfortable place for the children when they visit. So, in two weeks, two friends go with me to Bloomington. I do not involve the children. I want to spare them the pain. We work for eight hours, packing boxes and moving furniture. We take the furniture in a U-Haul to a small cabin owned by yet another friend. We move my clothes and a few books to Tina's house.

I can hardly believe my good fortune. I am now in a home where I am loved. From here, I will attempt to reassemble myself. I hope to soon resume my role as director of the counseling center and as a loving and consistent therapist for my clients. I hope to sleep at nights and not cry. I know I will eat, because Tina will cook with me and eat with me. I will rebuild my life. This is my goal.

It remains to be seen whether or not I will attain it.

5

Bursting Your Sides

Living with Tina is pure gift. She's one of those friends who holds you when you're sobbing, and then—after you've had your cry—is next to you as you're bursting your sides, watching an old *I Love Lucy* episode and snacking on popcorn and freshly squeezed lemonade.

Together, we cry and grieve. "What a jerk," I say. "And how boring is this? Another older man running off with his young student." Tina responds: "You'd at least think he would have found someone who was not his daughter's age." But then I cry again. "I just wanted to retire with him. To travel to Africa and China. I wanted to show grandchildren the Grand Canyon. All of that is gone."

Tina listens to my shame, to my feelings of being a "discarded woman" who has been "abandoned." It's like being cast into hell—always my greatest fear as a child. Shame, tainting the core of my being, is the quiet message I absorbed during the sex abuse as a child; now, the same shame roars back into my psyche. With her love, Tina pulls me out of that dark hole of shame—at least for a while. She talks me out of believing the accusations Louie pummeled me with when he was drunk, when he accused me of being nothing but a depressive and a careerist.

With Tina, it seems that there's always a party. For Nathan's 21st birthday, we fill her house with friends, banners and balloons. We bake bread, barbeque steaks and have our fill of ice-cream cake. With Tina's help, I feel like I am not failing as a mother. I worry at times, though, that Nathan will be damaged because I have not provided him with a stable father. Two divorces is something that no child should have to go through.

Tina expands my group of friends. She invites Wilson—a handsome, Scandinavian-looking man with light-green eyes—to her parties. Later, Wilson will become a very special friend, complicated though this will be. Tina's whole family welcomes me as one of their own—and they are quite the characters. Her mother is a 5-foot Serbian immigrant who takes frequent, mysterious trips to Serbia. Though petite and sweet, she is tough and not to be toyed with. Tina's stepfather is Mexican—20 years younger than her mother. He talks nonstop but he watches over Tina's mother like a hawk. You don't mess with him.

Most of all, it is Tina's bubbly personality that pulls me back when I start the spiral downward into the darkness. When Tina's cat escapes in a blustering snowstorm, the two of us chase her like wild women, giggling the whole way. When food is the only answer to pain, she seems to pull from her hat the world's best key-lime pie, made with fresh key limes. When we're too exhausted for anything but a movie, she pulls *Sister Act* from her shelf.

It is around this time that my mother becomes very sick. Tina is there to comfort me when I receive the call that she may be near death. For some time, my mother has had mini-strokes, but they quickly become totally debilitating. I am now 52 years old. I rush to Canada and have the good fortune of being with my mother when she dies. Her death is beautiful in its own sad way. She is in her bed at the retirement home where my parents have lived for 20 years; mother is 86 years old. On the morning of her death, my father is alone with her. Both know she is near death. She is too sick to talk very much, but at one point, she opens her eyes and whispers to him, "I love you, but it is time for me to go home and be with Jesus." My father responds: "I love you, too. I will pray that you will go soon to be with Jesus." Soon, my sister, Ruth, and I arrive at her bedside. We, too, know that she is near death. We decide to quietly sing to her. We sing her favorites: *Amazing Grace* and *How Great Thou Art*. At this point, we see that her breath is slowing down. We keep singing, but ever so quietly. Then, she takes her hands and folds them over her heart. Her face is profoundly peaceful. And she takes her last breath. My father, Ruth and

I sob quietly both for her loss and for gratitude that she is now free from pain and with Jesus.

I stay close to mother, holding her hand and touching her face. She is warm for a few minutes, but I can feel her warmth gradually seeping away. Soon, the undertaker comes to take her body. I hate that body bag, and I want to scream, "At least leave her head out!" The idea of having her stuffed into that bag revolts me. As the undertaker is taking her out the door, my sister, Rachel, arrives. She had had to leave mother's side earlier and is stricken because she was not able to be with her at her death. I feel very badly for her.

Two days later, at her viewing, I again caress mother's hand and her face, but the warmth is gone. I take pictures of her in her casket, with her pretty blue suit and white, ruffled blouse. She is so petite and delicate. When younger, she wore only dark, plain clothes, out of religious conviction. Now, those restrictions are lifted and she wears ruffled blouses. It makes my whole body smile.

At her funeral I sit with Aunt Edna, her only sibling, and Nathan, who has now arrived from Chicago. He puts his arm around my shoulders, holds my hand and squeezes it when I start to silently cry. His strength gives me strength. Yet on some level, I now feel like an orphan—a motherless child. Even though I have not spent much time with my mother in recent years, the time I have spent has been filled with love and support. I know the ways I have chosen to live are different from the ways she had taught; I know my beliefs are different from hers; I know my divorces caused her great pain. But at no time did she ever express blame or disapproval. I am profoundly grateful for this. Only later will I come to understand that this provided considerable healing to the perfectionist standards I had grown up with. Unfortunately, it is not enough to spare me from the fires of deep depression and self-condemnation.

With my mother, I am totally at peace; with my father—well, not totally. My feelings toward him are neutral, neither warm nor cold. When I later look back on this, I realize that there was a part of me that blamed him for not protecting me from Edmond. Most of the time I was not conscious of this, but I always had a certain emotional distance from him. But not so with my mother. After her funeral, I pass out little heart-shaped rocks that

I had collected in recent months. My nieces clearly cherish them. They are little tokens of their grandma's love and tokens of my love for my mother.

After the funeral, it is time for me to resume my life in Chicago. While I carry the pain of losing my mother, I am not devastated by it and I am able to face life there. Of course, Tina is with me and she is such a great comfort. But a problem soon arises: where should I go to church? Tina goes to a Serbian Orthodox church on occasion, but that doesn't work for me. For one thing, it's all in Serbian; for another, it's high church, with many rituals. I know nothing about it and I'm too fragile to take on even one more thing. I consider returning to First Congregational Church in Evanston, where I was ordained and where Louie and I went, but I'm stopped by shame and fear. What horrible thing do they think I did? Has Louie told them that I'm 'a depressive, a careerist and an unfit wife'? After all, the minister, Les, is a friend of Louie's. Les has not reached out to me in any way, so I only imagine the worst.

I take my woes to my dear friend Gloria—a friend now of 25 years. I've helped her through her divorce and through her phobias. She's helped me through my first divorce, and now she's here to help me through my second. She has a solution to my problem: "Come with me to Edgewater Presbyterian Church in Chicago, where you or Louie are not known. My church is small, and it is welcoming to all. There's no condemnation there. You'll find a place, I promise you. At least for now."

I'm scared that first Sunday. Will someone know me? What will they ask me? Will I tell them the truth? My fears are allayed even as I enter the front door. Rev. Gilbert Bladen welcomes me with a big smile. He lightly taps me on the shoulder and invites me to stay after church for coffee hour. He does not ask personal questions. Gilbert is a big, handsome man with a firm handshake that makes me feel safe.

In the worship service, Gilbert's warmth permeates. The sanctuary feels thick with love and acceptance. The faces in the pews are of all colors and social classes. Yet, most noticeable of all are the faces of many who appear emotionally, physically or mentally challenged. I feel strangely warmed to see them, and in the coffee hour after the service, I reach out to them. I learn that they all live in a halfway house for mentally challenged people, called Bryn Mawr Care, which is around the corner from the church. I meet Crystal, a large woman who walks with a limp and who talks slowly, with a mixture of warmth and fear on her face. I immediately like her. I meet Roy, who can barely speak: he says single words, not sentences. Yet, a certain innocence in his face captivates me. I go home that Sunday filled with hope, for I have found people who are clearly challenged, yet who have a place in the pews of Edgewater Presbyterian Church. With the exception of Gloria, no one yet knows of my own emotional challenges.

The second Sunday, I meet Jolene, an accountant, and Cliff, the church administrator. Soon, I become friends with them. I'm not threatened by them, and they do not ask about my past. I just tell them that I'm a therapist in Evanston and a friend of Gloria. I tell them that I am looking for a church. That second Sunday, in coffee hour, I sit at the table with the mentally challenged folks from Bryn Mawr Care. We chat until well after most others have left and gone home. Already, I know in my heart that I have found a church.

Gilbert, the minister, asks to meet with me. We immediately start to talk about ways to better serve the Bryn Mawr Care people. I tell him a bit about my divorce and my depression, though I do not reveal the severity of my depression. I tell him I'm a therapist with credentials as a psychologist and pastoral counselor, and that I'm a Congregational minister. He's thrilled to have someone with these credentials interested in the people from Bryn Mawr Care. Three weeks later, we begin offering Wednesday evening services aimed at meeting their needs. It's almost magical, really, the way it unfolds so quickly. It leaves me feeling like I am at the core of something truly good and right. I have the same feeling I had 15 years ago, when I helped to found the feminist magazine, *Daughters of Sarah*. I feel truly blessed and grateful.

I immediately become known in the church and to the Bryn Mawr Care residents as Rev. Lucille. I go to Bryn Mawr Care at 6:45 every Wednesday evening, and as soon as I arrive, an announcement is made over the intercom: "Rev. Lucille is here. It's time for church." About 20 people respond. I love walking across the street with them: I feel like a shepherd with my precious flock. I guard each lamb and lead them all through the busy intersection, then through the large, carved wooden doors of the church, up the stairs to the second floor and into the quiet chapel. There, we find a simple cross hanging above the altar, a piano on the right side and a pulpit on the left. The altar, with bread and wine on it, is ready for Communion.

Gilbert and I have crafted a worship service that meets the spiritual longings of our audience. We call ourselves "the Samaritans," based on the Bible story in which a man who was considered an outsider—a Samaritan—helped a wounded traveler. I compose a song for us Samaritans, and we sing it every week:

> *We are good Samaritans,*
> *we are good Samaritans,*
> *we are good Samaritans,*
>
> *God loves us and God cares.*
>
> *We are good Samaritans,*
> *we are good Samaritans,*
> *we are good Samaritans,*
>
> *We love each other and we share.*

Gilbert and I take turns preaching. This is the first time since my ordination that I have preached on a regular basis. While anxious at first, I soon relax. I preach about Jesus's love and acceptance of all people—all classes, all abilities and all problems, whether mental or physical. I preach about how Jesus especially loved and cherished those who seemed to be outcasts from society. "Jesus does not judge," I declare. "He just cares and cares and cares."

I preach about Jesus's acceptance of women as well as men. I tell about Mary Magdalene, Jesus's beloved friend who was with him at the cross; about the fact that Jesus appeared to Mary at his resurrection and told her to go and tell others that he had risen from the dead. As I tell the story, I notice that the women in the chapel are glowing with pride.

Praying together is a central part of our worship. The prayers of the Samaritans are so plaintive, full of joy and sorrow, and simple yet profound. One man prays about the scary voices he's been hearing for 30 years. Another prays for her children, whom she hasn't seen in five years. It sometimes brings tears to all.

We then serve Communion, and all of the Samaritans are invited to partake of that precious meal in which Jesus offered his love to his disciples and to the disciples of all times. In the chapel, the atmosphere is thick with love.

After the service, I again walk with the Samaritans, out the big doors of the church, across the busy street and into Bryn Mawr Care. Again I feel like a shepherd with her flock, guarding each precious lamb.

In my role as pastor, I wear clerical clothes. When I preach, I wear a long, white robe that makes me feel warm inside and out. Under it, I wear a clerical white collar and a black shirt. This provides me with a certain status that replaces some of the status of my former life. Out in the neighborhood, it brings respectful glances. One woman asks, "Are you a priest?" I respond proudly: "No, I'm not a priest, but I'm a minister." Later, I come to realize how good it feels to be on a clerical pedestal. When one lives with the demon of depression just under the skin, a clerical pedestal is absolutely perfect!

The Samaritan Program is my total preoccupation. It's a place where no one knows about my failed marriages, about my depression and about my loss of status in the Evanston community. By this time, I have resigned from my role as executive director, but I remain a therapist with a few clients. It will only be a few months before I stop counseling there, as well. In fact, it is like I'm slinking away from my Evanston roots and from my professional life there. Only a few colleagues reach out to me, and it's as if we all agree to silently ignore the pain of my divorce and professional failures. No one in my church, the Congregational Church in Evanston, contacts me. I contact them only to inform them of my new ministry at Edgewater Presbyterian Church and to get their formal stamp on it, for professional purposes. "Don't ask, don't tell" is the silent agreement.

I get an idea for expanding the ministry of my new church: I could open a counseling office for people in the church and community. Here, I could work again as a psychologist and a pastoral counselor, in addition to working in my ministry with the Samaritans. Gilbert loves the idea and the congregation approves of it immediately. So we set up a little nonprofit organization called Edgewater Lighthouse. We call it "Edgewater" because Edgewater is the community where we live, as well as the name of the church. We call it "Lighthouse" because it is a light and beacon for all in need of love and care. No one knows the extent to which it is a light-house for me. It helps keep at bay the darkness that lies within. I lovingly decorate my office with warm, variegated pinks and I have the ceiling painted with a soft blue. I am filled with hope.

With a counseling office now in place, I bring three clients from my Evanston office. Two of these are my favorites; the third is a burden to me. One of the favorites is Jim, a college professor. Jim has been with me for a year and he has found his footing after a difficult divorce. I have helped him analyze his destructive and unconscious patterns, and I have engaged him on a deeply spiritual level where grace and forgiveness abound and judgment and failure are absent. Through all of it, Jim has been able let go of a marriage that had no potential for success. Jim has also now been able to approach his college students with kindness, rather than condescension. Later, I come to realize that having success with a client who is a professor somehow diminishes my sense of failure in my two marriages, as both husbands were professors.

The other of my favorite clients from Evanston is Jenny, a single mother. She was shunned by her family for standing up to an abusive husband. She takes college classes and is headed for an internship in a girl's home while caring for her darling 3-year-old. Every day, Jenny moves one more step away from fear and into hope and strength. She is an inspiration to me.

A third client who comes with me from Evanston is Sharon, and I feel I am treading water with her. Sharon is depressed—very depressed—and has been ever since her only child, Thomas, was killed in a car accident several years ago. Her grief seems to never end. She has lost her job as a secretary because she simply cannot work. She barely cleans her house. She showers only on occasion. While I keep seeing her, she triggers in me my own despair. I later realize that I should have referred her to another therapist, but I did not. Perhaps I did not refer her because that would suggest some failure on my part, and more failure would only break my fragile sense of self.

It is now 18 months that I have worked at Edgewater Presbyterian Church and lived with Tina. She and her family have been simply won-derful, but Nathan and I decide it is time for me to live on my own. We believe that my mental health is now stable. While I will maintain close contact with Tina, I will rent a one-bedroom apartment across the street from the church. By being so close, I believe I will feel protected.

I find an apartment with big windows that face east, and the morning sun fills it with warmth. The sun and warmth, I believe, will repel any darkness that arises within me. For my bedroom windows, I buy bright curtains with big red, yellow and blue circles. Their cheer, I hope, will encircle any blues that lie within me. I buy a large, green pull-out sofa for Nathan when he visits from his college, the University of Chicago. I take from storage an oak table and chairs that I inherited from my grandparents. Sitting on those chairs, I hope, will remind me of the joy I felt when sitting on my grandfather's lap. I love that Nathan and I are establishing ourselves as a little family. Jimmy and Caroline, Louie's children, have pulled away from us, and while this hurts a lot, I try not to think about it. For I have my beloved son, Nathan.

Living in my apartment and working across the street in the Presbyterian church works beautifully for a year. The Samaritan program thrives. We throw birthday parties with a room full of balloons. We throw Christmas parties with gifts for all. We throw hair-cutting parties with an upper-end Evanston beauty salon that gives fancy cuts—spikes for men and wedges for women. In church on Sunday, we all sit together, proudly sporting our new hairdos.

My mood during all of this is generally good. I am helped by a counselor I am seeing—Donna, an older woman with a very motherly warmth. Donna has a strong presence and she gives me strength at times when I feel weak. She often prays with me, with the two of us kneeling at her sofa, and it is such a comfort. She reminds me of my own beloved mother.

Most of the time, my energy is endless. I'm also very attracted to Gilbert, the minister who is recently divorced. He responds very warmly to me—enough to make me believe that there is a possibility of a relationship with him. As it turns out, I come to realize that this warmth brings many other single women to hover around him, too. At one point, Gilbert explicitly tells me that our relationship is solely a professional one. I lie to him, saying, "That's fine with me. I have Wilson." Wilson, Tina's friend whom I met two years earlier, has been coming to church sometimes, and we have gone out afterward for coffee or to a movie. I do find Wilson attractive, but not as attractive as Gilbert. In the end, Gilbert marries one of the women of the church, and I am quite hurt. I realize much later that when a pastor marries a parishioner, it can be considered a form of abuse. This can mean that the church is not a "safe place."

Through all of this, however, my upbeat mood carries me through the disappointment with Gilbert. My relationship with the Samaritans thrives in every way and I am at an emotional all-time high. This leads me to big trouble, though. It keeps me from seeing the full reality of my emotional state, and grandiosity takes hold of me. I believe there is nothing I cannot achieve if I try, and my professional boundaries start to disintegrate.

Later, I will come to understand that this is a symptom of mania—the opposite end of depression. Mania leads you to think that you can accomplish anything; to think you are brilliant and beautiful and that you have endless amounts of money and good luck. You believe that you will always be loved. When the mania of manic depression is in full swing, you believe the depression is gone forever. Manic depression is also technically classified as bi-polar disorder. Unfortunately, my diagnosis does not come until much later. I will later look back at this and recognize it as the third symptom of mania that I have experienced: the first was that of plummeting into the "high" of an affair; the second was the "high" of spending sprees with Louie; and now it is about grandiosity.

In my manic phase, my grandiosity takes over and I believe I can rescue Crystal from Bryn Mawr Care. She has been begging me to help her find an apartment so that she can live on her own. I want to make her happy, so I find her an efficiency apartment. I buy some things for her: sheets, utensils, cleaning supplies and a green shower curtain with matching towels. I do not tell Gilbert about this. It soon becomes clear that Crystal is not doing well on her own, though, and so she moves back to Bryn Mawr Care. When Gilbert hears what I have done, he berates me for taking all of this on by myself and for not discussing it with him. He fires me soon afterward. I am immediately ashamed and stunned at my own lack of professionalism, as I know I should have consulted him before taking on the responsibility of moving Crystal. I berate myself: "You know better than that. You know you should have talked with him. Shame, *shame* on you."

Gilbert never again talks to me about my firing. He is silent. The Samaritans have a little going-away party for me, giving me a beautiful, hand-made clerical stole on which they paint their names. I cry when I receive it and I cry as I hug each one goodbye. Gilbert stands at a distance, giving me a perfunctory handshake.

After being dismissed from my work with my beloved Samaritans, I agonize. Now what am I to do? I have not only lost my ministry with them, but I am no longer able to do counseling in the office I had established at Edgewater Presbyterian Church. I am shattered. I talk with friends and family, and we decide that I should move out of the apartment across from the church and find one on the northwest side of Chicago. It should be an apartment that I can also use as an office, so that I can set up a small private practice.

After considerable searching, I find an apartment that seems just right. It has big windows and beautiful hardwood floors. I buy an antique sewing machine that reminds me of the one I used as a child. I buy a small, round kitchen table with a beautiful glass top and a fountain to soothe my restless soul. I do everything in my power to make this apartment my home as well as my office. After three weeks of setting up, I invite five of my clients from Edgewater to my new apartment office. I begin to settle into this, and it seems that it may work.

Soon after my move, my dear friend Gloria buys a condo five blocks from me. We all know that living near her is foundational to my stability. By this time, my friend Luke has moved back to his home in Pennsylvania and my friend Christa has moved back to her home in Louisiana. So, two people who were like family to Nathan and me are no longer in Chicago. I miss them terribly and of course we stay in touch, but it is Gloria who is now my anchor and longtime, beloved sister. Gloria and I assume we'll pall around together, as we've done for years—but my illness intervenes. Our time together is very short. I will soon move to a different state because of my mental condition.

I call Gloria almost daily for advice and support. One day, something strange happens in an afternoon call: she is not herself. I realize that she is lethargic—very lethargic. She is speaking in a whisper, with words so muffled I can hardly understand her. Gloria normally has a strong, clear voice, full of enthusiasm and fun, so I know that something is very wrong. She barely responds to my questions and what she says makes no sense. Somehow, I extract from her the name of her doctor, and I immediately call the doctor's office. I demand to speak to her doctor and I describe her symptoms. I am told to rush Gloria to Saint Francis Hospital, in Evanston. I remain calm on the outside, but on the inside I'm screaming from fear of losing her. As soon as we arrive at the hospital she is put on a heart monitor, for she is having heart failure. She is told she is not going home. As it all unfolds, Gloria is in the hospital for three days and she is given a pacemaker. We both realize this was a close call. If I had not called her at that time, she may be dead. I saved her life. As it turns out, she will save my life two years later.

Saving Gloria only deepens our relationship. For 28 years, we have been there for each other: I had helped her overcome her phobias years ago; I had driven her to appointments when she was too afraid to drive on her own; I had comforted her at her divorce; and she has comforted me in both of mine. I gladly helped her back then, and I gladly help her again. In some ways, she has given me a gift by allowing me to help her. I have been on the receiving end of so much love and support from so many people in recent years that to give back—through Gloria—is a deep joy.

Working in my at-home, private counseling practice goes very well at first. I have minor emotional ups and downs, but I am still in counseling myself and I am still taking Zoloft. It seems helpful—but then I begin to slip. New clients are sparse, and those who do come are irregular. For the first time in my career, I am low on clients. I gradually begin to slide into depression once again. I realize that a private practice in my home is mainly a mistake, for it does not provide me with a reason to leave my house. It does not give me any professional identity out in the community or in a church. I become very lonely, even though Gloria, Nathan, Tina and my siblings are very attentive.

I try to remedy the loneliness and isolation by volunteering to help with gardening at a girls' home. I teach these hurting, abused girls how to grow tomatoes, carrots and beans. It helps me a little. I realize later that in doing this, I was attempting to care for the hurting girl inside of me.

I also fill my time by trying to develop a relationship with Wilson. He and I spent time together during my work at Edgewater Lighthouse, but now I need more. Wilson is attractive in many ways: he is very handsome, with his light-green eyes and light-brown hair, and he is physically strong—he moves my Lay-Z-Boy chair with complete ease. He fixes my car when it won't start; he perfectly glues my wooden rocking chair when

its legs are wobbly. He's very intelligent, although not a seminary professor—instead, he works in the import business. This is a relief after two
academic husbands.

Yet Wilson is elusive. He is a widower who is still in love with his wife,
who died of cancer three years earlier. Sometimes he and I have glorious
days together, canoeing on the Illinois River or taking his grandchildren
on picnics. I cook elaborate Thai dinners for him, and he loves them. I
only realize later that he barely returns my favors. At Christmas I buy him
a Macy's sweater; he gets me a tiny box of chocolates. My moods start to
swing again: high and happy if I think my relationship with Wilson is
progressing, and sad and depressed if I think my relationship with him is
at a standstill.

My private practice has now dwindled to three clients. The depression
increases, and when I am not seeing clients, I simply stay in bed, isolated
and not eating. At age 55, I formally end my private practice. It is now five
years since Louie divorced me.

Soon after this, on a Saturday afternoon, I crawl out of bed and decide
to travel to Hyde Park on the south side of Chicago, where Nathan lives.
He is playing Frisbee, and I want to watch him. Maybe watching him will
give me a little lift, or maybe it will please him to have his mother watching him even though he is now a grown man. I arrive at the Frisbee game
an hour late because I got lost. Somehow, I had become very disoriented—
something that had never happened before. At the end of the game, I
start crying because I'm afraid I will again get lost going home. Nathan,
with tenderness in his voice and worry in his eyes, decides to drive his
car and have me follow him. About five blocks from my home, I get confused again. I stop, get out of my car and cry, "Where are you taking me?
I thought you were taking me home. Where are we?" Only when I arrive
home do I begin to understand how confused I really was.

I do not truly appreciate until a much later time how calm and caring
Nathan is in times like this, or how often I need him. But when I talk with
him about all of the love and care he has given me, he simply responds, "It
made me a better person." He also adds, "It brought me closer to you and
I wanted to do it."

I then come up with another idea about what to do. I decide to have
surgery on my back, as well as surgery on both hands. My back has been

hurting since my water-skiing accident at age 37, and I have a protruding disc that is badly in need of repair. I have tried every possible remedy for my back problems: physical therapy, medication, massage, acupuncture. Nothing has helped. Maybe surgery will solve my problem.

My hands have been hurting for three years, and I have severe carpal tunnel. Perhaps if I get relief from physical pain, my emotional pain will decrease. So in December of 2001, I have carpal tunnel surgery on one hand. The following February I have surgery on the other hand, and in March I have back surgery.

The carpal tunnel surgeries are successful, but when I'm faced with the implications for the back surgery, I have a big problem. The recovery for back surgery takes several months, and I realize I cannot live on my own for at least a month after the surgery. What am I to do? I agonize, but then my two beloved sisters, Ruth and Rachel, come to my rescue. They each offer to come from Canada for two weeks and take care of me. Nathan and I are deeply touched and profoundly grateful for their generosity. Their generosity seems to have no end.

The back surgery itself goes well, and when I arrive home from the hospital, Rachel is there. She is such a comfort. Two weeks later, Ruth arrives. They are both so loving, and they make me chicken soup, homemade bread and apple pie. They help me with my physical therapy. My back heals nicely and while they are with me, my depression seems to be gone.

But when I am alone once again in my apartment, my depression deepens. I have no appetite. I do not cook. I do not pay my bills. When I am with Gloria, my spirits are lifted somewhat, but when we part I sink into despair. Wilson is still in the picture but remains aloof. I fear I will never again have a man in my life who truly cares. I feel intensely shamed and discarded by my divorces. I feel that all of my education is a waste and that I am intellectually an inferior human being. I believe that the accomplishments I have achieved are superficial and transitory. My heart is hard and my body feels perpetually cold. I have no reason to live.

Nathan visits me as much as possible and he pours affection into me. He holds my hand when we walk down the street and he hugs me when I cry. He cooks for me. He takes me to movies and to parks. Yet it brings me little happiness. I know, intellectually, that he loves me, but it does not penetrate into the core of my being. What am I to do? The answer comes when I talk to Ruth and Rachel. They once again ask me to come to Canada and stay with them, as I had right after Louie asked for a divorce. They were just here in Chicago, helping me after my back surgery, and now they have invited me to come to Canada. I accept their invitation, of course, and our hope is that my family will love me back into health. I am now 56 years old, and it's been almost six years since Louie left me.

When I arrive back in Canada, however, I become very unsettled about Edmond. My fear of him abusing me again intensifies to the extent that I am unable to sleep when I stay overnight at his and Ruth's house. I struggle over what to do, because Ruth and Edmond have a big house while Rachel and her husband, Don, have just a small apartment.

I remember—rather vaguely—that eight years ago, I had told Rachel about Edmond's abuse. She totally believed me and never questioned a word. So when I tell her that I'm afraid of Edmond, she instantly says, "I understand, Lucille. You may stay at my apartment at night and go and be with Ruth during the day. That way, you will see very little of Edmond." But to work this out requires a tremendous sacrifice on Rachel's part. She does not have a bedroom for me, so she gives me her bedroom while she and her husband, Don, sleep on the living room floor.

My sisters devote all of their time and attention to me. They take me to get counseling, to see a psychiatrist and to get medication. At one point, a therapist even comes to Rachel's home. They cook my favorite meals— roast beef and mashed potatoes, and ham and scalloped potatoes. They have me help them bake bread and cookies. Ruth has me help her in the garden, working up the ground for spring planting and then planting peas and beans. They take me to church and pray with me. At home, they usually walk with me.

I am afraid to be alone. Rachel later tells me that at one point, she and Don needed to go out for a short time to run an errand. When they left, I was standing at the door; when they returned, I was still standing there, terrified of being alone. At first I have difficulty showering and I have to have Rachel stand at the door. Just knowing she is there gives me courage to shower by myself.

I turn to my faith and get some comfort there. Over and over I read the first verses of Psalm 41: *Blessed is he who has regard for the weak. The Lord*

delivers him in time of trouble. The Lord will protect him and preserve his life . . .
The Lord will sustain him on his sickbed and restore him from his bed of illness.

I am in Canada for three months. While I make a little progress, I am still very, very sick and profoundly depressed. My sister and their families are totally exhausted. Ruth later says, "Nothing we did seemed to really help. I felt so helpless."

They wrestle over what to do, and I am extremely anxious, too. I feel I have let them down by not getting better. They have been so committed to me: they have done everything in their power to help me heal, but it has not worked. I am acutely aware that I have an amazing support system in my family and friends, and I am deeply grateful. I thank them over and over again for their love and support, hugging and holding them. This gratitude does not make me better, though. It seems, in fact, that nothing will make me better. Finally, they drive me back to Chicago with no clear plan for the future. They agonize. They pray. They are tired. Their medicine of love has not helped.

Yet, back in Chicago, I miraculously recover. My energy returns. My desire for exercise returns and I treat myself to a pricey pair of rollerblades with all the paraphernalia: helmet, knee pads, elbow pads and a fancy bag for my water bottle and keys. I loved ice skating as a child, and I just know I will love rollerblading as much. I try it. I am at complete ease at it. Each morning, I get up and rollerblade along the shore of beautiful Lake Michigan. I feel like I'm up in the clouds as I glide along the lake. I meet people on the path and we stop and have a coffee before heading home. I later realize that this is just one manifestation of mania in my manic depression.

Back home, I start to cook once again. I make chicken soup for myself. I make stir-fry for Nathan, who visits me at least once a week. I throw dinner parties for my friends, cooking my standard dish: Pad Thai, with bean sprouts, peanuts, noodles and lime slices. Sometimes I cook my old-fashioned meatloaf, made with sausage, beef, roasted potatoes, carrots and onions. I've never been happier. My family and friends are relieved, but no one is more relieved than I am. Yet my dear friend Christa has doubts. She is a therapist and she quietly cautions, "Be careful, Lucille. This might be a flight into health." I ignore her advice.

With all of this energy and an upbeat mood, I decide to become a nanny. Within two months I have found two children whom I will care for. The parents are thrilled to have a grandmother-aged, English-speaking nanny with a Ph.D. in psychology.

I immediately take to it and it is clear that the children are delighted with me. I teach Mary, a 4-year-old, her ABCs, and I sing and dance with her: *The wheels on the bus go round and round, all through the town.* The parents of Ely, my 3-year-old, are happy because I somehow coax him to eat vegetables and I manage to get him to sleep in the afternoon—things they cannot do. I dance with him after his nap. My energy is at an all-time high, and I feel on top of the world. What I will come to understand later is that this is the mania, once again. Of course, I'll soon swing back to depression—though at the time, I am quite unaware of this. In the meantime, I sing and dance with the children.

6

Spiraling Downward

In three months, things begin to spiral downward. On the weekends, I stay in bed. When I care for the children, I'm lethargic—watching them, yes, but barely interacting with them. I'm acutely aware of my lack of care for them and I feel guilty, but I do not discuss this with their parents.

I am, however, in close contact with my family and friends. I have oblique conversations with my brother, Peter, about suicide. With all these mood swings, my family and my friends begin to suspect that I am suffering from manic depression. Yet my psychiatrist, Dr. Silvia Burn, will not hear of it. Dr. Burn is stern and cold, and there is no warmth in her eyes. This demeanor is matched by the drab, grey and brown suits she often wears. Dr. Burn is my age, and I am threatened by her power over me. She declares that I have major depression and not manic depression, even though she is not successful at treating me. She insists that this is somehow my fault, for she has never before had a patient who did not respond to her treatment. This, of course, deepens my sense of failure.

There is one good thing, however, that comes from my relationship with Dr. Burn: she provides information and records to establish the fact that I cannot work in my profession. The result is that I am eligible for both Medicare benefits and money from my own professional liability plan. With money from these two sources, I am able to live comfortably. Only later do I fully appreciate how fortunate I am to have this monthly income, which is about $2,600. Unfortunately, this does not spare me from depression. I continue to spiral downward, into that dark hole.

On September 25, I do not go to work as nanny of the children. I call the parents of the children and say that I am sick. They are understanding. I call my therapist and psychiatrist and reveal to both of them that I am considering suicide. They call my son, Nathan, and tell him to take me to Evanston Hospital. From there, I am immediately transferred to Chicago Lakeshore Hospital, because Lakeshore takes long-term clients. This is a hospital in which many of the people are clearly severely mentally ill but are too poor to afford sustaining care. They come in for a night, get their meds refilled, and leave again. I, however, stay there for four weeks. The drug that I am given is lithium—a well-known drug for manic depression—also technically known as bi-polar disorder. But it does not work. In fact, during two of these weeks I have psychotic episodes during which I am delusional about many things. This may or may not be related to the drug.

At a later time, Nathan—in tears—will tell me about some of these delusions: I believe my sisters are coming to visit me from Canada; I believe Wilson is declaring his love for me, and is saying we will get together as soon as I get out of the hospital; I believe that Dr. Paul, the kind psychiatrist from the hospital, has taken all of the patients to Campagnola, an all-organic, gourmet restaurant where Wilson took me on my birthday.

Nathan visits me in the hospital every day and keeps my family updated. He travels from Hyde Park, on the south side of Chicago, to where I am, on the north side—almost an hour away. He sits with me all evening, holding my hand and never criticizing me. He talks to the psychiatrist and explains my history of depression. Only later, when I am not absorbed in my problems, will I fully realize the depth and breadth of his care. My family and friends, however, simply marvel at it all. They see a 26-year-old man—starting his own career and with demanding work in a start-up computer software company—devoting tremendous amounts of time and affection to his mother.

After four weeks, I am discharged from the hospital and Nathan moves in with me, traveling to Hyde Park for work every day. The plan is for me to participate in the day treatment program at the hospital. I try it, but I am too nervous: all I do is pace. I'm dismissed from the program because

I cannot sit still. Yet, I cannot sit still at home, either, and I pace all night long while Nathan is trying to sleep. This agitation is the stuff of manic-depressive illness—one of the remaining symptoms that has not shown up until now.

After two weeks at home, I am taken to another hospital, Northwestern Memorial Hospital. Here, there is a more elaborate inpatient program that includes in-hospital counseling. They also offer ECT—electro-convulsive therapy. At this time, my family and I make the decision that I will receive ECT. Nothing else has worked.

ECT is a somewhat controversial treatment. Patients are briefly anaesthetized before being administered an electrical current to the brain. This induces a mild convulsion. It is believed that the convulsion scrambles the neurotransmitters in the brain, which gives them the opportunity to reassemble themselves in a healthy way and, thereby, help to diminish depression. ECT is successful for about 70 percent of the patients who use it to alleviate depression. Since no other form of treatment has worked for me, this is a last resort. The alternative would be to place me in a psychiatric institution—perhaps for the rest of my life.

The ECT treatment is brutal. Though I am anaesthetized temporarily, it leaves me feeling like a Mack truck has hit me. My body hurts from head to toe. My neck feels like it's been twisted and stretched. I'm very nauseous, but I don't throw up. My head feels like it wants to cave in on itself. When I walk, I lose my balance—sometimes even walking into walls. Most of all, I feel that at the core of my being I've been deeply abused and unmercifully shaken. It's not sexual abuse; it feels like violent physical and emotional abuse. All of these side effects last for several hours. Then everything lightens. The headache and nausea subside. I can walk straight again. My neck hurts, but not as much.

At first, my depressed mood does not seem to change, but after eight or nine treatments, the depression begins to lift. By treatment 12, I am feeling like my happy self. I look out the window and notice, for the first time in months, the fluffy clouds in the beautiful blue sky. I see my beloved son, with all the love in his eyes, and we hug and hug. I know deep in my soul that I'm the luckiest mother in the whole world.

But there is also something strange going on in my mind as a result of the ECT: I have severe memory loss. I've forgotten what my job was just two months ago, and I don't remember that Nathan lived with me before my hospital stay. I've forgotten random things from my distant past—that I once owned a boat, that I once knew how to cook Thai food and that I was a star basketball player in high school. Still, this is a small price to pay for the lifting of my depression. I have a life again. Light, and not darkness; hope, and not despair.

There is no discussion about the possibility of outpatient ECT treatments. In the future, I am to learn that I am a person who needs "maintenance treatments," as they are called. No one realizes it at this time.

After one month in the hospital, I return to my apartment and start to function like anyone else. I clean my house, pay my bills and get myself off to a movie with my dear friend Gloria. I know for sure that the ECT has worked and I'm bursting with gratitude and hope.

I jump into sewing projects. My sewing machine is heavy, 20 years old and hard to use. The antique machine that I recently bought looks beautiful, but it is dysfunctional. So Nathan and Gloria buy me a sweet, light-weight Singer sewing machine with the latest gadgets for fancy stitches. The machine purrs along like a happy cat, whether sewing through heavy denim or light silk. This is a $1,100 gift. The only other gift of this size that I have ever received was the ruby from my second husband, Louie. I am grateful, even to tears. I hug and hug and hug them.

My first sewing project is for Nathan. I make him elaborate, reversible aprons with matching oven mitts and pot holders. Then I make big, flowered cushions for my kitchen chairs and pink dresses for my cousin's baby. My life seems to be back on track. Keeping myself occupied seems to be the key, and right now, sewing is part of that preoccupation.

I also keep myself occupied by spending time with Wilson. He seems more accessible to me than he did in the past, but this is not to last long. In addition, the time with him is not with him alone—it is also with his granddaughters, age 3 and 5, and at times, with his son, Paul, who is in prison. The girls are adorable, as they chatter away in both Spanish and English. I spend endless hours shopping in thrift stores for girlish tops and pants for them. Wilson and I race around with the girls in the park, pushing them on swings and guiding them down the slides.

Visiting Wilson's son, Paul, is grueling yet fascinating. Only later do I understand what an amazing distraction this is for me, and in that way, it is a gift—temporary though it is. Never before have I been inside the gates of a prison or felt cruelty and hate of this proportion: it's thick in the air.

The guards bark orders to you and hate streams from their eyes. They do a complete body search, which is required before a visit. I take the little girls into a tiny room, strip them and myself of all clothes and wait for a female guard to come in and search us: we are stark naked. I try to soothe the little girls through all of this, wondering how much of this hate they are absorbing. After the body search, I dress them again and wait our turn to go out into a big, barren room where prisoners sit at small tables, ready for their 15-minute visit. Finally, it's our turn to visit Paul. He's nervous but oh-so-happy to see his girls. He doesn't pay much attention to his father and he totally ignores me. It doesn't occur to him to thank me for the effort and energy I have exerted to get his daughters here. But Wilson, in the two-hour car ride back to Chicago, is clearly (though quietly) grateful for my help. The intrigue of these prison visits and the fun of playing with the girls keeps me well occupied for a while.

By this time, Thanksgiving is upon us and I get enthused about making a big Thanksgiving meal. I have always loved preparing a feast for holidays, and this is no exception. Just the idea of it takes my mind off of my problems and sets me in the direction of pure delight. I will invite Gloria and Wilson, and my nephew and his wife, who are now in town.

I carefully plan the menu and start buying the food: the turkey, of course; the potatoes, asparagus, cranberry sauce, canned pumpkin, fresh fruit, onions, celery and applesauce; and the list goes on.

The best time is the night before Thanksgiving, when Nathan arrives. We have a long tradition of making this meal together. He is a man who loves to cook and bake, and by this time in his life, he is a pro at making a variety of dishes. Sourdough bread and spicy Indian dinners are just a few of his specialties. I love this about him. He has tried to teach me how to make sourdough bread by explaining both the mechanics of it and the chemistry, but I have never quite caught on.

The night before Thanksgiving we make pumpkin pie. Pumpkin pie is our specialty, for it is not your ordinary, heavy, dark pie. It is light and fluffy. But the key for me is the pure joy of doing it with Nathan. We've made this pie together for years, and as we work, things go as smoothly as though we were dancing across a ballroom floor. It's a ritual I can always count on. Tonight, more than ever, it provides me with some steadiness and grounding in a life that has too often felt like quicksand.

The recipe we use for making the pumpkin pie is from the *The Mennonite Community Cookbook*—the cookbook from my childhood. Since we love this pumpkin pie, we triple the recipe.

We happily walk through each step, to make our precious pies. The first step is to scald milk—an old-fashioned procedure in which you slowly bring your milk to a slight boil. Next, you take the eggs and carefully divide the yolks from the whites. You then stir the yolks and mix them with brown sugar and spices: ginger, cloves and cinnamon. Next, you gradually add the scalded milk. Then you beat the egg whites until stiff peaks form. (It is always fun to watch the gooey, slimy egg whites evolve into white, stiff peaks.) The last step of making the pie involves gradually and carefully folding the egg whites into the mixture of pumpkin, spices, brown sugar, milk and egg yolks. Nathan is the pro at this.

The best part of it all comes when the pies are baking in the oven and Nathan and I sit down and have a cup of tea. This time with him is priceless, and I savor every moment. I just wish it would never end.

On Thanksgiving morning, I set the table. I always love to set a pretty table. I have given my brown pottery to Nathan—which, with its orange placemats, would have been perfect for Thanksgiving. But I'm happy he is using it, and I can tell he is enjoying using it as much as I did.

So I set the table with my blue-and-white flowered dishes from Israel. They are certainly beautiful and delicate in their own way, as I set them on light-blue placemats complemented with linen napkins. The crystal water and wine glasses sparkle in the sun coming through the windows.

Just before our guests are due, Nathan sautés the asparagus in garlic and olive oil. We cut the bread he has made and I open the can of cranberries, placing it in a little crystal bowl. Nathan mashes the potatoes with my handheld mixer and I prepare the gravy. Nathan then carves the turkey, arranging it nicely on a platter.

At around noon, our guests arrive. We serve them wine and we gather around the table. I offer a short prayer of thanksgiving: "Thank you, O Lord, for this time together; for each person here at the table. Thank you for Nathan, who helped me prepare it. Thank you for good health and for this food. Amen." Never in my life have I been as thankful as I am now.

We dig in. Everybody is hungry and, in reality, we eat rather quickly and do not converse very much. It may not be all that polite, but it is gratifying to me. After the first course we take a short break, as we all need some time to digest the food before we have dessert. I happily go to the kitchen and cut the pumpkin pie, which is exactly the right consistency; it holds together firmly without being stiff. The egg whites have made the pie chiffon-like and lighter in color than the usual dark pumpkin pie. The guests ooh and aah over the pie, and I feel proud and appreciated. We all retire to the living room and chit-chat for an hour or so. The guests offer to help with the dishes, but I decline their offer. I have lots of time for dishes. I say, "Let us just be together."

Then the guests go home. I tell Nathan to go also. He has work to complete that he has put on hold for the occasion. I gladly do the dishes, working at them slowly and lovingly. I put the pretty plates back into the china cabinet.

The joy of Thanksgiving stays in my heart for about five days. Then the darkness starts to move in. I don't say anything about this to my friends and family. They have been so kind, and I don't want to upset them in any way. Fears creep in. Grief over losing my profession eats away at me. Living without a man who truly cares about me brings about feelings of intense loneliness. It is also now five months since my ECT treatments ended, and I will later learn that stopping them was a mistake. I am feeling really, really dark inside. But the Christmas season soon comes, and I decorate my apartment with blue lights and fancy wreathes adorned with red and gold balls. Nathan and I have a quiet Christmas with some of his friends. I smile on the outside, but inside I am screaming. I know I am getting very depressed again, and I feel desperate.

This is worsened by the fact that Nathan talks about moving to Washington, D.C. to fulfill his dream of working in international relations. On one hand, I want to encourage him: as I followed my dreams in my 20s, I want him to do the same. My mother had encouraged me to get my doctorate, and so I encourage him to move to D.C. On the other hand, I am terrified of living without him. He has been my anchor since my divorce seven years ago. I know it hasn't always been healthy, but it is how I survived. And so Nathan decides to leave.

Before he leaves, we learn about a day treatment program at yet another Chicago hospital—Rush-Presbyterian-St. Luke's Medical Center, on the west side. They have a great outpatient program. I'm interviewed and accepted. It is hard to get to, for it is on the west side of Chicago and I live on the north side, and driving there in rush-hour traffic would likely take two hours. Furthermore, I'd likely get lost. We conclude that I must take public transportation. Nathan patiently takes me for a dry run. It's long and complicated, and being early January, it's very cold.

On our dry run to the hospital, we first catch a bus across Devon Avenue. Next, we catch a train downtown, and there, we switch trains and head to the west side. Then we walk two blocks to the hospital. Nathan holds my hand as we walk, with tears in his eyes as he whispers, "You can do it, mother." I only partially believe him. Yet, with tears rolling down my cheeks, I assure him, "I can do it. I know this is the right thing for you and for me."

In a week, Nathan moves to Washington, D.C. I help him pack and then accompany him there to help him unpack. For four days, I am totally functional and happy. The two of us work together to assemble his apartment. From Target, we buy floor lamps and green towels with a matching shower curtain; from Whole Foods, we buy brown rice, flour for his bread and spices for his Indian dishes. Nathan has a perfect home and I know it is the right time for him to begin his career in D.C. I'm feeling happy for him as he drops me off at the airport, confident I can live my life without him. I am determined to be strong for Nathan as he has been for me. I am excited that he is now free to follow his dream, unencumbered by me. He has cared for me for seven years. What other young man has ever devoted so much love and patience to his mother? My family adores him and respects him as much as I do.

When Nathan drops me off at Washington Dulles International Airport, I see him for the first time as an adult man—not only as my son. He is a handsome man, about 5 feet 10 inches tall, and slender but strong. His years of playing Frisbee at the University of Chicago have made him an athlete. His dark-brown eyes and short, dark hair make him so attractive.

Yet in his former hippie-like days, with his thick hair reaching well below his shoulders, he looked just as handsome.

Now Nathan is staying in Washington, D.C. to begin a career in international relations. While I don't understand what this is really about, I know he will find his way. I am determined to make my way apart from him, so he can be unburdened by me.

When I return to Chicago, I again face the question, "Where will I go to church?" Two years ago I left Edgewater Presbyterian Church, having been fired because of my professional impropriety. Since moving to live near Gloria, I have tried several churches, but none of them have felt right. Then I come upon an evangelical church near my home. Perhaps, after all, I should dip back into my childhood tradition—the one that I left for liberal Protestant churches. It is worth a try. I jump headlong into it: I attend Sunday worship, Sunday school and Wednesday night classes. Somehow, I am encouraged to confess my sins. I am encouraged to make a list of my sins, and I do. I list arrogance, adultery, greed, rage and most of all, a lack of faith in God. I declare to my class that I have found a deeper trust in God than ever before and that I believe a renewed relationship with Jesus will protect me from the darkness of depression and the swings of mania. I believe that my old fears of being abandoned by God are gone. This church is my new preoccupation, and it works—briefly.

By this time, I am fully engaged in the day-treatment program at Rush-Presbyterian-St. Luke's. I bravely take public transportation down to the loop and out to the west side. It takes 90 minutes to get there and it is very cold—a cold that penetrates fleecy underwear and a fur coat. But I like the program. The group therapy is led by a social worker, David. He is clearly competent and he speaks the psychological language that I, myself, had used in my years of practice. In some ways he helps me understand my own diagnosis of manic-depression, yet I learn later that I still have not grasped the full import of it. David gives me hope. He believes I can learn to live with my illness and have a life in which I can be functional and productive. For me, productivity is the key. If I feel I am contributing to society—to the wellbeing of others—I feel good about myself. For three and a half months, I am happy. I feel like I am one of the patients who is experiencing personal growing. I am finally a success once again. I believe that it is only a matter of time before I will become productive in my profession.

I boost my sense of well-being by filling my apartment with nature. First, I buy a canary—a beautiful, yellow canary that sings all day long, it seems, and especially in the morning as I wake up. Its cheerful presence seems to drive away the blues that are so often there. I buy 10 African violets. I've always loved African violets, and my violets remind me of my mother, who also loved them. Caring for the African violets and the canary gives me a certain joy and purpose.

But come April, the downward spiral begins. I try to stop it by clinging to Wilson, but this only serves to distance him further from me. At one point, I muster the courage to ask him if he truly loves me. I ask him on the phone; I could never do it in person. When I ask, I am very aware that my voice is quiet and my words come slowly. When I ask, there is silence. Then, in a soft and caring voice, he responds, "I once was in love with a woman—a very lovely woman—but she was not in love with me. That was very hard for me. Very hard. So I understand your disappointment in me. I care about you, but I cannot say that I love you. And I know our relationship will not end in marriage." The conversation ends very quickly after that. I hang up the phone and start to cry. Yet I am not surprised with his answer. I knew all along that Wilson cared for me but did not love me.

I call Nathan and tell him what I have done. He says, "I'm so proud of you, mother—of your courage to ask Wilson this. I've been hoping you could do this. I've thought all along that Wilson did not care for you the way you did for him. But I know this is so hard for you. I just want you to know how much I love you." I am comforted by Nathan's love. I know deep within that his love will always be there.

The phone call with Wilson adds to the downward spiraling that had begun several days earlier. The spiraling happens fast—very fast—and it terrifies me. I now am so familiar with the pattern. It is a cold April week-end, and I'm home alone. It's Friday afternoon—days away from the next church service on Sunday, and the day treatment program on Monday. The darkness descends, darker and stronger than ever before. From within, I scream, "I am a discarded wife. I am a failed psychologist. I am a counterfeit minister. I carry secrets about abuse that I will never be able to heal. I am trapped in failure."

I feel like I am drowning in water beneath a layer of ice that I will never be able to break through. I look into the mirror and see a woman who appears 70 years old; who has no light left in her eyes, no shine in her skin, sagging shoulders and breasts and a hunched back. I barely recognize myself.

"Do I want to die?" I ask myself. The answer is "Yes—yes, if I am forever trapped." And it seems that I am forever trapped. No amount of love, and no amount of therapy, pills or ECT has spared me. I ask, "Is there no escape?"

I go back to bed to try to drown the misery in sleep. But I cannot sleep. I toss and turn. I get up and pace. The darkness only gets darker, heavier, blacker. I try again to sleep, but sleep is a million miles away—unreachable. I walk into the kitchen and see my pills—five bottles of pills—lined up on the first shelf of the kitchen cupboard. Suddenly, I know—it's like it is revealed to me from deep within—that the pills are my answer. I take them down from the shelf and place them on the kitchen counter. My spirit begins to lift, for I know I have found an answer—at least, an answer that will get me through the weekend. I will take enough pills to sleep until Sunday. I won't take enough to kill myself—I wouldn't want to do that, to put my family and friends through a suicide, when I have already caused so much pain. No, I could not do it—especially not to Nathan. Nathan is in D.C., making a life for himself, and I will not put him through a suicide. Furthermore, if I die by suicide, I might land in hell—the church I am now attending preaches that, and my childhood church preaches that. The liberal churches, however, do not preach that. They hold the belief that grace and forgiveness covers suicide. I am torn. Who is right?

At any rate, my plan is to take only enough pills to sleep through the weekend. So I stand at my kitchen counter and start pouring out pills— all white, but in different shapes. Some are oblong, some are round, some are thick and others are thin. I am faced with a dilemma: how many pills should I take to sleep through the weekend? I stand at the counter, trying to figure it out. Who can help me with this problem? No one. Whomever I call would destroy my plan. So I start taking pills. At first, I take five or six. Then I take a few more. I take another dozen or so, and I wait a bit. Soon, I start to get groggy, and know that relief is on its way. I'll be able to sleep for the weekend. I go to the bathroom, get into my fleecy, pink pajamas and crawl into bed. Just as I get into bed, the telephone rings. It is a friend from Florida whom I haven't talked to in a while, and since she is going through a hard time, I stay on the phone with her for a few minutes. But then I tell her I'm not feeling well and that I need to get to bed. I put the phone down, feeling myself drifting off. I am content.

But then—damn—my phone rings again. Should I answer it? No. Well, maybe I should. OK, I'll answer, but I'll say that I'm about to take a nap and will call back. So I pick up the phone. The voice says, "Hi Lucille, this is Peter, your brother." "Hello," I answer, in my groggy voice. "Lucille—you don't sound right. Are you OK?" I hear panic in his voice. I barely answer, but I mumble, "I just took a few pills to get to sleep for awhile." Peter answers, "I'm very worried." He hangs up the phone.

Later I learn that Peter immediately called Nathan. Nathan immediately called Gloria, who lives five blocks away. Gloria calls 911, saying, "My friend has overdosed—send medics right away." Gloria then races to my apartment, not even taking the time to slip on her shoes. She sprints barefoot. By the time Gloria arrives, the police are already there, finding a way to open my door. By this time I'm asleep, but I wake up when they come through the door. Gloria and the police rush to my room and walk me out of my apartment, down the stairs and into the medical van. They put me on a stretcher and race me to Swedish Covenant Hospital. I doze off to sleep during the ride.

I later learn that one policeman has stayed behind to collect my pills—the pills spread out on the counter, which number about 100, and the pills left in the bottles. They will be used at the hospital to determine how much I have taken.

When I arrive at the hospital, I am awakened again and am instructed to drink a black, chalky substance. Gloria is by my side. Her voice is very calm and her eyes are filled with both extreme fear and intense love. She and the nurse sit by me, and the two of them keep insisting that I continue to drink the black, chalky substance. I later learn that chalk absorbs the pills and somehow extracts them from the stomach. Apparently, stomachs are no longer pumped for overdoses; chalk works just as well.

Gloria later tells me that black chalk was dripping down my chin, but I was compliant in drinking it. I drank and I drank—I don't know how much, it seemed like a lot—and this goes on for a long time—maybe about an hour. Slowly, I regain some energy and, with the help of the nurses, I walk around a bit. Slowly, I begin to come to my senses and realize that I had been wrong to take all the pills and that I could have died with the amount of pills I had taken. I begin to realize that if my brother had not called me, I might have been dead; if Gloria had not been home and able to rescue me, I might not have been found in time.

I remember, at that time, that two years earlier, I had rescued Gloria when she had heart failure. I had heard the lethargy in her voice and had rushed her to the hospital. Now she has saved me. The bond between us becomes irrevocably as strong as iron, and we will be sisters at the deepest level for life—for we have saved each other while at death's doorway.

I stay at Swedish Covenant Hospital for three weeks. It is a nice enough hospital. Friends from my new church come to visit, and Gloria is there every day. Nathan calls daily. The psychiatrist is Dr. Taylor, a middle-age man who is rather nondescript but is in no way condescending or judgmental, as Dr. Burn was. Plus, he has a nice portion of warmth in him.

This hospital is the fourth hospital I have been in: Lakeshore, for four weeks; Northwestern, for four weeks; Rush-Presbyterian-St. Luke's, for three months; and now Swedish Covenant. So, the obvious dilemma is—what next? Is there any help for me? If so, what could it be? Must I be placed in a psychiatric institution for the rest of my life? My son agonizes. My family and friends worry. I am terrified at the thought of spending the rest of my life in a psychiatric institution. I have heard horror stories of people locked in rooms, drugged and never visited by family or friends. I believe that my family would never abandon me, but I also realize that their energy is not limitless.

Finally, my family finds one more possible solution: Gould Farm, in Massachusetts. Gould Farm is a rehabilitation center whose philosophy is based on work—work on a 650-acre farm.

Gould Farm is a self-sustaining farm with many work teams for the guests. (The patients at Gould Farm are called "guests," and that fact alone is deeply inviting, with no hint of condescension.) The literature from the farm contains a quote from a former guest that captures my attention: "When I came to the farm I was in a hole that I truthfully wasn't sure I'd ever be able to climb out of." The literature also states, "We harvest hope." Another guest writes, "I do feel as though that was big for me:

experiencing hope. Really, the difference is just night and day: I was in such a bad place when I got here and going forward I'm just so hopeful and enthusiastic … It's really remarkable. I'm grateful."

The possibility of going to Gould Farm provides me with a ray of hope, a ray of light. Getting to Gould Farm, I realize, will be a process. It will not happen immediately. But it gives me hope. *Hope.*

7

Unstinting Kindness

I know I can no longer live by myself. My family knows this, too. While in the hospital recovering from my overdose, we decide that I will go to Philadelphia to stay with my brother, Peter, and his wife, Eunice. Peter later tells me how profoundly sad he felt about my condition; that my sisters had tried to help. Now it was his turn, even though he had no idea how to help me. He said that Eunice—being a therapist herself—gladly joined him in his commitment, although she, too, was baffled by my condition.

I am in Chicago, in the hospital for exactly three weeks. Gloria visits me faithfully, of course. She later tells me how my illness affected her. "I just felt so powerless. It left me with a sense of helplessness." But Gloria does what she can. Upon my release from the hospital, she takes me to my apartment, helps me pack two suitcases and puts me on a plane to Philadelphia. I am barely in Philadelphia a day before I pour over the literature I have received from Gould Farm, which is located in the Berkshires of Massachusetts. The mission statement of Gould Farm is deeply inviting: "Emotional rehabilitation based on the principles of respectful discipline, wholesome work and unstinting kindness." I love the term "unstinting kindness." These are such healing words; such hopeful words.

I also find immense hope in the possibility of rehabilitation through work. Work has, for me, always been central to a sense of self. If I'm working, I feel good. Furthermore, it is the philosophy of Gould Farm that rehabilitation is not fast: it does not happen in a few weeks, or even a few months. It might take years. At Gould Farm, patients may stay for up to three years.

A week after I arrive in Philadelphia, Peter and Eunice take me to Gould Farm for a visit and for an interview for possible admission. We learn that Gould Farm was founded in 1913 and is the first and oldest rehabilitation center based on the principles of work. We stay overnight in the guest house—a lovely space with big windows and oak floors. I experience firsthand that the patients at Gould Farm are called guests, just as the literature had said. My heart is warmed. I've been a patient for years, but here, I would be a guest.

I learn at this time that Gould Farm is affordable for me. I do not have the money to pay the full fee but will be allowed to pay what is within my budget. This sliding-scale option is available for two primary reasons: one, because some members of the staff are volunteers; and two, because of substantial fundraising. For this I am deeply grateful. At this time I have $10,000 in medical bills from Chicago, but Peter oversees my finances and, as a result, I only end up having to pay $2,000.

In the visit to the farm, I learn that there are 40 guests and 60 staff members. The staff includes family members, which means that children and spouses are considered part of the Gould Farm family. The guests and staff are assigned to eight work teams. First, there is the garden team. This team is already at work planting beans, corn, tomatoes, kale, carrots and much more. Then there is the baking team, which bakes bread, cakes, pies and cookies. We sample the banana nut bread, and it is scrumptious! There is the kitchen team—the team that plans and prepares food for the guests and staff. The kitchen team makes and uses healthy food—spinach, couscous and organic beef—and it is very much unlike hospital food. There is the child care team, which cares for the young children of the staff. The farm team milks the cows, shovels the manure, plows the land and brings in the hay.

In early spring, there is the maple syrup team—the team that collects sap from 200 trees, boils it into syrup and bottles the syrup for sale. There is the cleaning team, which cleans the dining hall, the common rooms in the guest houses and the large meeting rooms. Finally, there is the Roadside Café team, which operates a small restaurant that serves the larger community. Peter, Eunice and I stop at the cafe for tea and cookies, and we are impressed not only with the food but with the proficiency and warmth of the guests. We are already absorbing "unstinting kindness."

I'm intrigued by it all. I've never seen anything like it, and it gives me hope. I'm accepted into the program, but I must go back to Philadelphia with Peter and Eunice until an opening is available. Back in Philadelphia, I am faced with a new obstacle: what to do with everything I left in Chicago. My apartment is still filled with everything I own, with the exception of what I brought to Philadelphia in two suitcases. The apartment must be attended to. So on the third weekend in Philadelphia, Nathan flies from Washington, D.C. to Chicago and assembles a team to pack up my apartment. He brings two friends from Hyde Park, and Gloria and Wilson join them. They work nonstop all weekend. The men carry the furniture while Gloria packs my precious, hand-painted dishes from Israel, my mother's china teacups, my lifetime collection of knickknacks and my family photos. She packs the photo of Grandpa Cline, who rocked me for hours, and the photo of Cherry, my beloved childhood cousin. It will not be long until Cherry will offer me a gift too large to even totally comprehend.

With my apartment packed, Nathan drives the U-Haul truck to Philadelphia, drops off some of my belongings and furniture, and takes other furniture with him to D.C. It is a whirlwind weekend for him—an exhausting labor of love. But for him, also, it is a labor full of hope. He has long been nagged with the question, "Will my mother ever recover?"

I move to Gould Farm in May of 2003. I am 57 years old. It is now more than seven years since the separation from Louie and since my first depressive episode. The room I am assigned to at Gould Farm is not really inviting. It is small, with a single bed, a desk, a dresser and a small closet. The walls are painted an institutional off-white and there is a small window. Pictures of Nathan and my family, however, help to make this room my own. The building I am in has just one floor and 12 rooms, including two bathrooms. The other guests in my building are in their 20s and 30s, and while they are friendly, I'm not really drawn to develop a relationship with any of them.

In contrast to the bleakness of my bedroom is a nearby building with a large dining room—and this is totally inviting. It has lots of windows and various nooks and crannies. Adjoining the dining room is the living room. The living room is smaller than the dining room, but it has lots of cushy chairs and sofas and a beautiful stone fireplace with a wood mantle. Jutting out from the living room is a small, rounded space just big enough to fit a baby grand piano and eight people, who can stand around it and sing. From the very beginning I often sit in the living room—sometimes with others, or just by myself—people watching ... wondering about their stories, their struggles, their strengths. The psychologist in me is always at work: analyzing, analyzing. The Gould Farm guests are very fascinating people, and I am certain from the beginning that this is a place where I can belong. It is a place where I will not fear being abandoned.

The team that I am invited to join is the garden team. I love it immediately. The peas, planted in March, are already peeking through the ground and are in need of tender weeding. Gently pulling out these weeds, on my knees, is deeply satisfying. The earth itself is so accepting of my body. The sun, shining above, dispels the darkness of my soul.

In the summer we harvest all of the vegetables—peppers and beans, carrots and onions, lettuce and kale, and many more. Most of all I love picking the cherry tomatoes, as hundreds of them drip from the vines. I pop scores of them in my mouth, and their sweetness ascends to my spirit.

Our days at Gould Farm are not filled only with work. Each day begins with a post-breakfast morning meeting that includes announcements, a poem and some group songs. The songs are uplifting—*We Shall Overcome* or *Oh, What a Beautiful Mornin'*, to name a couple. Poetry and singing have never been part of any other rehabilitation I have had over the years. I take to it straightaway. Saturdays are a day for outings, and we go to the movie theater, the mall and the bookstore. My routine on those trips soon becomes that of stopping at the ice cream stand to get a peach smoothie made with fresh peaches.

Come fall, when the garden is tucked away for the winter, I join the child care team. There are six children, ages 3 to 6, and within a day I am playing peek-a-boo and singing *Twinkle, Twinkle, Little Star*. The second day I build towers with the children, using brightly colored red, green, blue and yellow blocks. We hold our breath when the tower gets high and we clap when it falls down.

All of this works well for me until late October. Then I begin a downward spiral. I become lethargic, have sudden, crying outbursts and withdraw from both staff and guests. It happens very quickly, and there seems to be no precipitating event. Perhaps it is the coming of winter; perhaps it is a certain loneliness, for at that time I do not have any close friends. Whatever the reason, it is clear I cannot function on the farm. I am terrified that work rehabilitation, even with "unstinting kindness," will not work for me. After considerable struggling, my family and I turn, once again, to ECT. After all, it had worked back in Chicago. So I am admitted to Berkshire Medical Center—located nearby, in Pittston—to begin ECT. I will have 12 treatments—three a week for one month.

I am comfortable in the hospital, as I was at Northwestern Memorial in Chicago. The walls are decorated with inviting artwork of the four seasons of the year, and the staff and patients are friendly. The psychiatrist for administering the ECT is young, warm and confident. The nurse who is present for the treatments caresses my feet as the treatment begins. The beginning of the ECT treatment is always the same: receiving an injection that quickly puts me to sleep. When asleep, an electrical shock is administered to the brain, which causes the "convulsion" that is believed to scramble the neurotransmitters and give them the opportunity to reassemble themselves in a healthy way.

Awakening from ECT is brutal. This is similar to the experiences I'd had after receiving ECT two years earlier, in Chicago. The only difference is that this time, there is no long-term memory loss. It does not, in any way, wipe out memories from my childhood or my later years. For this I am deeply grateful.

ECT works its magic, and in four weeks I'm back on the farm. This time, I join the bread-making team. I immediately take to it. There is nothing more sensual to the touch than kneading a gigantic bowl of bread; nothing like the magic of yeast rising to raise your spirit. And there is nothing like biting into a slice of freshly baked bread, slathered with butter, to feed your body and soul so sweetly.

When I return to the farm, it seems significantly easier to make friends with other guests. I don't know why I had not done this earlier, but I am finding friends now. There is Jenny, who gives me a lovely children's book she has written about a maple tree that falls in love with an oak tree. Jenny is such a tender soul. I get to know John, a Jewish doctor who emotionally collapsed under the stress of residency. He is profoundly depressed, but a lovely human being. There is Albert, a rising musician who will soon enjoy a national reputation. Most of all there is Tim, the owner of a small shop of creams and oils of his own creation. All of these people are wounded, struggling with severe mental illness. All have received years of treatment that have not worked. All, along with their families, are hoping that work rehabilitation and unstinting kindness will be the answer.

My psychiatrist, Dr. Taylor, adjusts my medication. First he puts me on Lamictal, which is a mood stabilizer. I am given the diagnosis of bipolar disorder—the common name of which is manic depression. As I look back, it is clear that I have suffered from manic depression, although the majority of my swings have been due to depression. This diagnosis just feels right in the core of my being. It gives me hope that I can truly stabilize.

Dr. Taylor also adjusts my medication in two other ways. He gives me a small dose of Risperdal, which is sometimes used to keep the edge off of depression. He also increases the dosages of my sleeping medications, Temazepam and Ambien. This is such a relief, for now I am getting a solid night's sleep. I hate lying awake at night, trying to fall asleep, as I have done ever since my first depressive episode. None of that deep breathing, soothing music or melatonin has ever worked for me. So now, taking plenty of sleep medication eliminates the dread of trying to fall asleep.

Soon after returning to the farm, I find a new therapist. I have been seeing Katy, the woman assigned to me when I arrived. She is warm and friendly, but our conversations have never really had enough purpose or direction. Our conversations have not probed the depths of the psyche and the wisdom of the unconscious. I need this, so I insist that I find a therapist who can provide it. I am given Mary, who lives in the community. I like her immediately. She helps me analyze the meaning of my dreams, which are often dark, chaotic and threatening, with men chasing and overpowering me. Dream interpretation is enhanced by hypnosis. In the hypnotic trances I continue to probe the pain of being abandoned by Louie and the fears I still carry about my childhood religious teachings of hell and God's judgment. I find hypnosis fascinating, both from the perspective of myself, as a psychologist, and as a client. With this therapy I know I am making progress in both understanding and healing the shadows of my past. But I do not focus on the sexual abuse of my childhood.

My family, as always, is supportive of me. Nathan visits faithfully from Washington, D.C., and when he cannot come he arranges ways for me to visit him. He introduces me to his D.C. friends and does not seem ashamed that his mother suffers from a mental illness, is divorced twice and is not functional, professionally. He clearly does not hold this against me. I am the only one who holds this against myself. At the core of my being I carry a stigma—a prejudice—perhaps even a hatred—for myself and for others who have a mental illness. On an intellectual level I know that I am wrong, but my intellect does not override my psyche. I do not share this prejudice with anyone—not even my therapist.

While Nathan is absolutely loving with me, he tells me later how hard all of this was for him. One time, after visiting me, I called him when he was driving back to D.C. I scolded him for not calling me, when the reality is that he was calling me every day. After I scolded him, he tells me, "I just pulled my car over to the side of the road and cried." Yet when talking with him about my illness and expressing my sorrow about everything he had to do for me, he replies, "It made me a better person." What an amazing person!

Other family members stay in close touch. My brother, Peter, and his wife, Eunice, come from Philadelphia to visit me at the farm, and they sometimes invite me to stay at their house on weekends. The next summer, they invite me to their cottage in Maine—and it is in Maine that I bare my secrets. I tell them about the sexual abuse by the hired man when I was 6 years old; about the fact that he threw manure on me and that mother wanted him fired but father would not hear of it. I tell them about Edmond sexually abusing me when I was 15. I tell them that I had told our parents about this abuse, but that they did nothing but pray. Peter and Eunice believe me: they do not question whether or not this is true. In fact, Eunice, a therapist, asks me if I would consider exposing this to the family and taking Edmond to court. The whole idea is completely overwhelming, and I decline. But the seed has been planted.

My younger brother, Benny, and his wife, Laura, travel from Canada to Massachusetts to visit me at the farm. This is the brother, I now realize, who is like my beloved grandfather: quiet, but sturdy and wise. I tell him and his wife about the sexual abuse by the hired man on the farm and about the abuse by Edmond. They listen; they believe me; and I am affirmed. This now means that all of my siblings—with the exception of Ruth—know about the sexual abuse. It will be six years until I tell her.

Back at the farm, I begin to find that I am artistically creative. Gould Farm has a 3-mile walk, and on my evening walks—usually with another guest or two—I begin to notice the brilliant fall leaves that have fallen onto the ground. I collect them—dozens of them, a full array of them—in shades of green, orange, brown and gold; in shapes of maple, oak, ash and apple leaves. As I did as a child, I press the leaves between pages of my books and then carefully iron them between sheets of wax paper, thereby preserving them. I tenderly cherish each leaf. I buy thick construction paper and rubber cement glue. I arrange the leaves artistically on the paper and glue them to it. As it turns out, I create three lovely pieces of art.

One of my pieces of art is large—18 by 20 inches—and the theme is maple leaves, inspired by the maple leaf of my native country, Canada. Many colors of leaves are layered, with only parts of each leaf showing. The stems of the leaves are pointed toward the center of the paper, and in the center is a tiny, red leaf that highlights and consolidates the whole piece of art. I am delighted with it. I buy a light, wooden frame for it and show it to Danielle, my favorite staff member. She is immediately taken by it and insists that it be hung in the dining hall. I am very proud and I get many compliments from both fellow guests and staff members.

My two other pieces of art are smaller, with different themes. One is organized around a huge oak leaf. For this piece I cut out the center of the leaf—except for the arteries—and weave smaller leaves around the large oak leaf. I am thrilled with the result.

My third piece of art is a collection of a variety of small leaves—maple, ash, oak and willow—in addition to leaves from flowers that I found along the road. The leaves are layered so that the contrasting colors and shapes are highlighted; all are pointed down and to the left, leaving the feeling of movement and purpose.

In years to come I will hang this art in my house and will receive many, many compliments about it. I later come to realize how immersing myself into nature, as I did in choosing those leaves and then arranging them artistically, is healing. It unites me with nature and, in a mystical way, lifts me into a deep communion with the divine.

At Gould Farm I rediscover my love of music, especially playing the piano. I start to practice every day and soon, I find a small number of guests joining me around the piano every morning after breakfast. As we did in my family 50 years ago, we sing in four-part harmony, with me carrying the alto. I like the sound of my voice. It is strong yet tender, and full of emotion.

I rediscover the hymn I had learned at Yale Divinity School, and it speaks to me deeply: *God of my life, through all the circling years, we trust in Thee; in all the past, through all our hopes and fear, Thy hand we see. With each new day, when morning lifts the veil, we own Thy mercies, Lord, which never fail.* It is clear that, despite the pain I have been through in recent years, my faith in God has helped sustain me. It still does. Even though my early childhood was full of fear of God—especially of being abandoned by God—somehow, miraculously, a faith in God's love has always been there. I have never turned my back on God, even with all the pain. And so I sing and sing the hymn. *God of my life, through all the circling years, we trust in Thee.*

Not only do I find myself singing old, familiar hymns, but I also learn some new ones. The one that I sing and play over and over again is *O God, in Restless Living*, composed by Harry Everson Fosdick, pastor of the famous Riverside Church in New York City. I sing: *O God, in restless living, we lose our spirit's peace. Calm our unwise confusion, Bid thou our clamor cease. Let anxious hearts grow quiet, like pools at evening still, till thy reflected heaven, all our spirits fill.* So often, I find myself playing and singing this hymn and finding an inner peace.

I join the evening campfires and listen to Jason on his violin, playing everything from Beethoven's *Symphony No. 5* to *You Are My Sunshine*. He plays with such deep feeling that it brings me close to tears. I listen to Tim, playing his guitar, and I join in singing the song he had composed for his son: *It's a ba, ba, beautiful day, it's a ba, ba, beautiful day. The skies are blue, and I'm with you. It's a ba, ba, beautiful day.*

I find a special friend in Tim. He is my age, unlike most guests, who are considerably younger. Like me, he has a son. Like me, he struggles with manic depression, although his swings are usually in the direction of mania instead of depression. Like my family, his family—including his wife—has stood by him. Their last resort for finding help for Tim was with Gould Farm.

Tim is soft-spoken, with kind eyes and a gentle smile. His sweet soul—his very being—draws me to him. He has a head of thick, white hair and a dense, white beard. He is a medium-large man with a strong body, which has the effect of providing a certain protective quality. Tim explains the founding of his store in Tennessee that sells creams and oils. The massage cream that he created is widely used in that part of the country. Tim gives me lavender oil from his shop and tells me to put a drop or two on my pillow each night; he says it will have a quieting effect. It seems to work for me. When I tell him about my mother and her love for rose perfume, he gives me rose oil. Wearing it makes me feel close to my mother, and at this time I badly need that comfort. While my relationship with Tim is sweet and tender, there are never any sexual innuendos between us. He is a perfectly safe man to be with. Our relationship is rooted in a deep kinship. He, like me, knows insanity and is fighting for his life to be freed from its grips. This is survival bonding.

Having a special friend like Tim always gives me a person to sit with at meals. While the staff and guests are friendly, I sometimes feel anxious when entering the dining hall, wondering just where to sit. If Tim gets there before I arrive, he always saves a place for me; if I am there before him, I save a place for him.

At Gould Farm, all the men—both guests and staff—are safe to be around. None are smarmy in any way. One of the farmers smells a bit—he obviously doesn't take enough showers after shoveling manure—but he is not smarmy. The only time I am faced with a smarmy man is when I go to Canada and I have to be around my brother-in-law, Edmond. I stay far away from him, not allowing him to hug me. But this does not prevent him from staring at my breasts. I truly despise him, and at times, I feel a bit guilty for my hatred.

I settle into a church near Gould Farm: United Church of Christ, which is very much like the church in which I was ordained. I am comfortable there. I like the minister, Kate, who is very warm and inviting. She is a graduate of Harvard Divinity School. With my seminary training at Yale Divinity School, I feel a kinship with her. Much, much more important, however, is the fact that mental illness is understood and accepted in this church. I do not feel outcast because I am at Gould Farm, and I am soon invited to participate in Bible studies and other church functions. I make contributions to the discussions and feel that my education and experience are being used. So often during my illness, I have felt that my education and experience were wasted. Now it is once again valued by others, and more importantly, it is valued by me.

Another benefit of this church is that one of the two psychiatrists from Gould Farm, Dr. Gable, attends there. He is the minister's husband. Like his wife, the pastor, he was educated at Harvard. One morning after church, I ask him a question that has been nagging at me for some time—a question with two parts: "What is the rate of success of the treatment of people with severe mental illness?" And: "How does the success rate at Gould Farm compare to the success rate at the other psychiatric center where you work?" (The other center that Dr. Gable works at is more psychoanalytic in approach than Gould Farm.)

Dr. Gable pauses before he responds to my questions. He appears hesitant, but the answer he gives is sobering. "The two rehabilitation programs where I work have a similar success rate. About one-third of the patients recover significantly; about one-third move in and out of functional living; and about one-third become very sick and are permanently severely mentally ill." I quietly thank him for this information, and move away from him quickly. I hope and pray that I am in the one-third group that recovers significantly. That statistic becomes firmly lodged in my mind, and in future years I recall it, determined to be part of that one-third that recovers significantly.

It is now seven months since I have been at Gould Farm, and Christmas is approaching. I am afraid about where I will be at Christmas and whether or not I will be with family. As always, I am in close touch with Nathan. At one point I ask him gingerly what we will do. Immediately, he replies, "Of course I will be with you at Christmas! We are always together at Christmas. I will come to Gould Farm." I am so relieved. Tears of gratitude for my son fill my eyes. I know I am the luckiest mother in the whole world. For Christmas dinner, Nathan and I join many other guests and staff member for a feast of turkey and all of the typical trimmings. When it is time for Nathan to return home, my eyes are again filled with tears—some tears of gratitude, but some of sorrow for our need to be apart. When he returns to Washington, D.C., I am forlorn. The staff at Gould Farm is aware of this, though, and they spend extra time with me and engage me in additional work.

Six days after Christmas, I receive a call from Canada; my father has died. I am shaken, but not stricken. Though his health had declined in recent months, with mini-strokes and kidney problems, I am still shocked. As soon as I learn of his death, I call Nathan. He immediately comes to Gould Farm, and together we travel to Canada. At the visitation, 300 people come to pay respects to him and to console us in our grief. At the funeral, I join my four siblings in singing. We sing his favorite hymn, *Amazing Grace.*

At my father's funeral, most of my memories are focused on his success in ministry and his kindness to all served: his unwavering commitment to anyone in need, whether physically or spiritually. My siblings talk about his care for them. I mainly agree. Yet there is a part of me that is ambivalent about him. I remember the harshness in his preaching that penetrated my soul as a child—even though, in his later years, he had mellowed. I remember, also, that he did not defend me at age 6 when the hired man threw mature on me. And he did not defend me at age 15 when I told him about the abuse of my brother-in-law, Edmond. While I had also told both of my parents—I hold him mainly responsible, based on the experience that he did not fire the hired man when he threw manure on me. But I do not dwell on this ambivalence. I put it out of my conscious mind, and it returns to my unconscious mind, where it has resided for most of my life.

At my mother's funeral, I had brought a sack of heart-shaped rocks to pass out to my nieces—little mementos to remind them of my mother's love. I do not take them to my father's funeral. One of my nieces asks for them, but I clearly have never had a relationship with him that would evoke this kind of tender reminder.

I return to Gould Farm after my father's funeral and continue to thrive, though when I seriously take stock of myself, I see clearly that I have manic tendencies. This is especially evident when the pond freezes over and it is announced that it is safe for skating and playing hockey. As a child in Canada I loved to play hockey, and I relish the opportunity to do it again. I join the young guests at the farm, playing with great gusto, speed and aggression. I am in heaven. But soon, everything changes. I fall on the ice, hit my head hard and am rushed to the hospital. It turns out that I have a serious concussion. I am sobered by my foolishness in playing hockey as if I were a child or a teenager. I make a promise to myself. I repeat this over and over again until I am sure it is lodged solidly in my mind: "I will never again act foolishly in sports. I will always act my age." In the future, when I am tempted to participate in some activity that is dangerous, I always return to this promise.

After the deep winter at Gould Farm comes early spring, which is the time for making maple syrup. I'm assigned to the maple syrup team, and I love it: trudging through the many paths, over the rolling hills, in the woods; carrying the one-gallon pails, filled with sap, to the trucks that hold small tanks for it. There is a light covering of snow on the ground on most days, and in the rolling hills of the Berkshires, it is truly a winter wonderland. The sap runs well on the days when the nights are cold and the days are warm. The joy of the whole maple syrup experience is heightened by the fact that Tim is working alongside me. His very presence is a comfort, and often, he helps carry my pails of sap if they are too heavy for me.

Being on the maple syrup team is also a joy because the team leader is Tom, a man truly of "unstinting kindness." While I have experienced kindness in all of the staff members, kindness permeates Tom in every pore. His kindness is enhanced by a very high intelligence, and when you're around him you know you are in the presence of a truly amazing human being.

Spring passes quickly, as does the rest of the year. In the summer I work on the kitchen team and learn to wilt kale in olive oil and garlic—wilt it to the point of softness, but not mushiness. I wash a tub of lettuce from the garden and I scrub pots and pans that have the remains of macaroni and cheese superglued to them. It's not all fun, but doing it together and producing a healthy meal for 100 people provides its own satisfaction.

Fall passes and winter arrives, and my mental health is superb. I have not been this stable since my divorce. Thanksgiving and Christmas come and go, with Nathan at my side. In January, a new opportunity presents itself. The farm has just developed a program in Boston that is designed to help people transition from farm life to the outside world. I am a good candidate because I am doing so well. So I move to Boston and live in a large house, called Fellside, with seven other guests. As always, I carefully follow through in cleaning and cooking. I specialize in making banana bread, using the Gould Farm recipe. It is perfectly moist, not at all crumbly and contains exactly the right amount of bananas.

The staff member that is in charge of this program is Danielle—truly a woman of "unstinting kindness." She has that perfect combination of warmth and strength that helps you feel secure when you're unsure of yourself. Danielle is my rock when I'm faced with navigating Boston using the subway system. I am very shaky about this at first. Chicago's subway system seemed so straightforward in comparison to Boston's, and it takes me a month to feel like I won't miss my train or get lost. Danielle helps me through it.

Part of the Fellside program involves working out in the community, and I am assigned to work at a bakery. Having worked on the bakery team at Gould Farm, I feel confident that I can do this. But from the beginning, I clash with my boss. I feel she is condescending to me, treating me like a "mentally ill" person. I talk to Danielle about this and she suggests that I discuss my discomfort with my boss. I, with trepidation, try to talk to her, but it only makes matters worse. After that she seems even more condescending. She criticizes me for—of all things—the way I make cookies. I am very hurt by it. Not getting along with bosses or colleagues is highly unusual for me and it wears on my self-confidence.

After work at the bakery one day, I head to Harvard Divinity School. Since I graduated from Yale Divinity School I feel a sense of belonging at another Ivy League school, and that lifts my spirits. I find the bookstore, filled with many books and authors that are familiar to me—my favorite philosopher, Soren Kierkegaard, and Henri Nouwen, the modern-day mystic who is very sophisticated psychologically but who also struggles with depression. Nouwen does not try to hide this in his writing, and that somehow serves to lessen my own stigma about those of us who suffer from depression.

I meander my way through the bookstore for a good hour—and suddenly, I am startled by a book I see. It is a book by Stephen, a fellow Ph.D. student from 25 years ago. While I liked Stephen, I had not particularly thought of him as an outstanding intellect—but now, before my very eyes, I see a book written by him—a book that is being sold at Harvard Divinity

School! It's as if I have been hit by a brick. I'm stunned. I hurt. I want to cry. Furthermore, I'm ashamed. I'm working in a bakery, in a program for mentally ill people, and here is Stephen's book—glaring at me, telling me how absolutely inferior I am as a person and that I am an utter failure; telling me that all of my education has been wasted and that I am likely never going to work anywhere again, except at a bakery—and even at that I am functioning minimally. I race out of the bookstore in tears. I don't want anyone to see me. With difficulty, I find my way through the complicated subway system and arrive back at Fellside. Danielle is there when I arrive, and she sees the agony in my face and hears the trembling in my voice. She listens and listens and listens. Yet the spiraling downward into the dark hole of depression is well on its way. In the next couple of days, I am unable to function at work. I get lost on the subway. It soon becomes clear to everyone that I cannot stay in that program and I must return to the farm. Danielle herself drives me back, and she listens and listens as I tell her of my failures—including my divorces. I tell her I was married to two seminary professors and that both of them would be shocked if they knew the state I am in.

Back at the farm, I am immediately assessed by my psychiatrist, Dr. Taylor, who recommends that I return to the hospital in Pittston for a course of ECT. He also recommends that, after I return from the hospital, I continue ECT on a maintenance, outpatient basis. He says that I am clearly a person who needs maintenance ECT. I receive this news with a sense of shame and failure. I had thought that if I just tried hard enough, I could overcome my illness once and for all. If only I had the right therapist and the right doses of medication; if I stayed on a good exercise program and ate healthy food; perhaps then I could be free of this awful disease. I am shocked that Dr. Taylor thinks I will need ongoing ECT. I agree to it, but in the back of my mind I am determined to prove him wrong. To stay on maintenance ECT for life is a stigma I cannot bear.

The ECT works its wonders. I am stable once again and I resume my life at the farm. I am part of the baking team again. There is a big decision to face, however, as my time at Gould Farm nears an end: where do I go after Gould Farm? I have been here over two years. Do I return to Chicago—where I left in shame? Do I join my son in Washington, D.C., and somehow try to hitch a ride on his life? Do I go to Canada once again

and rely on my sisters to help me make a fresh start? Do I go to Philadelphia, to live with Peter and Eunice? While they are extremely loving
people who truly care for me, I cannot bear the thought of living with
them because their success in life would be a constant reminder of my
failure. They are happily married—never divorced. Peter is a seminary professor, like my two husbands, and his very presence reminds me of what
I have lost. Peter is a prolific writer with 15 books under his belt and he
is a very popular speaker in the evangelical world—a world I do not feel
comfortable in. To top it off, Eunice is a therapist—obviously competent,
as she runs her own private practice. I had failed at this, and just seeing her
so successful in it hurts me. I do not share these feelings about Peter and
Eunice with anyone, but I know within myself that it would not be good
for me to live with them.

My cousin, Cherry, provides me one other option. Cherry was my best
friend when I was a little girl, and we have grown apart over the years.
There was never any problem between us—we just went separate ways,
with her becoming a nurse and marrying an IBM computer expert and
living in Binghamton, New York. I lived in three different places in all of
this: Connecticut, for seminary; Kentucky, for another graduate degree;
then on to Chicago. Through it all I was married twice, divorced twice,
had developed a career and then lost it when becoming sick.

About six months earlier, Cherry had come to Gould Farm and taken
me to her summer home in Pennsylvania. This home was along beautiful
waterfalls and set in the charming hills of Pennsylvania. I loved it. I found
it deeply healing. I also found that I was totally comfortable with Cherry
and her husband, Gabe.

So when it is time for me to move from Gould Farm, Cherry and Gabe
invite me to live with them in Binghamton, New York—about a one-hour
drive north of their summer home in Pennsylvania. Binghamton is a small
city, but it has its own charm. Binghamton is halfway between New York
City and the Canadian border at Buffalo, New York. Being closer to my
sisters in Canada would be a huge plus; Chicago is so far away from them.
Plus, Binghamton is just a six-hour drive to Washington, D.C., where
Nathan lives.

Binghamton is set between two mountains, with the Susquehanna
River running through the heart of it. It has a big university, Binghamton

University, which provides concerts and lectures for the entire community. Binghamton has an opera house and a community theater. It has outstanding hospitals and social services for people with mental illness.

So when Cherry and Gabe ask me to come and live with them, I immediately accept the invitation. It feels exactly right. They say they will reconstruct their attic in such a way that I will have my own quarters. I will, however, eat my meals with them and be able to join in family activities as much as I want. It sounds perfect.

Cherry has worked in social services for years and is well acquainted with the resources I will need in moving to a new place. She seems comfortable in helping me cope with my illness. In fact, her own son struggles with such issues. In this way, I don't feel like an anomaly.

On September 11, 2005, Peter comes to Gould Farm to help me pack up my belongings and take me to Binghamton, New York. I am ready to begin a new life with Cherry, Gabe and their family. I am exceedingly grateful. Nathan and everyone else in my family, is exceedingly grateful. But will it work? Only time will tell. We all hold our breath.

8

Giving Us Brightness

It is clear from the very beginning that moving to Binghamton, New York and living with Cherry and her family is absolutely the right thing to do. There are only minor hitches here and there. It is quite an adjustment, however, as the household is full of both people and pets. Living there is Cherry's 27-year-old daughter, Danielle, and her 18-month-old son, Justin. Danielle is a loving mother, and Justin, happy and curious, pulls us into his world of Legos and fairytales. He brings brightness to us all.

Also living in the household is Charlie, Cherry and Gabe's 29-year-old son. Charlie is a sweet man and often loves to chitchat. But he has a mental illness, which drives him to pace around the house or yard. He appears to be talking to someone else, somewhere else. With my own mental illness, I feel a certain camaraderie with Charlie—yet at the same time, it unsettles me, for I wonder if my depression will escalate into delusional behavior, like his. Two of Charlie's friends are often visiting. I hear that one of them gambles a lot and the other one drinks too much, but I am never uneasy around them. They are gentle and respectful young men.

Gabe, Cherry's husband, is retired from IBM. He is a very kind and interesting man, and he will do almost anything anyone asks of him and then some. He loves to show me his collections of coins and miniature cars, and he tells me stories about scuba-diving—a hobby he has now given up. Gabe would spend all of his time at their home in Pennsylvania, where I first visited them, if only Cherry would retire and move with him. I, too, had fallen in love with the paradise there. The 60-foot cascading waterfalls and gentle flowing creek never fail to soothe a weary body and soul. I totally understand Gabe's wish to be there full time, but the thought frightens me. What would happen to me if they moved away from Binghamton? Could I survive without them? I don't dwell on it, though.

As for Cherry, she is an RN who now supervises 60 home health care aids at the Family & Children's Society—a health care facility of considerable repute. Cherry is the glue that holds both work and home together. She is gentle and kind, has endless energy, and above all is a peacemaker and rescuer. She cannot tolerate conflict, so she intervenes at the slightest tension. There is tension at home, at times, between Danielle and me: While Danielle is very bright and knowledgeable about everything from politics to gardening, she is sometimes rigid and so am I. Of all things, we clash over how the table should be set, with me insisting on the formal, traditional placement of silverware and her setting it in haphazard arrangements.

Living with Cherry and Gabe also includes living with countless pets. When I arrive, Cherry kindly but sternly informs me, "The pets are members of the family." I respond quietly, "I hear you. I'll adjust." But I really have no idea what this means. Coco, the retriever, and Jack, the curly-haired cocker spaniel, are usually on the sofa watching TV with Gabe, and at night they sleep with Cherry and Gabe. The long-haired, white cat, Precious, is in and out of the house; sometimes she even walks on the dining room table, which sends me aghast. But Cherry doesn't mind. She simply wipes off the table with bleach.

There is a tank full of fish, including a 12-inch shark, which apparently will grow to 5 feet long. There are three parakeets—pretty enough with their red, yellow and green, but they are noisy little things and are always chirping away. Yet they do provide background noise that blends in well with the TV. There is also an African grey parrot, named Trouble. He greets you as you enter or leave the house with a raspy "Hello," and at any old time, he'll blurt out, "Want a peanut?" I find his voice grating and irritating. For me, having grown up on a farm where animals were confined to the barn or yard, this menagerie of pets is shocking. Yet, they are entertaining in their own way. But I keep them at arm's length, emotionally.

This household, with all of its humans and creatures, is a joy and is so much better than trying to live alone—at least for now. What a gift it is. Sometimes it seems like the heavens open up and drop you a treasure that is absolutely priceless, and living with Cherry and Gabe is clearly one of those treasures. Furthermore, what is absolutely delightful is the beautiful suite that they have built just for me. I later learn that this cost them $11,000. The rent they charge me is $325 a month, for room and board. At times I am overwhelmed by their kindness.

The suite seems to smile at you when you enter, with its yellow walls and big windows. It is spacious, with plenty of room for a desk and bookshelves, a TV and a computer, and—most of all—my precious rockers. I have taken my rockers out of storage from Peter's house, and this signals to me that I am returning to a normal way of life. I am emerging from being a "mental patient."

I retreat to my suite at any time. I invite family members and friends whenever I wish. As soon as I move in, I gather an array of blocks, trucks, Legos and books for Justin. We bond from the beginning. He loves to be rocked, and I sing to him a version of the song my grandpa sang to me 55 years ago. *Sweet little Justin boy, sweet little Justin boy, you're my sweet little Justin boy.* I feel completely at peace when I rock him. As I hold him, it's as if Grandpa is holding me. Any inner chaos subsides and the activities of the rest of the house fade. What I do not realize at the time is that Justin and his sister, who will be born two years later, will become like grandchildren to me, gracing and delighting me for many years.

Often, Cherry comes to my suite for tea. Sometimes I join her at the dining room table, when the house is quiet. She has such a calming presence; a wise word. She still has those soft, blue eyes, the round, warm cheeks and the thick, golden hair—even though her hair is now cut short and dyed. I feel utterly blessed to be part of Cherry's life. The rest of my family, whom I keep in close touch with, feels exactly the same.

As Cherry and I will talk about at a later time, we both agree that I had some bumpy times when I first settled into her household. Sometimes I'd awaken feeling quite depressed, and I'd become very frightened that I was sinking into the dark hole of depression. But I'd go downstairs and tell Cherry, and she'd invariably say, "Let's go for a little walk, Lucille, and we'll talk about this." She gets to work a little later than usual on those days, but by the end of our walks, I'm always feeling better and able to face my day.

At a much later time, I ask her: "How did you ever manage to handle all of my ups and downs?" She calmly answers, "I'm a rescuer. I love to help people through tough times. I never really questioned whether or not you were too much for me to handle. And I just knew that it was right for you to live with us."

After a week of settling into the household, Cherry kindly but sternly says, "You need to venture out now. I will go with you at first, and show you how to get around." I respond firmly, but on the inside I am shaking. "I agree with you wholeheartedly," I say. "I will learn to get around on my own." By this time I have my own car, which was stored with Peter in Philadelphia. While it is scary driving in a new city, I am struck by how small Binghamton is in comparison to Chicago. You can get anywhere in 15 or 20 minutes, with no real traffic jams. Cherry is exceedingly patient in giving me directions and making suggestions about what I might do.

Her first suggestion is that I explore a program at Catholic Charities: an outpatient program designed for people with mental disabilities. Like Gould Farm, it is work-oriented. I apply and am immediately accepted. I'm assigned to the team that runs a community thrift store, called Wares Like New. I help sort through the clothes, shoes and purses that are donated. I price items and hang them on the racks. Members are allowed to shop, and I find a grey tweed jacket, two blouses and an array of silk scarves—all for a total of $12. What a deal! It becomes an adventure to sort through clothes, knowing that I have the option to buy them. Furthermore, the staff leader is generous and often gives members clothes for half-price or even for free.

I run into a glitch, however, when I try to work the cash register. I find this task overwhelming and cannot remember which keys to push when. I am deeply embarrassed. With all of my degrees and experience, I am incapable of working the cash register! Although my supervisor in no way pressures me to continue, I berate and even despise myself for not being able to master it. I hate that I cannot function as a normal, healthy adult. I just hope and pray that this is a temporary state out of which I will soon emerge.

At Catholic Charities, I also struggle with the social and educational level of my fellow members. Most of them do not have a high-school diploma. This is in sharp contrast to the members of Gould Farm, with whom I easily blended in. Here I am, a misfit—something I have struggled with my entire life. Yet, I am grateful to be here. The members are always kind, and that's what counts the most. And helping to run a thrift store that is functioning within the larger community is a step up from working at the farm, where work was primarily confined to endeavors on its property.

As soon as I arrive in Binghamton, I also begin searching for a church. It seems that I've been searching for a church my whole life. My childhood church is long behind me; I am an ordained congregational minister; I have worked in a Presbyterian church; and I have worshipped with the Quakers. The question remains the same: where can my soul be fed and where can I find loving, accepting people? This has always been my bedrock requirement—the denomination is quite irrelevant.

At first I go with Cherry and Gabe to their church, the First Assembly of God. But this church is Pentecostal, charismatic in worship and fundamentalist in theology, and I clearly do not belong. I decide to check out the liberal Protestant churches that are lined up on the main street of Binghamton.

It is Monday morning of my third week in Binghamton, and today I will stop at various church offices to gather information. I begin at the United Church of Christ but find a secretary who is cold, unwelcoming and not really knowledgeable about the programs of the church. I ask her if there are any small groups within the church, and she doesn't seem to know. So I cross that church off my list.

I then stop at a Presbyterian church. The minister is there, but again I do not find the warmth that I am looking for—the warmth that will draw me back to this church on Sunday, to hear him preach. Plus, he says nothing about small groups within the church.

So I knock at the door of the Methodist church, which is just two blocks away. A smiling woman opens the door. "Come in, let me tell you about our church." She then tells me about a community meal on Wednesday nights, which is open to anyone who is hungry. She tells me about AA groups, NA groups and Al-Anon groups. She then says, "And we have small groups." Without divulging too much about myself, I tell her that I have a background in psychology and theology. She responds immediately: "Come back on Sunday at 9 a.m. for Will's group. You belong there." She just seems to know what is right for me.

The following Sunday at 9 o'clock sharp, I walk into Will's group. He pops up from his chair, shakes my hand and asks my name. He then introduces me to the group and asks the 10 women sitting in the circle to tell me theirs. They all smile warmly. They already feel like sisters. When Will leads the group, I immediately realize that he is coming from a place that is psychologically and theologically similar to mine. He explicitly draws me into the discussion and I feel proud to share some of the knowledge that is inside of me. To top it off, after the class Will asks me to meet him for lunch on Thursday at Cyber Café, just down the street. On Thursday, when we begin to talk, I learn that he is a minister and that he graduated from Yale Divinity School—five years after me. He tells me that he is in private practice as a pastoral counselor and a social worker. It is immediately clear to me that I have found a church home. The following Sunday, I talk further with a few women from the group—most especially Kate, who is a professor at Binghamton University. Like me, she is looking for a church. I sense in her a camaraderie, which soon grows into a friendship. Three months later, Kate and I will stand together, formally becoming members. Like other church members, we will call our church Tab, the affectionate name for Tabernacle United Methodist Church.

As the secretary had said on that first day, Tab is a church that is committed to serving the needs of the community in a whole array of ways. I immediately gravitate toward the Wednesday night community meal. I learn that for 20 years, Tab has served meals every Wednesday evening to more than 100 poor and destitute people from the neighborhood.

I go the following Wednesday to help serve the meal. That first night, when I walk into the dining hall, I find it startling and heartbreaking to look into the strained, gaunt faces of hungry people. But I am invited into the kitchen to put bread into baskets, make salad and then serve the food.

The second week there I am drawn to a girl who is 13 years old. I sit down beside her and begin to chat. "Is this your mother you're sitting beside?" I ask. "No," she says quietly, "I come by myself." I am shocked and determined to get to know her. Her name is Kimberley. She is a big girl for her age—about 5-foot-8 and 180 pounds, with wide shoulders. Her T-shirt has stains on it and her long, brown hair is unwashed and uncombed. Yet there is a sweetness about her that captures me, and I want to know more. What I do not realize is that this is the beginning of a relationship that will last well into her 20s. Kimberley will become like a daughter to me: a daughter to worry about, to shop with, to gently chide—and to deeply love.

I go home after meeting Kimberley and am profoundly grateful. It is just three weeks after my arrival in Binghamton, and already I have found a safe home with Cherry and Gabe, where there is a toddler to love; I have found a church, complete with a small group of caring women and a teenage girl to love; and I have found Catholic Charities, where I work in the thrift store—a place to go every day. How blessed am I. I pause to thank God.

This is not enough, though. Cherry makes it clear to me—and I fully agree—that I need a therapist and a psychiatrist, and I need to continue ECT. She recommends that I begin my search for a psychiatrist by seeing Dr. Shane, the doctor her son, Charlie, is seeing. I take to Dr. Shane right away. He is tall and handsome; dark-skinned, and from India. He greets me with a warm handshake. His waiting room has a flowing fountain and his walls are decorated with flowers and sunsets. There is tranquility every-where. His business card has a smiley face on it. Now that's stepping out of the psychiatrist box! Dr. Shane is gentle yet assertive. I feel safe with him. We discuss ECT; he believes in it. In fact, he does it. But I do not feel comfortable getting ECT in a small area like Binghamton. I felt so confi-dent about it in Massachusetts, where the staff was exceedingly friendly. I just can't imagine it being as good in Binghamton. I tell him this, and he is in no way defensive. I tell him that I will return to Massachusetts for ECT.

I am also in search of a therapist. Cherry suggests the counseling center where Charlie goes. It is a Christian counseling center, and I'm skeptical at first because this center is housed in a very conservative church. But Char-lie tells me that one of the therapists, Donna, has struggled deeply with depression—and so I decide to try her out. I tell her up front: "I believe you are much more conservative than me on theological issues and that concerns me." She replies, "I suggest you try me for three sessions. And then, if you think we're not a fit, we'll stop." By the second session I know that this will work, because I sense no need in her to impose her ideas on me. At the beginning, she shares some of her history with depression. I quickly find that she is a therapist who is very practical in her approach. She has me make a list of concrete things I can do at the onset of feelings of depression: walk, have tea with Cherry, sing, play with Justin, call my sister. She says, "When depressed, it's hard to think of what to do. But if you have a ready-made list, your chances of sinking into it are greatly decreased." Somehow, in all my years as a client and as a counselor, I had not come up a method that was so practical and accessible.

At the beginning of my counseling, I tell Donna about my sexual abuse: the abuse at age 6, by the hired man, and the abuse at age 15, by my brother-in-law, Edmond. In all my years in therapy, this is the first time that I have divulged those dark secrets. Donna listens intently and compassionately to my stories and writes them down, and I learn that they are fixed in her mind. In the next weeks she makes connections between my childhood abuse and the emotional abuse I experienced in my second marriage.

About three months into the counseling, I mention Nathan's last name. Lights go off in her head and she quickly asks, "Are you the Lucille I knew from seminary—where your husband taught and where my husband was a student? Are you the Lucille I so admired, when you presented your views on feminism—women leaders in history and in the Bible?" Neither of us could believe the synchronicity of our meeting. Over 20 years ago I had helped her develop the courage to assert her own abilities as a woman. Now she is helping me find my stability after the ravages of divorce and mental illness. What an amazing gift!

One of the first issues Donna and I address is the problem related to ECT. I tell her I need ECT, but that I will not have it in Binghamton; that I do not trust the quality of the treatments in Binghamton (although the reality is that I have no evidence on which to make this judgment). Like Dr. Shane, she is not defensive in any way and she does not try to persuade me to try it here. I feel I must return to Massachusetts for treatments, but that is four hours away. What will I do? I agonize about this with Donna, and she suggests that I talk with Cherry. Cherry, too, is not critical of me. She talks with Gabe about this, and they offer a solution: Gabe will drive me to Massachusetts for my treatments. I am again very touched by the generosity of Cherry and Gabe.

So this is what I do for four months: Gabe and I leave at 8 a.m. We arrive in Massachusetts at noon. My treatment and recovery last for two hours, and then we drive back. I lie in the backseat of the car as I emerge from the confusing and brutal side effects of ECT. As before, it leaves me with a pounding headache, an upset stomach, a neck that feels twisted sideways and a balance deprivation that leaves me sometimes walking into walls. Gabe in no way complains about these trips, but 10-hour days are clearly grueling for us both.

After four months, and with encouragement from Donna, I decide to try ECT in Binghamton. I am totally surprised. The staff there is very kind—even more so than in Massachusetts—and Dr. Shane is obviously very competent. The treatments seem to be a little less brutal. And so I decide to continue to do "maintenance" ECT, as was recommended at Gould Farm. While I hate ECT, it seems to keep me stable. Nathan absolutely agrees and is adamant that I not stop it. So I will tough it out, at least for now.

My life is going so well, and I have so much to be thankful for. I have my church, my new friends there and the young girl, Kimberley, whom I see on Wednesday nights at the community meal. I have Catholic Charities, to which I go to work every day. I have a good therapist and psychiatrist and, most of all, I have a beautiful family life with Cherry and Gabe.

On some weekends, I go with Cherry and Gabe to their summer home in Pennsylvania, where I visited them over a year ago while at Gould Farm. The three of us often sit at the foot of the waterfalls, which reach 60 feet high. Sometimes we chat. Sometimes we're quiet. The flowing water has a cleansing effect.

When we are not sitting at the waterfalls, Cherry and I work in her garden. Working side by side, we talk about our childhood with Grandpa and our many trips to the altar; about rebelling against our parents and cutting our hair. Cherry was my very best childhood friend. She knew all of my secrets. Now she is becoming my best friend once again.

I tell her about the trauma of two divorces and about the winding and terrifying road of mental illness. Most important of all, I tell her about the sexual abuse by the hired man and about Edmond. In tears, I tell her that I told my parents about Edmond, but that they only prayed. I tell her that I felt totally unprotected and abandoned by them. I am struck by the fact that none of this seems to shock or frighten her. Perhaps the mental illness of her son, Charlie, has schooled her well. Or perhaps her accepting me so deeply is simply because she, at the core of her being, is an incredibly kind and accepting person. Time and time again, I am moved by her kindness. She had a dream for me: that I could recover from my illness by moving to Binghamton and living with her and her family. No one else had had a viable plan for me when I was ready to leave Gould Farm, and now here I am, working side by side with her and chattering away in her garden.

Cherry is clearly the stabilizing person in my life. Nathan is there for me also, of course, but he is in Washington, D.C., pursuing his career in international relations. I am soon to realize that my relationship with him is starting to change. He is falling in love with Erin, the woman whom he will marry in three years. He emails a picture of her and writes, "This is my new girlfriend. I'm smitten." Nathan has never talked this way about any other woman. I'm delighted for him, but a little scared, too.

I meet Erin at Thanksgiving, and I understand why Nathan is smitten. She's beautiful—warm eyes, a pretty face and petite. She has long, wavy, dark-brown hair that flows gracefully down her back. More important is Erin's intellect and enormous range of interests and knowledge. She is brilliant, like Nathan—an intellectual equal. They met at a University of Chicago alumni gathering in Washington. She has been accepted into law school at the University of Chicago, and she makes it clear to Nathan that she will pursue her law degree there: she will be quite content to live in D.C. a couple of weekends a month, but she will travel to Chicago for law school.

When I return home after Thanksgiving, I find myself mostly delighted by Nathan's new girlfriend. Yet, I'm a little worried, too. How will I fit into their relationship? Will the intimacy and support system I have had with Nathan be altered? It seems, from that first meeting with Erin, that it will not change. In the future I will learn that it will change somewhat, but in the moment I simply glow with them in their newfound love.

Back home, I talk to my counselor, Donna, about Nathan and Erin. She is very supportive of me in my delight for them, but she also hints that the future might require some adjustments on my part. I put this out of my mind for the time being. I spend Christmas with Nathan and Erin, and I feel nothing but total love and support.

Spring soon arrives, and I return to Pennsylvania with Cherry and Gabe on many weekends. Every weekend there, I grow to love it more: the waterfalls, the woods, the gardens, the birds … it is an absolute paradise. Then I get an idea: I would like to buy a trailer and sit it on Cherry and Gabe's property. I could have my own, separate space, but still be close to them. I keep this idea to myself for at least one week, as I don't even have an estimate of what a trailer might cost. But one day, when Cherry is out shopping, I casually mention my idea about a trailer to Gabe. He replies without delay. "Let's check into it. I'll go into town and get the paper that has the sales in it." In 20 minutes he is back and we are pouring over the advertisements of used trailers in the surrounding towns. This is Friday night. There are two trailers selling for $5,000 or below. I call and set up appointments to see them the next day. I can't believe this is happening. On Saturday morning, Cherry, Gabe and I set out to see these trailers. The first one is junk. Gabe immediately tells me to not even consider buying it.

The second trailer, however, is a totally different story. It is 11 years old and the only thing that shows wear and tear is the carpeting. Unlike many trailers, there are many windows, so one feels like a part of the outer world and not trapped from it. There is a sliding glass door that leads out to the deck. On the inside there are big mirrors, which give the illusion of spaciousness. The trailer has a sweet little kitchen and dinette area and a medium-sized sitting area with a pull-out couch. This means that with the double bed in the bedroom, the trailer can easily sleep four people. The bathroom is small, and the shower can hardly be turned around in, but it is adequate and it is certainly better than an outhouse and showering in the river. The cost of this trailer is $5,000. We talk to the sellers, and they tell us that they have 10 more potential buyers. We go back home and sit on it. Four hours later, I call the sellers and tell them that I want the trailer. I can get $1,000 to them on Monday and I will pay the rest when we pick it up, a week later. In two more hours, I call the sellers again. I tell them that I would also like to buy the deck that is in front of the trailer. They agree to sell it to me for an additional $400.

I talk with Gabe and Cherry about where we might set the trailer on their property, and Gabe knows instantly. It should be on the cliff that overlooks the stream and the gorgeous waterfalls. We go over to that spot; the view from it is magnificent. I will have my own little Niagara Falls, and I will have my own little house. It's not a rental; it's my very own. All for $5,400! I also agree to pay Cherry and Gabe $2,000 a year for rental space on their property and for the upkeep of the trailer. What a small price to pay for the paradise I have walked into! I am elated and I am deeply grateful. This is one of those times, once again, when I feel like God's heaven has opened up and showered me with a priceless gift. It is pure grace.

Part of moving into my trailer entails a trip to Philadelphia. My brother has been storing the belongings that Nathan had packed almost four years ago, when I had overdosed and could no longer live on my own. While the trailer is fully furnished, I bring back some of my artwork, all of my books and my precious set of dishes—the hand-painted set of Jerusalem pottery that Louie and I had carried from Nazareth. I cherish each piece as I unpack it, each with its unique floral design in shades of blue, soft yellow, light red, green and white. I can already see the dishes arranged on my little table, with blue placemats and white linen napkins. I can't wait to see them filled with food once again. My first guests, of course, will be Cherry and Gabe.

With my trailer in Pennsylvania and all my good fortune in Binghamton, I feel very stable, emotionally. Symptoms of depression are gone. I feel I have conquered the disease that has held me captive for 10 years. By this time I have been doing ECT in Binghamton for eight months. I feel so good that I insist I stop treatments. Nathan tells me not to stop; my sister, Ruth—who calls me every Tuesday night—strongly hints that I should not stop. But I am shamed by what ECT seems to say about me: that I am a person with a severe and chronic mental illness. I hate that label. I feel shame about this label and about the fact that I have suffered for so long from chronic mental illness. Many, many people have been betrayed by their husbands and sexually abused, and they did not fall apart. Why me? What I do not notice is that I am the only one who holds any stigma about ECT or about mental illness. I talk to my psychiatrist, Dr. Shane, and while I sense that he thinks I should continue ECT on a maintenance plan, he agrees that I can stop. It is my choice. His only requirement is that I immediately resume ECT if my depression should return. I agree to this.

It is around this time that something strange and wonderful begins to emerge in me. I start to write short stories. These stories are about two pages long and can be can read in 10 minutes. They just start to flow out of me. Through my life I have written only term papers or scholarly papers—papers for which a case is argued, point by point, and at the end, summarized to convince the reader of its value. I was very good at that type of writing. It brought me a great education. Yet, now creativity is flowing and stories seem to emerge from some place deep inside of me. I am shocked, but elated.

My first story is about William and his short arm. William comes from a perfect-looking family. His two brothers are handsome, brilliant and star athletes. But William is born with a short arm. He is a misfit. While his parents try to accept him, it is really only his grandfather who gives him unconditional love. His grandfather rocks him and sings the song my grandfather sang to me 54 years ago: *Sweet little William boy, sweet little William boy. Sweet little William boy ... You're my sweet little William boy.*

Another story is entitled *The Essence of Zucchini*. It is about Molly, a child zucchini who cries to her mother about being so different from cousin green cucumber, and from her friends, yellow zucchini and orange pumpkin. Her wise mother confides in Molly that she, too, struggles with being "different." Her mother reminds Molly that zucchinis are perfect for zucchini bread, curry zucchini soup and much more. By the end of the story Molly and her mother are dancing around the garden, loving themselves just as they are; they are perfect, just as they are.

It is obvious that my stories grow out of my struggle with my own limitations and my own determination to heal. I read some of these stories to Cherry and she encourages me to keep writing. I meet Carolyn, and my writing continues to flourish.

I meet Carolyn at coffee hour at church. She appears out of the blue. She has that look of a person who suffers from a severe mental illness, and sometimes her mind seems to be off on another planet. She tells me that 20 years ago, she was declared "schizophrenic." Her 5-year-old son was taken from her and she was forcefully transported to the state psychiatric hospital, where she was incarcerated for four months.

Carol is overweight, has whiskers and is missing two teeth. I'm a bit uneasy with her at first, but she is warm and articulate. She tells me that she is a writer and a former teacher of creative writing at Broome Community College. She shows me some of her poetry, and I am stunned by both the imagery and the depth of meaning. I tell her about my little stories and she invites me to coffee the next day to talk about them.

We meet at McDonald's and I buy us coffee. I shyly read her my story about William and his short arm. She comments right away: "It's beautiful. You're a writer." I'm shocked, and I don't believe her. I tell her that I only know how to write term papers and scholarly articles. She ignores my protests and, in the next few weeks, proceeds to give me informal lessons in creative writing. In the first lesson, we talk about the pros and cons of writing in the present tense and the past. Do you write, "The sky *IS* a gorgeous blue?" or "The sky *WAS* a gorgeous blue?" I'm fascinated. I've never thought about this sort of thing before. Week after week, Carolyn and I meet at McDonald's; and week after week, I read my stories to her and she consistently responds, "You're a writer."

After a couple of months of this, I get an idea: perhaps I could lead a spirituality group at Catholic Charities, where I could read my stories. I ask Carolyn what she thinks about this. She says, "Of course, go for it." So I write a proposal to Catholic Charities—an academic-like proposal that argues my fitness for leading such a group. It is accepted immediately. In two weeks, I start the spirituality group. Stories, silent meditation, discussion and singing are all a part of the group sessions. I end each time by having everyone hold hands and sing *We Shall Overcome*. The group is successful and about six people attend regularly.

Two months into this, I get in touch with my friend Luke. I want to tell him about the spirituality group and my stories. He is now living in Williamsport, Pennsylvania—about two and a half hours away. We have been in touch since my illness began, and I have felt only deep love and understanding from him. I still feel close to him, emotionally: for it was Luke and Christa who met with Nathan and me every Sunday night, 30 years ago, to pray and meditate. Luke was my original teacher of meditation. So I invite him to visit me in Pennsylvania, to show him my trailer and paradise there. We sit at the foot of the waterfalls. We chat. I tell him about my spirituality group and my stories, and I let him know that I have them with me. He asks me to read one. I'm scared, but I agree. He swiftly responds, "It's great. Keep writing. I want to hear more." And so I continue to write.

A month later, Luke asks me to join him and his friends for a day of meditation. I'm hesitant at first. With the agitation that is still within me, I don't know if I will be able to sit still. But, of course, I agree to join him. I trust that his calming presence will carry me through any agitation. The quaint meditation that Luke and his friends are doing involves sitting on chairs in a shallow stream. I am wary of this, but I join them. Fifteen minutes into the meditation, I become aware of the fear that I am holding in regard to my son, Nathan. While he is in love with Erin, he is without steady work. He seems to be floundering in his profession, and I'm scared. He's always been my stability, and to have him unstable is deeply disturbing.

Yet, as I sit in the stream with my fellow meditators, I begin to notice the little ripples of water gently coming my way, passing by me and moving down the stream. Those ripples draw me in, and I effortlessly begin to silently repeat: "Let it come; let it go. Let it come; let it flow." I immediately know that this is a teaching I'm receiving about my son. "Let him come, let him go; let him come, let him flow." By this teaching I am deeply calmed and comforted. The burden of Nathan's faltering is flowing away from me, and I am free.

After we come out of the stream and onto the shore, I tell Luke about my chant. He quickly adds to it: "All is well." He tells me that he is paraphrasing Julian of Norwich, a 14th-century female mystic who said, "All shall be well. All shall be well. All manner of things shall be well."

When I return home, a tune to Julian's chant comes into my mind. I write it down. I call Luke and sing it to him over the phone. He soon joins in, singing it with me. This chant will, in the future, carry me through times of despair. When I believe that I am saddled with a darkness that will never go away. It will carry me through more times of anxiety about my son. It will later become a chant that will be embedded in a story I write. I will use it in my spirituality group at Catholic Charities. Luke and I will use it in workshops we host in the future. I will teach it to my church. It will, in fact, become a lifelong chant of letting go of fear, anger, envy and disappointment. It will give me hope that all will be well. It is light through the darkness.

I later come to realize that part of the magic of this chant came to me because I was immersed in nature. I was sitting in a stream, listening to and seeing the ripples of water flowing between my feet and down the stream. I was hearing the birds and seeing the trees, as the sun was glistening through it all. This was the first of several mystical experiences in which I would feel as one with nature, hearing the voice of God in a quiet way and experiencing an inner wisdom that is not just my own.

Then a very disturbing change emerges, in regard to Cherry and Gabe. Cherry decides to retire and move from Binghamton, as Gabe has wanted her to. They will move to Pennsylvania, to live on their beautiful property with the waterfalls. I am in shock. Will I move with them, living in my trailer? Will I stay in Binghamton, living in their house with Danielle, Justin, Charlie and all of those pets? Or—and this is a very scary thought—might I get my own apartment and try, once again, to live by myself? It is now 18 months that I have lived in Binghamton. I have a church with friends, a group that nurtures me every Sunday, a community meal where I help feed the hungry, and a little girl, Kimberley, to love and care for. I have a therapist and a psychiatrist. I have the program at Catholic Charities, where I lead a spirituality group. This would be a lot to leave behind.

I talk with my therapist and psychiatrist about all of this—and most especially about living by myself. I talk with Nathan and my siblings. They all encourage me to try it, and yet I seem to hear some anxiety in their voices—though in reality, I don't know if it is their anxiety or if it is my own. For two weeks, I go back and forth in my mind. Should I move? Should I risk living by myself? Or will I get depressed? Finally, I decide to do it. I listen to the confidence that others seem to have in me, and this gives me confidence.

Also by this time I am in touch with Mike, my favorite boyfriend from high school. He recently tracked me down and, in his own way, is still in love with me. Mike is a very practical man, and I ask him about living on my own. He, like Nathan and my siblings, encourages me to move into my own apartment.

In March of 2007, I search the newspaper for apartments. There is only one that I'm drawn to. I call the landlady, Andrea, and tell her that I want an apartment that has lots of windows—for I know that without sunshine, my depression will surely return. She replies, "There are large, south-side windows in the kitchen, dining room and living room, and there is a porch that is open on three sides. There are small windows in two bedrooms on the north side." She informs me that the apartment comes with a garage, a washing machine, a dryer and air conditioning. It sounds perfect. I take Cherry and Gabe with me to look at the apartment, and I rent it on the spot. I will move in one month.

In that month I order a cushy, taupe sofa and a cherry dining room set with six padded chairs. I purchase a corner desk with lots of space for a computer and printer. I buy a slate coffee table with a matching end table. I buy standing lamps and table lamps for my desk and dresser. I'm very excited, but also very scared. Can I live by myself? It was while living by myself that I overdosed four years ago. I try to shelve these doubts and continue with the process of moving.

To add to the furniture I'm buying, I go to Philadelphia to get the furniture that has been stored at Peter's house. Gabe and I travel to Peter's house in his truck, and I am again struck by his kindness and support. When I bought my trailer, I had picked up books, a few pieces of art and household items. Now I take the rest of my furniture—the furniture that Nathan had lovingly brought from Chicago. Now I am reunited with my cedar chest, given to me by my parents upon my high school graduation; I am reunited with my antique oak dresser, my chest of drawers and my corner china cabinet. I am also reunited with all of my precious artwork. I adore the mother-and-child Mary Cassatt print from France. The mother in the picture has her enlarged arm around her child, protecting her. I somehow feel that protection now. I unpack the 3-foot by 4-foot charcoal etching that I had traced from a cathedral in England 38 years ago, featuring a man and a woman bowing respectfully to each other. I am reunited with the photographs of my family, and it is such a comfort to have them back.

While embarking on this challenge of living alone, I feel deeply supported by my family. My sister, Rachel, tells me that she prays for me every single day. When my parents were alive, they prayed for all of their children and grandchildren every day. Now my sister has stepped into their place, and by this I am greatly comforted. Also praying for me every day is my dear friend, Gloria, from Chicago. Gloria and I have journeyed together now for over 35 years. She comprehends the depth of my depression, and we talk about her anxiety and phobias. Our relationship grows deeper and deeper.

Others stay in close contact. My sister, Ruth, calls me every Tuesday night. While part of our conversations are simple, revolving around such things as gardens or decorating, we move to in-depth sharing at times, too. What I like most about Ruth is that I can always count on her to cry with me. If I'm feeling edgy about living alone, I call her and cry. She never tries to talk me out of it; she simply joins me in my crying, thereby absorbing some of my pain. There is one thing that I never tell her about, though, and that is the abuse by her husband, Edmond.

By this time, I have told Cherry about the abuse by the hired man when I was 6 and the abuse by Edmond when I was 15. We're mystified by Ruth. Does she not know? Does she not see all the subtle ways he stalks me—and others? My fear runs very high when Ruth tells me that they would like to come to Pennsylvania and see my trailer. I want to show it off, of course, so I agree. But before they arrive, I'm in agony and fear. I tell Cherry and she invites me to stay at her house for the night. I decline, though, because I'm afraid that Ruth would wonder why I'm not staying with them. I want to protect her. What I do for myself, though, is make a very specific plan about how to respond to Edmond if he should approach me. My plan is that I will shout, "Stop!" and jerk away from him. I decide—for the first time in my life—that I will not be victimized by him. This is the beginning of my release from the power he has had over me for most of my life.

True to form, Edmond tries to abuse me. Ruth is in the shower and I am at the kitchen sink, washing dishes. Edmond approaches. He puts his arm around my shoulders and I jump away, hollering, "Stop!" He is clearly surprised and he moves away. In a small way, I feel elated. I have given him the message that he cannot stalk me. Yet I am shaken by the whole experience and I determine that I will never again sleep in the same trailer or house with him. My hatred of Edmond continues to grow. I tell Cherry what happened and she consoles me in her tender, supportive way. When I see my therapist the next week, I tell her my story—in detail—and I come to understand, in a deeper way than ever before, that Edmond truly is a predator. We talk about me discussing this with Ruth and exposing

Edmond as the predator that he is. But I am not ready; not yet. I want to protect Ruth from the pain of it all. And soon, once again, I tuck the abuse far back into my consciousness, and I go on with my life.

Back in Binghamton, I am truly content and joyful. From March to August of that first year in my apartment, my spirits are high. I delight in my furniture, both the old and new. I love the way the light from the windows bathes the apartment. I invite friends for meals, making them mushroom-beef stroganoff spiced just-so with paprika. The food looks perfect on my beautiful, hand-painted dishes.

I continue to deepen relationships at church. I see my little girl, Kimberley, weekly. I am writing stories that seem to magically flow out of me and which are received warmly in the spirituality group at Catholic Charities. This makes my being a member of a program for mentally ill people less painful. It gives me special status within it.

Yet, I want more. I wonder if I am ready to return, in some way, to my counseling profession. I shyly bring this up to Dr. Shane, my psychiatrist, and he encourages me—he even suggests that I take clients released from the inpatient program at Binghamton Hospital. These patients have severe mental illness, though, and I'm not sure I can handle them. I then talk to Will, the Sunday group leader, who is a therapist and a minister. He says, "Go for it!" I take one step further and ask if he will supervise me. Instantly, he says, "I'm happy to supervise you, and I will give you my office on the days I'm not there."

It all happens quickly. I go to the local printer and have cards made, which read "Lucille Sider, Ph.D." It feels so good to be "Dr. Sider" again. It feels like I am regaining the profession I lost so long ago.

In a month I'm set up and have two clients from the psychiatric unit at Binghamton Hospital. But it doesn't go well. The two clients come erratically and do not settle into therapy. I try to resolve this problem by visiting professionals in the area who might refer clients with less severe problems—the kind of clients I worked with during my years as a psychologist. One professional I meet is Patricia. We connect immediately, delving into conversations about psychology and spirituality. As it will turn out, I do not receive any referrals from her, but in two months I will receive a recommendation from her that sets me on a whole new path, professionally.

Come October, my spirits suddenly and unexpectedly begin to decline. I have only two clients, which is disheartening; and fall presses in upon me, as the sun begins setting by 6 o'clock. On Wednesday nights, when I work in the community kitchen and see Kimberley, I am just fine. Sometimes I go to Cherry's family home, and I play with Justin. He drives away the blues for a couple of hours, but they come marching back as soon as I return home.

One night, when I'm feeling very blue, I call Cherry. I hear deep compassion and concern in her voice. Within minutes of the start of our conversation, I'm sobbing. She hears my despair and offers to come the next day, at which time she insists that I make an appointment with Dr. Shane. Cherry offers to accompany me when I see him. One year ago I had stopped ECT, and Cherry had questioned the wisdom of this at the time; so had my son, my sister and Dr. Shane. But I had felt healed. And ECT is such a stigma—such a sign that I am severely mentally ill. It signifies a fact that I desperately want to deny.

Dr. Shane sees me and Cherry the next day. He immediately asks me to resume ECT and he sets up two treatments in that same week. The kindness and compassion in his voice makes me want to follow his advice. There is not a bit of "I told you so" attitude in him; there is only compassion. Cherry goes with me for the treatments. I am scheduled to have 12 treatments in the next three weeks, and then to have maintenance ECT each month after that. By the fifth treatment, the darkness begins to lift. At one point, it is very dramatic: I am sitting on my sofa, looking out the window into the sky, and I am stunned at the sheer beauty that I see. The sky is a soft blue and the big, white clouds are perfectly puffy. This picture brings me deep joy and delight. Just two weeks ago, when I looked out that same window, I saw only grey—even though the sky was just as blue and the clouds were just as puffy. At this point I know that the ECT is helping and I have hope that I can once again become a person who is not depressed; that I can become a person living a normal, successful life. As my ECT treatments continue, I come to experience even more joy in looking at the clouds, in playing with Justin and in going to church. I even feel increased competence in counseling my clients. Yet I do not feel that my clients are well anchored into therapy, even with Will's supervision and support.

During all of this time, I continue to write stories and to lead my spirituality group at Catholic Charities. I spend some time with Carolyn, who had originally encouraged my writing. Things with Carolyn get complicated, however, and her own pathology surfaces. She has seven cats, a cruel landlady and big financial problems. I give her $700 to move to a new apartment. I try to help her move, but she is so disorganized that it overwhelms me. She calls me daily, subtly pressuring me for transportation and more money. I begin to withdraw from her. I feel badly about this, but it is a matter of self-preservation, and Cherry and my therapist support me in this decision.

Yet a startling thing happens in regards to Carolyn. At this time I am doing some hypnosis therapy in addition to my traditional therapy with Donna. The therapist is Mary, from the Gould Farm community. Luke and I had visited Gould Farm two months earlier, and I had connected with her while there. She offered to do some hypnosis counseling with me over the phone, and I was intrigued. I decided to do it. While seeing two therapists at one time is totally unconventional, it just seems right at this time. The two therapists stay in contact with each other to coordinate their work with me.

Five weeks into hypnosis therapy, I have a vision that is very powerful. In the vision, I see myself going across a bridge. Around my waist is a golden belt that steadies me as I cross the bridge, into the unknown. Ahead of me is light, and in my trance I know it is the light of God. Behind me, supporting me, is Carolyn: I see her face, with her big, blue, compassionate eyes. In my trance I am irritated that Carolyn is there, because I want her out of my life. She has become a burden to me. What I later come to know, however, is that she has been like a midwife to me—she has helped me give birth to my creative impulse, to a creative part of me that had thus far been dormant and totally unknown to me. What I will remember time and again in later years is Carolyn's compassionate eyes in the vision: they will comfort me when I question my own ability to write. On a whole deeper level than ever before, I will cherish the place she has had in my life.

As I later reflect on this vision, I am so aware that in it, I was crossing a bridge—a bridge to a new life. I am cognizant that a golden belt was steadying me, and that God, in the form of light, was guiding and welcoming me. Time after time—especially when going through times of darkness—I remember this vision and am sustained by it.

By this time, the course of ECT—that is, 12 treatments—is behind me, and I am feeling healthy and whole. I wonder if I could stop it again, because the treatments are so brutal. I dread them, and it takes a full day to recover from each one. Furthermore, the stigma of needing them surges in me. Dr. Shane strongly advises that I continue on a monthly maintenance basis, though. My family—especially Nathan—is adamant that I continue. So I continue, at least for now.

In mid-December, I get a telephone call. It is Patricia, one of the professionals I had visited when beginning my private practice. We had clearly connected in a deep way. She calls to ask if I would consider interviewing for the position of "pastor of visitation" at Northminster Presbyterian Church. They had asked her to apply, but she was not interested. She told them, however, that she knows someone else who is well qualified. Thus a whole new door to my professional life opens.

9

Loving My Seniors

Pastor of visitation. What is that? I've never heard of such a position! That's what I'm thinking, but I'm more restrained in my response to Patricia. "Perhaps I'm interested, but I've actually never heard of a 'pastor of visitation.' Please tell me about it." She carefully explains, "It's a part-time position at Northminster Presbyterian Church, close to where you live. Northminster is deeply committed to ministering to their seniors, and they have a separate, part-time pastor just for them. I know you'd be great at it."

Patricia then goes on to explain, "There are about 30 seniors to visit each month. Some are just retired and others are quite elderly and often very frail, physically and emotionally." She then says that it's a matter of accompanying them, wherever they are in their journey. At first I'm taken aback: I have had no training in the field of geriatrics. I tell her this upfront, but she insists that I should apply. She's sure I'd be good at it. With her confidence in me, I agree to apply.

Patricia says she'll call the church and give them my phone number; I'll need to meet with the personnel committee and then the pastor, Rev. Louise. The next day, Danielle, from the personnel committee, calls. She says the committee would like to interview me in five days and that I need to send a resume as soon as possible. The requirement of a resume sends me into a tailspin. What do I say about the years of my life since I was dismissed from my position at Edgewater Presbyterian Church? How can I craft my resume in such a way that it looks like I've been a fully functioning professional? I realize I'll have to tweak it just a bit.

That evening I sit at my computer, wondering how to write my resume. Yet, I find that it flows nicely. I state that I am currently in private practice, even though the reality is that it is failing. I include in the resume the private practice I held in Chicago during the three years I wrestled with mental illness—although during the last years, this was very, *very* part-time. I include volunteer experiences—most especially my volunteer leadership of the spirituality group at Catholic Charities. I do not, of course, say that I am a "patient" there. I include a spirituality group that I am attempting to establish at the Mental Health Association, even though it is currently failing. I do not address the four-year gap in my resume between 2003 and 2007. I do not mention Gould Farm.

I send my resume and am ready for interviews. I am interviewed first by the personnel committee—two lovely and warm women. We connect immediately. They are clearly impressed with my resume, with all of my education and my experience. They then ask me to take the next step in the hiring process and be interviewed by the senior minister, Rev. Louise. Two days later, I meet with her. She is warm and engaging and clearly very intelligent. I like her immediately. She asks, "And what brought you to Binghamton after all those years in Chicago?" I casually respond, "I wanted to be near my favorite cousin after a difficult divorce. And it was time to retire." She does not pursue my response in any way.

A day later, Rev. Louise calls me and says that she would like to hire me. She just has to take her recommendation to the session, the governing body of the congregation. A week later she calls once again, and says, "The session has agreed with my recommendation and would like you to begin work on January 4." This is in two weeks. She also casually mentions that in the future I will need to meet with the Presbytery, the regional body in the Binghamton area that gives final approval for any minister serving in a Presbyterian Church. She is so casual about this, I don't give it a second thought—although soon enough, a glitch will arise in this area.

Rev. Louise and I meet again, and I have many questions for her. "What do I call myself?" I ask. She says, "I suggest you be called Rev. Lucille. I'm called Rev. Louise, and I think you should be Rev. Lucille." This feels just right. I was called Rev. Lucille at Edgewater Presbyterian Church, when doing the ministry there, and now I'm at another Presbyterian church—and the title is very affirming. It feels fine not to be called "doctor," because I'm not functioning as a psychologist in this setting. I'm functioning as a minister.

I then ask, "How is visiting people in their homes—or in a retirement home—different than meeting them in a counseling office?" Rev. Louise says, "Pastoral visits of this kind likely include a prayer, a Bible reading, maybe a song and some physical touch—a handshake or even a hug. The visits will also include serving communion to those who are homebound." I've never served communion in a home, and I'm a bit anxious about that. But she assures me that there is a specific, simple ritual provided in the Presbyterian guidelines, and she is sure that I can do it. This calms my anxiety, and I leave her office excited about my new profession and eager to get started.

On January 4, I set out to visit my first senior: Colette. Like all seniors at the church, Colette has been assigned a deacon whose goal it is to help her in any way that is needed. Colette's deacon is Nina, and she offers to go with me on this first visit. When Nina and I arrive, Colette is sitting at her kitchen table. Her hand is shaking—an uncontrollable tremor. Her back is stooped, even when sitting, due to constant pain. She can hardly hear, so we literally shout as we speak. Her voice is high, soft and squeaky. Yet she is eager to talk when I say, "I'm interested in getting to know you."

Colette explains that her parents were immigrants from Italy in 1922, and that she was born the day after they arrived in America. Her father eked out a small income by doing lawn work for a doctor and, later, working on an assembly line at a shoe factory. Colette, now 88, lives alone. Her daughter lives in Florida and her son lives in Washington, D.C.—but they call every day. I soon learn that Deacon Nina watches over Colette very carefully, taking her grocery shopping and to her doctor's appointments. Colette's husband died suddenly 12 years ago from a heart attack while driving. Collette, in tears, says, "When the police called I went into the living room and screamed—I don't know how long."

Colette is very unsteady on her feet and has fallen several times, even though she faithfully uses her walker. After the falls she is rescued by the emergency squad, which arrives after she pushes the medical alert button that she always wears. She tells me that four years ago, her family per-suaded her to go into a nursing home, but she hated it and, after three weeks, she made her son bring her home. Her daughter has asked her to move to Florida, but Colette won't hear of it. "Everything is set up here. I've lived here my whole life and in this house for 60 years, which my hus-band and I built. Why would I move?"

Colette spends most of her time crocheting—a craft she inherited from her mother. She shows me a 4-foot by 6-foot hanging she made of the Lord's Supper and a lacy, cream-colored bedspread. She now cro-chets yellow daffodils and white doilies. But she complains, "This thread is uneven—sometimes thick, and sometimes thin. That's because it's made in China and not in the U.S. anymore. Everything's changing and now it's hard to crochet." This difficulty in crocheting is compounded by the fact that Colette's hands shake so much that she can barely get the tiny crochet hook through the loops. Yet she plods along.

A vase of the crocheted yellow daffodils, which sits on her kitchen table, brightens the room that is otherwise rather dark and cluttered. In six months there will be a special luncheon for retirees and I will ask Colette if she will provide daffodils for the centerpiece of each table. As it turns out, she will be thrilled to give them, and after the luncheon, every-one will take one home. She says, "Crocheting gives me purpose. I give my work to my family and friends."

Colette teaches me from the outset that having a purpose is crucial to the well-being of each of my seniors. It is, in fact, one of their greatest challenges. How does one spend time after a profession is over and chil-dren are raised; after a house is sold and there is no yard to care for? I will help many seniors who struggle with this issue. Collette has many chal-lenges, but she has found purpose—and this will enliven her for several years.

After hearing Colette's stories, I ask, "Would you like to sing a hymn with me?" She hesitates a bit, but we soon decide on *Amazing Grace*. I find it in the hymnbook I brought. Nina, Colette and I sing heartily. I see a tear flowing down Colette's cheek. We then repeat Psalm 23, and at the fourth verse, tears again trickle down her cheek: *Even though I walk through the valley of the shadow of death, I will fear no evil, for you are with me; your rod and your staff, they comfort me.* After we repeat the psalm, I ask Colette if she would like me to say a prayer. She nods. It's a short prayer: "Oh Lord, I thank you for this time today with Colette. Please be with each of her family members—give them wisdom as they face the challenges of life that are always before them. And be with Colette, O God. Keep her safe, and help her to know at all times that you love and care for her and that we love her. Amen." I put a little kiss on her forehead, and Nina and I are on our way.

I leave feeling very good. I know that I have helped to soothe Colette and have encouraged her in her faith. Perhaps I am suited to this job. I pause in gratitude, so blessed to have this new position that seems to have miraculously dropped into my lap. It's another case of light shining in the darkness.

My second visit is with Lila, at Willowpoint Nursing Home. Lila had a stoke eight years ago and cannot talk or walk. She sits in a wheelchair most of the day, but she is able to wheel around using her right hand; her left arm is in a sling and her left hand is closed and unusable—another side effect of the stroke. The left side of Lila's mouth droops slightly. Her husband is dead and Lila has no children. She will spend the rest of her life at Willowpoint Nursing Home. Willowpoint is the county nursing home—the place where Medicaid patients live; a place that sometimes smells of urine. Lila is watching a cooking TV show when the deacon, Katy, and I arrive. Katy has told me that Lila used to be a great cook and that all day long she watches cooking channels.

After we greet each other, I tell Lila that I have an all-time favorite recipe. I ask, "Would you like to hear it?" She lights up and nods her head. So I explain, "The recipe is from *The Mennonite Community Cookbook*—the Mennonites are similar to the Amish." Hearing this, Lila gestures "Wow." So I begin: "This is a Christmas cookie recipe, and it has the ingredients of an old-fashioned fruit cake: walnuts, dates, raisins, candied cherries, pineapple and citron. The cookies are spicy, with nutmeg and cloves, vanilla and lemon extract. In all, there are 18 ingredients in the recipe." Lila and Katy seem to be impressed by my recipe. Lila makes a high-five motion, with a big smile on her face. She emits a friendly grunt and I know I have made a good connection with her.

After about 20 minutes of Katy and me telling Lila more cooking secrets and reporting on the ice storm that is kicking up, I ask her if we might sing. She immediately nods, and I ask if she would like us to sing *Amazing Grace*. Her whole face lights up at this thought. So Katy and I begin to sing—and to our amazement, Lila joins us! She sings off-key and she says only a few syllables (which are essentially indiscernible), but she sings with such joy and confidence that she sounds like an angel. Katy and I are stunned and almost swept off our feet. Katy thinks that I'm a miracle worker, and I am inclined to agree. When I had asked Lila about singing, I certainly had not expected her to join us. Back at church, Katy spreads the word about my getting Lila to sing. I quickly acquire the reputation of being almost magical in my ability to relate to the seniors. Singing with them—or to them—becomes my signature pastoral gift.

While I have clearly ministered to Lila, it will soon become apparent that she is ministering to me. She shows me, through her sweet spirit, that she is happy and content. She evidently has accepted her life as it is. She is not depressed, and she is loved by the caregivers at her nursing home. I later say to Rev. Louise, "How can she not be depressed? She amazes me. I so admire her!" I will come to admire many of my retirees, and I will often comment to them, "You teach me how I want to be when I grow up."

During the next four weeks, I visit 25 more seniors. The visits are highly rewarding, for I know I have made a good connection with each one. I am now very optimistic that I can thrive in this position, as pastor of visitation. By this time I have met with Rev. Louise to review each visit and I have met with the board of deacons to give an overall report of my work. This has all gone well.

This optimism and hope is severely challenged, though, when I visit with George and Nelly. Deacon Paul and I go to their home. Nelly is in her chair, and she reaches out to me in a warm handshake. George stands, and quickly—almost desperately—pulls me to himself for a hug. I am immediately on guard: it is too tight of a hug. The visit then proceeds as would be expected. We learn that George was a founding member of the church, 70 years ago. We learn that they have six children and 20 grand-children, and that they have lived in their house for 60 years. The house is charming: The fireplace is graced with a carefully carved wood mantel, and the trim around the doors is chestnut wood—a wood that is now rare. The dining room table is a perfectly preserved oak, and George proudly reports that they've had it for 60 years and there isn't a scratch on it.

Then I ask George and Nelly if they'd like to sing. They immediately respond: "Yes, please." I ask if they have a favorite, and George requests *The Church in the Wildwood*. This is an old hymn that is no longer in the hymn book, but I remember it from my childhood. So I begin, and they join in heartily: *O come to the church by the wildwood, the little brown church in the vale. No thought is so dear to my childhood as the little brown church in the vale.* I then offer a short prayer, thanking God for this time together and for the many children and grandchildren that they enjoy so much. I pray for Nelly because she has memory problems and for George because he has acute back pain.

At the end of the visit I stand up, go over to Nelly, shake her hand and give a gentle tap on her shoulder. I then go to George. He stands up and instantly leans toward me, putting a quick kiss on my cheek. I pull away and quickly leave the house. The deacon with me does not notice—and I say nothing to anyone about this visit—but I am enraged with George.

In two months, I visit Nelly and George again. This time, the deacon is not with me. When I arrive I greet George, extending my arm stiffly and keeping him—literally—at arm's length. He tries to pull me to him but does not succeed. I leave, repulsed and angry. I tell Rev. Louise what George has done and she immediately apologizes, saying, "Oh, Lucille, I'm sorry, I should have warned you. George has been a problem in this church. In fact, when he comes to worship we have a male deacon stand by him to prevent inappropriate advances to women. I apologize for not mentioning this to you. And I don't want you to ever visit him alone again. I will go with you."

I appreciate Rev. Louise's support, yet I'm very disturbed that she had failed to discuss this with me ahead of time. Moreover, I am appalled that the church tolerates George at all; that it somehow feels an obligation to visit him, and that this obligation is now falling on me. I accept it with quiet resignation, though, telling myself, "It's part of the job—the job you truly love otherwise." As I later reflect on this, it is clear that Northminster is not a safe church. A predator is there. The church has taken some measure by having a male deacon watch over him, but in my situation, I was not protected.

At a later visit with George and Nelly—even though Rev. Louise is with me—George quietly asks, "Have you ever been sexually abused?" I curtly respond, "I refuse to answer that." I remain calm outwardly, but I am stunned and repulsed. Somehow, the question has evoked in me a sense of shame and of feeling dirty. It is a trigger that has taken me back to feelings of shame and a fear of helplessness, even though I have, in fact, defended myself. I discuss all of this with my counselor, even adding a few extra sessions to cope with it.

I wonder, in all of this, what Nelly is feeling and thinking. Does she notice her husband's behavior? I was told that she is suffering from early Alzheimer's, and perhaps this prevents her from truly seeing and absorbing his behavior. Or perhaps she has just resigned herself to his behavior. Like many wives of her era, she has shoved his shameful behavior under the rug and has chosen instead to see his "good points."

Already, so early in this new job, I have had to cope with a predator. As it turns out, George's son will advise me, years from now: "Never visit my father alone. Always take someone with you." I thank him for that suggestion, but I do not tell him what has already transpired. Our conversation ends quickly, yet I'm appalled that he had not warned me sooner. I realize, once again, that hiding family secrets is more the norm than the exception. My own family—and I, myself—have done the same in covering the abuse by Edmond.

Two months into my work, however, another glitch arises. At the time I was hired, Rev. Louise told me that I would need to meet with the local Presbytery for final approval for my position. She had explained it as standard procedure for any minister that is appointed in the area. The Presbytery functions much like the office of the bishops in other liberal Protestant denominations, although it consists of both clergy and laity. So when I receive an email from Rev. Ely, the head Presbyter, I'm not surprised. I tell her I'm available at the time the Presbytery is scheduled and that I look forward to meeting her and the other members of the Presbytery.

I don't think too much about this upcoming interview. I've successfully passed many examinations of many varieties in my lifetime, so I assume that this one will be the same. A day before the interview, Rev. Louise asks, "Are you nervous?" I respond, "Not really." But her question raises some doubt. When I arrive at the meeting, I realize that 16 people—all seated around a huge table—will question me on my doctrine, my spiritual

journey and my professional life. I become very anxious. While I'm waiting for the interview, I cannot sit still; I begin to slowly pace. I find a book
on a shelf about God's compassion and desire to provide us with all that
is good. I then remember how miraculous it was that I was sought out for
this position. I pray for wisdom in the interview and for a calm mind, and
by the time I am ushered into the meeting, I have gained composure. I
have a big smile on my face when I'm introduced to each of the 16 people
sitting around that huge table.

I am asked the first question. "What is your favorite Scripture passage?"
I hesitate only a moment before replying, "I have many, many favorite
Scripture passages. But my very favorites are the parables Jesus told. Those
beautiful stories with lessons that reach across the centuries. Perhaps I
love, most of all, the parable of the prodigal son—the son who had spent
all of his inheritance in debauchery. When his money was gone, he was
homeless and hungry. He returned to his father's house, fearing rejection
and comparing himself to his brother who had saved his money. What the
prodigal son found when he returned home is a father who was forgiving,
a father who was overjoyed to see his son. The brother of the prodigal son
was judgmental, unforgiving." I then compassionately ask, "Haven't we all
been at times prodigal sons and daughters, who have been forgiven and
loved unconditionally by God? And it is in this 'generosity of spirit' that
we are called to give to others and to those we serve."

The Presbytery seems to affirm my response to their question about my
favorite Bible passages. Then they ask about my understanding of communion, because my job description includes providing at-home communion
to shut-ins. I'm well prepared for this question, so I respond confidently:
"Communion is a symbol of the powerful presence of God in our lives.
Bread and wine represent the basic sustenance we need constantly. So
God's presence is always with us."

I then continue, "Communion also speaks of being reconciled to God,
forgiven, receiving grace and receiving unmerited favor from God. This is
the meaning of Jesus's words, 'My body is broken for you and my blood
is shed for you.'" The presbyters sitting around that huge table seem to
nod approval to my response, so I continue confidently. "The communion
table is also a meal with fellow believers. We are not eating alone, but we
have the love and support of fellow Christians." At this point several more

presbyters nod their heads in approval. I know I have connected with them.

A glitch arises in this interview, however, when I am questioned about the church I was ordained in, which is the First Congregational Church of Evanston. My church is an independent congregational church and is not part of the wider denomination, the United Church of Christ. It is part of an "association," with each congregation being independent. Yet the doctrines are essentially the same as those of the United Church of Christ denomination. But my not being part of a "denomination" is where the problem occurs.

When I leave the Presbytery meeting, I am generally pleased with my interview. I assume I will be accepted as a fully functioning clergyperson. But after I leave, it is decided that I cannot serve home communion as part of my ministry. They report this to Rev. Louise, but not to me. In fact, they will never make contact with me. When I meet with Rev. Louise, she is clearly upset with the decision of the Presbytery; she assures me by saying, "You can certainly do this ministry without communion. In fact, you are." I agree, but I am seething inside. I cannot believe that I am barred from serving at-home communion simply because I am from a church that does not belong to a denomination that has been officially approved by the Presbyterian Church. But I love my job, and I will not be stopped in my ministry to the precious seniors by a legalistic decision of the Presbytery. My work with the seniors hums along very nicely.

I engage my seniors on so many levels: about the painful and difficult slope of aging, and about the need to let go of friends and family as they are dying, one by one. I engage them about the pain of losing their youthfulness and the professions that have been so much at the core of their identity. I talk with them also about death itself: the fears of it that we all have, and the hope we have about an afterlife with God and with our loved ones. When I talk with my seniors about their mortality, I later come to realize that all of this is helping me to face and embrace my own mortality.

As I look back at my professional life as a psychologist, I am aware that being a pastor affords me a deeper intimacy with parishioners than I had with clients in a clinical setting. I am enjoying this intimacy tremendously. While I clearly am the pastor, my seniors are teaching profound lessons in letting go of others and living each moment to the fullest. As it turns out, one of the songs we often sing together is: *One day at a time, sweet Jesus. That's all I'm asking of you. Just give me the strength to do every day what I have to do. Yesterday's gone, sweet Jesus, and tomorrow may never be mine. But help me today, show me the way, one day at a time.* This becomes almost a theme song for my ministry and it speaks as profoundly to me as it does to my retirees. Plus, this whole ministry is giving me a deep sense of purpose, professionally.

In my other work—my private practice—nothing good is happening. It is clearly not taking off. I have only two clients, Pete and Dan. Both have recently been hospitalized in the psychiatric unit of Binghamton General Hospital. Dan is single, 21 years old and slight of build. He is a computer whiz who can't keep a job. Pete, a 6-foot, wide-shouldered man, is an accountant who is in deep internal turmoil. He believes his problems are rooted in his abusive mother, who still criticizes him mercilessly.

For five months, both of my clients come to therapy—but irregularly. I receive some help in my work with them through supervision by Will, but although Will is obviously competent in his supervision, it does not substantially change the fact that neither of my clients is becoming anchored. This is very hard on me, because I've never had problems in working with clients. I'm baffled and disappointed. This disappointment increases, week after week, and my clients come less and less often.

One morning, I get a call from Pete—he is canceling our session once again. I confront him over the phone, saying, "For you to resolve your problems with your mother, you must come to therapy regularly." He reluctantly agrees to come to the session. Two hours later I receive a call from his wife, who says that he has attempted suicide. Instead of coming to therapy, he attempted to hang himself. The timing of the attempt was such that his mother would have found him—dead, and hanging from a rope. But the rope broke and his life was spared. His mother had arrived just after this happened, and he was taken by ambulance back to the hospital.

I am in shock after this phone call. I sit at my kitchen table, staring into space for a good hour. In my mind, I see my client crawling up a ladder and tying a rope to the beam in the ceiling of his garage. I see him tying the rope around his neck. I see him hesitate, but the despair about his life and the anger toward his mother overwhelms him. I then remember my drug overdose six years ago, and the fact that my own despair had over-ridden my hope.

I call my supervisor, Will, and we agree that I will no longer see Pete as a client. This is a tremendous relief, yet the picture I have in my mind—of him actually jumping off the ladder and having the rope break—remains with me. Later that day I receive a call from Pete's social worker, and I tell him that I will no longer be seeing Pete as a client. I explain, "Pete needs a therapist who is part of a larger network, rather than someone in private practice." He agrees with this decision and says that he will convey this to Pete. I never again hear from Pete or his wife.

The next day I call my other client, Dan, and tell him that I will not be continuing to see him. He has not shown up for the last three sessions, so this is no loss for him. Thus my private practice ends. I feel like an utter failure. Will and I talk about how hard it is to establish a private practice in an area where one is unknown and with clients who endure such severe problems. He assures me that I am a competent therapist, but believes that private practice is not for me at this time. I agree, though it still hurts a lot.

After my private practice ends, I continue to see Will. Our relation-ship quickly develops into a client-therapist relationship. His approach to therapy is very much like my own, and he is a perfect fit even though I continue to see Donna, the therapist I've had since moving to Bingham-ton. I know that having two therapists at the same time is unorthodox, but they consult with each other. Furthermore, I realize that having both a male and a female therapist provides a strong mother figure and a pro-tective father figure. As a child, I had neither of these. I also realize that I am healing on a deeper level than ever before. For this I feel most grateful.

While losing my private practice was hard, my successful ministry with seniors mitigates the pain. Furthermore, other areas of my life are humming along beautifully. I'm in close contact with Nathan and am just delighted in the way his life is unfolding. He continues to date Erin, and it is clear that they are a good match. In only a few months he will give her an engagement ring, and they will plan a December wedding. They are attending church regularly—something Nathan has not done before. He and Erin are fast becoming gourmet cooks, and I love visiting them and experiencing new tastes. In one visit, they serve me braised pork wrapped in banana leaves. In another, they serve homemade cardamom-flavored ice cream. It becomes a standard request: "When I come to visit, I want to experience a new taste." They always deliver.

My life at church also continues to thrive. I'm still attending the Sunday morning class, where I continue to deepen relationships with the women there. I am still working in the community kitchen on Wednesday nights, and I regularly see Kimberley, the young girl I met three years ago. I often take her to McDonald's for ice cream after the meal. We just sit and talk. She tells me she hates school because she has to go to special classes; some of the kids tell her she's stupid and that she smells. I assure Kimberley that I will help her with her hygiene.

The next week we go to Wal-Mart and we have a shopping spree. We buy body soap, shampoo, conditioner, hair dye, toothpaste, deodorant, perfume, combs, brushes, socks, bras, panties, T-shirts and running shoes. We are both elated. The next week she says, "You're like a mother to me. I love this church. It shows me that I have a place in the world." With tears in my eyes, I respond, "Yes, you have a place in the world, and it is in this church. You will always be welcome here."

Six months later, Kimberley is baptized and joins the church. I buy her a long, black skirt, a black sweater and a gold scarf for the occasion. At the baptism, she kneels at the altar and I stand at her side. Pastor Stan sprinkles water on her forehead, and when she stands up, the whole church claps. I remain with her when she takes her vows to live a life of service to those in need, and to follow Jesus's teachings to the best of her ability. Tears are rolling down my cheeks as she takes these vows. Afterward, many church members come forward from their pews and welcome her into the church. They hug her, and they hug me. Pam whispers, "Congratulations. Good job."

While I am at church most Sundays, I still frequently go to Pennsylvania, also—to my beautiful trailer and to visit with dear Cherry and Gabe. By this time, their granddaughter, Ella, is born—a sister to Justin. With her blue eyes and blonde hair, she reminds me of her grandmother, Cherry, when she was a little girl. Her personality is just as sweet, too. Justin, by this time, is constantly looking for bugs, toads and snakes and is always eager to show them to me. I love to have Justin and Ella over—for them to visit me in my trailer. I have assembled a whole cupboard full of toys for them. They love my colored blocks and finger paints most of all. Together we stack the blocks as high as possible, holding our breath until they fall down. Then we turn to finger painting. Justin has, since a very young age, shown remarkable artistic ability, and it appears that Ella has the same. So the three of us sit on the deck, painting with our fingers—and then we proudly take our masterpieces to Cherry to be hung on her refrigerator. After delivering the art to Cherry, I pause to give thanks for these children, for this beautiful place and for all the other joys in my life.

Now I have yet one more joy: a new friendship with my landlady, Andrea. Andrea is a woman of considerable means and is well respected in the community. She lives in the building next to me and, like me, she is on the second floor. At night I look out of my window and see her in her apartment—often watching TV on her big flat-screen. When I pull into my driveway, I invariably look over to her building to see if she is there. It is such a comfort to see her. When she is not there, I feel a twinge of unease and loneliness, and—not quite safe. She has a wise and warm aura, which seems to reach from her apartment to mine.

By this time, Andrea and I often sit and chat in her living room. I tell her about my divorces, a bit about my mental illness and about my sexual abuse. I do not mention ECT, even though I am receiving it on a monthly basis; I believe that to divulge this would send her the message that I am currently very ill, mentally, and I want her to believe that I am psychologically healthy.

Andrea tells me about the death of her beloved husband, 19 years ago, and about the recent necessity of ending a relationship with another gentleman. We are both grieving, and this creates a bond between us—a bond that will only get stronger in upcoming years.

I tell Andrea about Nathan and Erin: how proud I am of them, and how hopeful I am for their future. She tells me about her daughters and their families, and especially about her six teenage grandchildren, whom she has helped nurture from the time they were babies. I realize that Andrea is not just an ordinary grandmother. She reads their term papers and teaches them how to work around her properties; she is the matriarch, in the best sense of this role, and is respected by all; she consistently offers steadiness, strength and wisdom. I soon realize that I am the fortunate recipient of her strength and wisdom, and I am deeply grateful.

With my newfound friend, Andrea, two therapists, a successful pastoral profession and a deeply satisfying community at my church, I once again address the issue of ECT. I am clearly very stable and healthy. I'm feeling so healthy that I persuade myself that I no longer need ECT; I am now absolutely functional. I discuss my desire to stop ECT with my therapist and my psychiatrist; with Nathan and other family members. They are all hesitant about my stopping, yet because of my persistence, they agree—as long as I promise to resume it at the smallest sign of depression. I agree.

It is shortly after I stop ECT that Nathan and Erin set their wedding date. It is for December 29—a Christmas wedding. We're all excited, and they start to make plans. The bridesmaids will be Erin's twin sister and younger sister. The best man will be a political buddy of Nathan's—a young Jewish man—and the groomsman will be a friend from Nathan's college days at the University of Chicago—a brilliant mathematician from India.

The summer before the wedding, Erin asks me to go with her to shop for a wedding gown. I'm thrilled, although I feel a bit sad that her mother, who lives in Baton Rouge, is too far away to join us. Erin has carefully researched wedding boutiques and has chosen two to visit. We go to the first one and have no success at finding a gown. In the second boutique, however—after considerable hunting—we find a simple but elegant gown. It is made of soft chiffon, and while it does not have a crinoline, it flows gracefully down her slender body into a 4-foot train. The gown is absolutely beautiful, and we both sense right away that this is the one for her. We go home thrilled. I go home deeply moved that I have been able to be part of this once-in-a-life moment for my daughter-in-law-to-be. I feel like I am now a mother with two children, rather than just one. What I do not comprehend is that at times, I will have to share these children with another set of parents—and that at times, Nathan's attention will be solely on Erin and not with me.

The wedding itself, on December 29, is nothing short of beautiful. The bridesmaids' dresses are strapless—a deep red that magnificently complements Erin's gown. It was planned that the men would wear standard tuxedos with black cummerbunds and bow ties. The best man appears as planned, but the groomsman appears in his formal Indian attire—which is a long, turquoise gown with a long, tan-colored scarf, pants and brown sandals. He is clearly wearing his traditional garb. When Nathan and Erin see him, they are delighted. In the wedding itself, when all the parties are lined up across the front of the church, the colors are stunning: Erin in her white gown, her sisters in red, Nathan and the best man in black and the groomsman in turquoise.

Ninety people attend the wedding. Not a large wedding, really, and yet as I greet them at the reception, I am struck by how far and wide they have travelled. Erin's family and friends have travelled from Louisiana, New Mexico, Arkansas, Ohio, Texas, New Jersey and Virginia. Nathan's family and friends have travelled from Canada, Pennsylvania, Illinois and Alabama.

Luke has come from Chicago, and he plays the organ for the wedding. Christa has travelled from Louisiana. The bond I feel with them is as strong as it was 25 years ago, when we—along with Nathan—met every Sunday night to play, eat, pray and meditate together.

When Nathan and Erin take their wedding vows, I see such compassion and love in their eyes. The wedding vows, while crafted especially for them, are also traditional in some ways. When the minister turns to Nathan, quiet tears role down my cheeks. She asks, "Nathan, will you have this woman to be your wedded wife, to live together in the holy state of matrimony? Will you love her, comfort her, honor her and keep her, in sickness and in health, and forsaking all others, keep only unto her, as long as you both shall live?" I feel a twinge of fear when she says, "forsaking all others": Nathan has been a pillar for me since my illness eight years ago, and I cannot bear the thought of losing him in any way. Over time I come to realize and know that I will never lose him, although at times I will have to adjust to the fact that I do, indeed, share him with his wife and with her parents. Nathan will always remain a central pillar, though.

The reality is that I also have many other pillars in my life: Andrea, Cherry, two therapists, Luke, my siblings and others. It is around this time that Luke and I develop a deeper relationship than ever before. We are in weekly contact, even though he has now left Pennsylvania and has moved back to Chicago. As it unfolds, we talk on the phone every Monday morning at 9 a.m. Throughout the week, we email each other and often talk again. When either one of us has a crisis—whether large or small—the other provides a listening ear. He tells me about conflict with his former foster son; I tell him about my struggle concerning ECT and the stigma it still holds for me. I also tell him that I am having some trouble in my faith: it seems harder than ever before to believe that God is guiding me. It seems, also, that the presence of God is more distant. I confide all of this to Luke, saying, "I feel like I am losing my faith." He quickly responds: "That's okay, I will hold your faith for you." That is such a relief. There is no hint of fear or accusation in his voice. He simply offers to hold my fears about feeling distant from God. What a gift! And soon my faith is totally restored and I feel the presence of God in a deeper way than ever before.

Luke is an avid reader, and as always, he shares with me what he is reading. I call him my librarian because after he reads a book, he often gives it to me. At the moment he is studying the work of Neil Douglass-Klotz, a scholar of Middle Eastern languages. Douglass-Klotz has recently written about Jesus's teachings as they are portrayed in the The Lord's Prayer and the Beatitudes. He explains the meaning of the words of Jesus from the Aramaic, the language Jesus would have spoken.

The Beatitudes are at the core of Jesus's teaching. Luke is especially focused on the first Beatitude, and it is here that he engages me. It is found in Matthew, 5:3: *Blessed are the poor in spirit, for theirs is the kingdom of heaven.* I learn that this Beatitude is about trusting the spirit of God that breathes within us. It is about letting go of the fear, anger and grief that overwhelm us. It is about leaning into God's care—and in this, we bring heaven to earth. "Mature are those who can let go" is the central meaning of this Beatitude.

As Luke is explaining all of this to me, I immediately connect it with one of the stories I had written two years ago for my spirituality group at Catholic Charities. It's almost magical the way I so quickly remember the story and relate it to this *Beatitude*. My story is about a woman who was in deep despair over her son's disabilities caused by post-traumatic stress disorder from the Vietnam War. I remember how I had embedded into that story the song Luke and I composed three years ago: *Let it come, let it go; let it come, let it flow. All is well.* This story and song are resonating with me now. It seems that I am letting go in a more profound way than ever before: letting go of the pain of my divorce, the agony of my mental illness and the sexual abuse. I am embracing God's love in a whole new way. I feel like I am experiencing heaven on earth.

Luke then has an idea. He suggests that we design a series of retreats around the Beatitudes as we now understand them. I'm very hesitant. While I used to be comfortable and confident in such settings, I am now fearful. Luke is patient with me, yet at the same time, he is persistent. He believes, beyond a doubt, that we can offer meaningful experiences not only for participants but for ourselves, as well. And so, a few months later, he schedules a retreat with a Lutheran congregation in Chicago.

I fly to Chicago and stay with Luke for a day before we travel to the retreat center. I'm very anxious, but his calm presence and reassuring words give me confidence. It has now been 10 years since I have done a public presentation with highly educated, functional people. (I later realize that I disregard the storytelling I have done with the members at Catholic Charities.) With the exception of Catholic Charities, most of my presentations have been more like a scholarly paper, in which I argued a case. In this setting, I would be reading a story and teaching a song. I'm very scared. I practice it over and over again. When I read it, though, the participants relate to my story. Through my story and song, it is clear that they are inspired to attempt to let go of pain and lean into the love of God—the love that is always flowing and is ready to receive them and renew their spirits. In this, they experience heaven on earth.

As it unfolds, Luke and I are invited back two more times to provide retreats on the Beatitudes. The result is that I gain considerable confidence in making public presentations. In doing so, my own inner healing and stability continues.

My stability is so strong that I will soon have the confidence to take another huge step in my life—something I never thought I would be able to do. I will buy my own house.

10

Cracking Open
the Darkness

The next six months is a time when the heavens seem to open and drop into my life a gift I'd never dreamed possible: a beautiful house. My very own house. Also, however, a series of events are set off—events that crack open the darkness in me and in my family. Yet through these cracks light flows in and slowly heals my innermost wounds—the wounds of a lifetime.

Buying the house happens quickly, really. Just three weeks from the time I start looking for a house, I put in a bid on the one I will buy. I am 64 years old. Spring is here, and I'm getting a little restless in my apartment. By now I've lived there for three years. Then Mike says to me, "Why don't you buy a house?" I can't get the idea out of my mind. (Mike was my favorite high school boyfriend, and he tracked me down four years ago. He lives in Canada, but we talk often.)

A year ago, Mike had encouraged me to buy a new car. He helped walk me through the process of purchasing my brand-new, light-blue Hyundai Accent, which I now love. Now, Mike is asking, "Why don't you buy a house?" While I protest—"I'd never be able to handle a house by myself!"—I silently wonder if I might be stable enough to buy one and live alone. After all, my mental illness is being managed successfully with medication and counseling. It's risky, but I know I must check it out. So I drive around the neighborhood where I had lived with Cherry and her family when I first moved to Binghamton. It soon becomes crystal clear that if I am to buy a house, I must be close to Cherry's grandchildren, Justin and Ella. As it is now, I see them on occasion, and my grandmother hormones are running wild.

When I drive around the old neighborhood, there are only three houses for sale—and two of them are on the very street where Cherry's grandchildren live. One is right beside their house and the other is six doors down. I call the realtor and set up appointments to see both houses. I take Andrea with me, as I know I can count on her knowledge and common sense. We look at the first house—the one next to Justin and Ella— but I don't like it because the windows are small and the layout feels cramped.

The second house we look at is quite the opposite. It has many windows, and there is a big, sliding glass door that leads out to a big deck and lawn. The layout is open, with the rooms flowing into one another. The living room is spacious and has a beautiful stone fireplace, floor-to-ceiling, crafted with rounded riverbed stones. I can already hear the wood crackling, the flames dancing and the warmth caressing my cheek. I can see Justin and Ella sitting beside me on the sofa, all of us crunching popcorn. The dining room, like the living room, is large and looks even larger because of the sliding glass door. The kitchen is a little smaller, but it has a big island. I can already see my friends gathered around the island, chatting away as I prepare food—pesto, guacamole or curry stew.

The front entrance to the house leads through a rounded, wooden door—clearly the original door from when the house was built in 1938. Like the fireplace, it is truly stunning. I so prefer rounded things to square, for round provides a certain flow of energy that seems to permeate the soul. On the opposite end of the house is a small, portico-like carport. It, too, is rounded, providing perfect symmetry. Below the living room window is a dark-red, wooden window box, waiting to be filled with flowers: to be filled with red and white geraniums, yellow marigolds, lacey blue lyceum and mint-green ivy. I can't wait to get to the nursery and buy flowers!

Inside, on the second floor of the house, are three bedrooms—all small. There is only one bathroom in the house, and it is on the second floor. The bathroom is mainly a disaster: the bathtub, sink and toilet do not match, and the floor is a dirtied white linoleum with holes in it. I can already imagine that Andrea and I, in the future, will tackle it and manage to pull it all together in some miraculous way. She's such a pro at this kind of thing and together, we're magical at turning disaster into beauty.

The road the house is set on is busy and without sidewalks, and the neighborhood emergency squad is a block away. As a result, sirens blast both day and night. The neighborhood has some houses that are medium-size and well kept, and others that are shabby and small. It is this fact that makes the asking price of the house one that I can consider: $94,000.

After going through the house with Andrea, I ask Cherry to accompany me on the second visit. Cherry likes the house and would love to have me near her grandchildren. I then have the good fortune of having my brother, Benny, and his wife, Laura, visit the house. They are traveling from Canada to visit their daughters in Pennsylvania. Having built or rehabilitated their own houses, they know what to look for. They see problems with the bathroom and the roof, but they also see the classic beauty of the house. They encourage me to bid on it. While Benny and Laura do not say it directly, they let me know that they think I am stable enough, emotionally, to have my own house. Their confidence adds to my own.

Benny and Laura even offer to loan me part of the down payment, if I should need it. As it turns out, I will borrow $8,000 from them. As I calculate my finances, I find that I can well afford this house. Combining my salary from working with the seniors, my disability insurance and my savings, I am surprised by how manageable all of this is.

I will realize later that, at some point, I had put myself in the category of being irresponsible with money—even though all reality points to the opposite. When one has an emotional breakdown, it tricks you into believing that you are inadequate in all areas of life—finances, profession, friendships, parenting. But this simply is not true. With this new awareness, I put in a bid of $80,000. After two more bids and counter offers, I settle at $87,500. I then go through the lengthy process of getting a loan and insurance. It seems to take forever, and it is not until late August that I actually take possession of the house.

I am in close contact with Nathan and Erin during all of this. Erin asks how far the house is from the Susquehanna River and, when learning that it is just one block away, she insists—absolutely insists—that I buy flood insurance. She is originally from Louisiana and she knows the devastation of floods. My house is not on a flood plane, although it is near one. So I buy flood insurance, mainly to assuage her. It is only $300.

Nathan and Erin also talk to me about getting a cat. Three months earlier, when I had seen their cat roll over on its back to have its belly rubbed, I casually remarked, "I'd get a cat, too, if there was one like that." Their cat is Tonkinese—a breed that is part Siamese and part Burmese. As soon as I put the down payment on the house, they offer to buy me a cat as a housewarming gift. Nathan says, "It will enrich the quality of your life— immeasurably." While I'm sure he's exaggerating, I agree. I'd love a cat, if they would find one for me. I'm very touched that they want to enrich my life in this way. I soon learn that they have located a breeder of Tonkinese cats and have purchased a kitten, which they will bring to me right after I move into my house.

We then discuss the name for my cat. Since it is from a prestigious Tonkinese heritage, it's been named "Panama Jack, the Third." I definitely don't want to say "Panama Jack, the Third" every time I speak to him, so I choose a shortened name: his initials, PJ. That name, PJ, turns out to fit him perfectly.

In the meantime, I get busy packing. For me, moving—although hard work—is exhilarating. It's a time for re-imagining life; for getting rid of baggage that no longer serves you and buying new things that offer a whole new way of living. Moving day itself is easy. A moving company handles the furniture and I, with four girlfriends from church, handle the rest. Cara, 75 years old, carries 30-pound boxes of books up the stairs to the second floor. I'm stunned. I thank her profusely and whisper a prayer of gratitude for all the goodness that is in my life. In two hours we women are sitting on my precious deck, snacking on cheese and crackers and drinking lemonade. The champagne will come later.

After my friends leave, I make my bed, sort out some toiletries and find my pajamas. Initially, I'm scared of that first night. Can I really be safe in a home all by myself? What if someone breaks in? I check the locks on my three doors two different times. I take my sleeping pills, and soon I fall asleep. I sleep soundly and awaken peacefully the next morning, feeling quite sure that I can live alone in a house. My confidence in this only grows over time. I feel stable, emotionally—more stable than I have felt since my emotional collapse 14 years ago.

I spend a week settling in before it is time to receive my cat. I can't wait to see PJ. When Nathan and Erin arrive, Erin is carrying him. She hands him to me, and without hesitation, he snuggles into my arms. He is adorable. When it's time to go to bed, I assume that PJ will settle in with Nathan and Erin. When I awaken at 6 a.m. the next morning, though, I feel a little furry creature under the covers at my feet. I'm elated. PJ has sought me out. I do not realize that the bonding had occurred last night, when he arrived, and that he will be my constant little companion for years to come. I soon understand that what Nathan had said to me is absolutely true: "A cat will enrich your life immeasurably." What I do not realize is the heartache and fear that will come in the future, when PJ runs away.

Three days after PJ arrives, Benny and Laura travel from Canada to help me with minor repairs and with painting the first floor of the house. Benny works on repairing the bathroom floor, as it has a tile missing. Laura and I head to Lowe's to get paint. I have already decided that I want dark-red accent walls for both the living room and the dining room. The dark red we choose matches the red in two Mediterranean area rugs that I had purchased a month earlier.

I've always loved painting. I love the smell of paint and I love to pour it from the can, into the paint tray, and test its thickness. The high-quality paint we get from Lowe's is thick and creamy, elastic and sticky, which means it easily adheres to the surface of the walls.

It's so rewarding to see the walls transformed before my eyes. Laura says that she finds painting monotonous, but somehow it is not monotonous for me. It feels like a miracle—spreading the paint and watching the new colors emerge. The dark-red walls require three coats, but the result is stunning. The fireplace is graced with the red on each side, and it almost takes your breath away.

Painting and working with Benny and Laura is deeply satisfying. We had never worked side-by-side like this—and in fact, we had never spent much time together in any setting since I was 13 years old. I had gone off to high school, and then to college, and never returned except to visit. Benny's manner reminds me of my grandfather: mild, yet strong and wise. In the future, Benny will quietly convey his love for me in ways that I could never have imagined. Laura is also strong and wise. Sometimes she is a bit more forceful than Benny, but he always holds his ground with her. I love the way they work together and I love to work alongside them. What I do not realize at the time is that in just one year, I will be spending months working alongside them.

Benny and Laura return home and I continue to settle into my house, loving every minute of it. I hang my precious pieces of art: the Mary Cassatt print of a mother protecting her little girl; the grave rubbing in which a man and woman are slightly bowing to each other in deep respect; my family pictures. As always, my favorite family photo is the one of my grandfather and grandmother. My beloved grandfather, who held and rocked me when I was a child being sexually abused by the hired man on our farm. It seems that some of his love has stayed in my heart ever since, and it sometimes embraces me when I feel unprotected and vulnerable.

As I settle into my house, I find that I love it even more than I had imagined when I first saw it. The flow of rooms creates a warm spaciousness that subtly enfolds me. The riverbed stones in the fireplace pop out and greet me as I walk into the living room. The deck, which is a large extension of the dining room, is ready for a big housewarming party. I pay no attention to the flaws in the house; the beauty of it all far exceeds the flaws. I'm incredibly grateful for it all and I know, deep within, that I have made the right decision in buying the house. I feel so stable, emotionally—so much so, in fact, that I am surprised at how stable I truly feel.

In the second week in my new house, I turn to planting flowers. I will make the outside as beautiful and as inviting as the inside. I head to Russell Gardens Wholesale, down the street, and start buying flowers. I'm in heaven. I start with the window box in the front of the house, which gets full sun. I buy exactly what I had imagined on the day I first saw the house: red and white geraniums, yellow marigolds, green ivy and blue and white alyssum.

For my deck, which has little sun, I choose shade-loving plants—mainly impatiens. I buy a whole array of colors—red, white, light pink, dark pink, coral and mauve. I soon develop the habit of going to my deck every evening, swinging on the new glider and soaking up the beauty of it all. I sometimes get lost in the beauty, and it is a lusciousness in which I am incomprehensibly "found," in some primal, mystical and fundamental way. It is a universe that is full of love.

Other parts of my life are purring along beautifully. I love my work with seniors, and my reputation for ministering to them continues to grow. I work at the soup kitchen at my church every Wednesday night. I see my young girl, Kimberley, and continue to help her with her hygiene and listen to her pain. I spend time with my female church friends. I have my trailer in Pennsylvania along the beautiful waterfalls, where I see my beloved cousin, Cherry. I have Mike, my high school boyfriend, with whom I chat often. And most of all, I have Justin and Ella, who come to my house often to play with PJ and with the dolls and trucks I have bought for them.

I am still seeing two counselors: Donna, the counselor I started with when moving to Binghamton, and Will, the Sunday group leader who had supervised me when I was trying to set up my private practice. I also have my psychiatrist, Dr. Shane. I am not currently receiving ECT, but am prepared to resume it if I begin to fall into depression. ECT still represents a stigma for me: it screams out, "You are severely mentally ill!" I just can't bear to think of myself in this way. I realize that I have accepted the fact that I will need counseling and psychiatric medications for the rest of my life. That does not hold any stigma to me. The stigma comes with the need for ECT.

But then … but then a whole new era in my life begins. Events start happening that crack open the wounds within me and the dark secrets within my family. Gradually, though, light finds its way through the darkness and the healing begins. While I have, over the years, attempted to face the pain of my childhood, it is only now that I have to stare it down head-on.

It is set off with a call from my sister, Ruth, just three weeks after I move into my new house. When I walk into my house that Thursday afternoon, I see that there is a message on my answering machine. The light is blinking. Without thinking, I push the button to see who has called. I hear Ruth's voice. It's quiet; muffled. She sounds stricken. She says, "We've had a family tragedy and I need to talk to you. Call as soon as you can." Her message is short but desperate. When I hear it, I know—I have a strong sense of knowing that this is about Edmond. I feel it in the pit of my stomach. I know he has abused someone. I simply know it. I do not call Ruth immediately; I need time to settle myself.

In 30 minutes, I call. "Ruth, tell me what has happened." Her voice is weak and still stricken. She responds, "Edmond has been arrested for sexually abusing a girl—15 years old." My mind flashes to Edmond abusing me, also at age 15. Ruth continues, "He told me he shouldn't have done it. He knew as soon as it happened that he shouldn't have done it." I ask Ruth, "What did he do?" She goes on, "There were some youth at our farm and he touched one of the girls, Katie—a girl from our church, who is like a granddaughter to him." Ruth does not tell me exactly how Edmond had touched the girl. I can only imagine. But one of Katie's friends saw it. Ruth goes on to explain, "Katie called her mother. Her mother called the police and Edmond was arrested." This occurred on September 21, 2010.

Ruth says, "I don't know what the truth is. But I hope that the truth will be found." I pause after I hear her say this. I totally agree with her. I intensely and desperately want the truth about Edmond to be known. I tell her, "And I will pray that the truth will come to the light—that it will be revealed. It is truth we need." I hang up the phone and am shaken at the core of my being. I know the truth. I know Edmond abused that girl. But I feel deep pain for Ruth. I dread the future that is ahead of her. I wonder about the future of all of us. What will happen? What will it mean?

I decide to make two other calls. The first is to Mike. When I tell him about my conversation with Ruth and how upset I am, he does not understand me. He doesn't hear my pain. Instead, he talks about the shame that this will bring to Ruth and about the money Ruth and Edmond will need for legal fees. He guesses that it will be at least $100,000. I put down the telephone, thoroughly disappointed and disgusted. This is the beginning of the end of my friendship with Mike.

Then I call my sister, Rachel. She is extremely distraught and totally humiliated. Edmond's arrest has been all over the news, both on the radio and in the local newspapers. She says that this is bringing shame to the entire family—not just to Ruth. At the same time, she feels utter pain for what Ruth is going through.

I remember how kind Rachel was to me when I was so mentally ill. She protected me from Edmond by asking me to stay at her house every night rather than go to Edmond and Ruth's. Rachel has this same compassion now.

Rachel then tells me about an article in the newspaper about Edmond's arrest. It says that he is 72 years old and is charged with sexual assault and sexual interference of a 15-year-old female who knows him, but who is not a family member. Edmond will appear in court in late November. The article also says that the investigation is ongoing and that police are asking anyone who may have any information to contact them. It is that sentence about asking for information about Edmond that totally unnerves me. I don't say anything to Rachel, but I begin to agonize: should I report him?

In the next week, I am in constant contact with my brothers and their wives. While at Gould Farm, I had told them about Edmond and his abuse of me. They had been so accepting, never doubting the truth of it in any way. I remember how Eunice had asked if I wanted to bring this all to light, and how I had declined; I hadn't had the strength to do it. But now an opportunity has presented itself, and I have a strong hunch that I should seize it.

I'm also in close contact with my niece, Joy—Ruth and Edmond's daughter. I've always had a special bond with Joy. We have both suffered with depression, and she is currently struggling with a dysfunctional marriage. She reminds me that, long ago, I had told her that she should never leave her daughter, Sandy, with Edmond. Joy has followed this advice painstakingly and is greatly relieved that she has. When Sandy was a little girl, Joy read her a children's book about "wrong touching." Joy firmly instructed Sandy that if anyone were to ever touch her in that way, she must tell her immediately. Joy had also carefully instructed Ruth to never let Edmond pick up Sandy at the bus stop and never let him be alone with her. Joy had not told Ruth why she must keep Edmond from Sandy and Ruth did not ask. She was diligent, though, in never letting Sandy be alone with Edmond.

Joy also tells me for the first time that Edmond had abused her when she was 13 years old. I am shocked and thoroughly disgusted that he had even assaulted his own daughter. After school one day, Edmond took her to a bedroom and touched her sexually.

Joy later tells me that she had a special boyfriend at this time. She was in love in that profound and sweet 13-year-old way. She tells me that her boyfriend had asked her to marry him, but she had declined because she did not feel she could trust any boy. This was because of her horrible experience with her father.

I then tell Joy about Edmond's abuse of me. "He abused me at age 15, when he came into my bedroom, touched my breasts and declared his love to me." Joy is silent, but I know she believes me. I continue, "In both subtle and explicit ways, he has been stalking me my whole life." And then it dawns on Joy and me that Edmond has been abusing young girls for 50 years. We are shocked, appalled and enraged. While the bond between Joy and me has always been there, it has now become a bond stronger than superglue. It is no longer just a relationship between an aunt and niece; it is between two adult women who will walk together in all of the murky and horrendous days ahead. In that walking together, light comes into each of us and we begin to heal.

A couple of days later, I receive a telephone call from Detective Gilbert, from Kitchener, Ontario, where Edmond was arrested. I have never before talked with a detective and it is fascinating, in a certain way. Detective Gilbert has a soft and caring way about him, yet his voice is determined and strong. He says, "I am investigating the case of Mr. Edmond Galter and it has been suggested to me that you have some information about him." He hints at the fact that my name has been reported to him as a possible victim, but he is careful to not accuse Edmond. I tell him the truth directly, and my voice is clear and strong. "Yes, Detective Gilbert, Edmond Galter has sexually abused me, as well as his daughter." He then asks if I would be willing to share this information. While I sense that he is being careful to not pressure me, he, in fact, is. In some way, I greatly appreciate it.

When I am finished talking with the detective, I call Joy. I ask her if she is going to testify against her father. She says that she is seriously considering it, although she is heartbroken for her mother, Ruth. Ruth still believes that Edmond is innocent. We think that Ruth has no idea about the extent of the abuse, although we're not certain of that.

I then call Rachel. She says to me, "I have heard that Edmond has abused many, many women through the years and that at least one of these women has decided to come forward and testify against him." I then ask her, "Do you think I should testify?" She does not answer me directly, but I can tell by her firm voice that she thinks I should. Yet she is also trying to be neutral, feeling very torn between Ruth and me. I hang up the phone, knowing she believes I should testify. I then call my brother, Peter, and he seems to have the same opinion—although he, too, is utterly pained for Ruth and for all of the disgrace this will bring to her.

Finally I call Benny, and his opinion is absolutely clear. He says, "To not testify is to repeat the pattern of hiding the truth, which is what mother and dad did with you 50 years ago. When you told mother and dad about Edmond's abuse of you, they remained silent. I do not think you should continue that silence." By the end of this conversation, I am quite sure that I will testify. I call Nathan. He thinks I should testify. I talk with my two therapists and my psychiatrist, and while they all encourage me to testify, they are hesitant to push me. My psychiatrist, Dr. Shane, wonders whether or not I am strong enough to travel to Canada for the trial. He asks if I could testify in Binghamton, and have the testimony forwarded to Canada. As soon as he says this, I realize that he is right. I am still too fragile, emotionally, to face Edmond in court.

I call Detective Gilbert and tell him that I am quite sure I will testify, but that I am not able, emotionally, to travel to Canada and testify there. "We can easily make arrangements to accommodate that," he says. "Just tell me where you live and I will contact the local police force so they can do the investigation there."

He explains that I will eventually talk with a detective, but before that meeting, a police officer will come to my house to explain to me the nature of the questioning that I will receive. Detective Gilbert explains that the testimony itself will be given at the local police headquarters.

I wrestle with all of this for several days. I try to provide a distraction by throwing myself into work or into a house project. It doesn't really work. I find that I am angrier at Edmond than ever before. I want him prosecuted and I want him put in jail, where he can never again touch a little girl. Yet I am still feeling protective of my sister, for she still has no idea about the extent of Edmond's abuse. I am also just plain scared of the whole process, as I know that it will be traumatic. Will I have the emotional stamina to testify and tell my story about Edmond? Will it stir in me such pain that I will collapse? About 30 percent of me is deeply afraid, the other 70 percent is strong, determined—actually delighted—for the opportunity to tell my story to the world. I am deeply relieved that finally, after 50 years, there is the real possibility that Edmond will be stopped and that he will be punished for what he has done.

I also find myself reliving the original assault by Edmond when I was 15 year old. I feel, once again, the fear of the night when I was staying at Edmond and Ruth's to help them paint and get ready for their baby; I remember how hard we worked that day, and how good it felt to go upstairs and get in bed. I remember how I awakened at 2 a.m. to Edmond standing over me, fondling my breasts and telling me he loved me. I remember how I fought back: how I swatted at him, but I did not scream. How he backed off and went downstairs. I remember how I lay there the rest of the night, fearing his return; how I got up the next morning and did not say a word to Ruth. I had felt that I had to protect her.

The next day I had painted ferociously, but did not finish; this meant I would have to stay another night. I remember how terrified I was that second night, as there was no wooden door into the bedroom; there was only a curtain hanging over the doorway. What was I to do to keep out Edmond? I panicked at first, but then I found some straight pins. I reasoned that if I could fasten the curtain into the molding around the door with these pins, Edmond would not come into my bedroom. I knew this was no real protection, of course, but it was all I had. So that night I lay awake, ready to fight Edmond off. I lay awake, despising him for what he had done to me. But he did not return. The next morning, Ruth and I finished the painting and then I returned home.

I remember arriving home, so relieved to be away from Edmond. Though frightened, I knew I wanted to tell my parents. Pressure was building inside of me and it had to come out or I would burst. I told them that something terrible had happened at Ruth and Edmond's house. They had me sit down at the kitchen table to talk. The table was in front of the kitchen window. Crying, I told my parents what had happened.

I remember how, when I told my parents, my father's face had filled with rage. My mother's face was white, appalled. At first, they were silent. Then my father said, "We need to pray." So the three of us bowed our heads. I did not hear what they prayed; I only hoped that their prayer would be answered. After the prayer, we silently left the table. We never again talked about this. Never. I carried the secret—the darkness—all by myself.

I remember how, over the years, I have endured hugs from Edmond. The hugs were always too tight and too long. I remember how I have tried to never sit by him at a table, though it seemed that, wherever I sat, I always felt his eyes on my breasts.

Other memories come floating back also: the time when my dear friend, Christa, visited my family in Canada and was in the barn, looking at the goats, when Edmond came up from behind and grabbed her. She pulled away in utter disgust and never again allowed herself to be near him again.

I remember how, just a few years ago, Edmond had tried to grab me in my trailer in Pennsylvania. I remember how I was ready for him and hollered for him to stop. In tears, I had told Cherry what happened. We talked about telling Ruth, but I did not want to hurt her. I wanted to protect her—even at my own expense.

And now I find that I truly hate Edmond—for what he has done to me, and what he has been doing to women all of these years. I'm aware that hate is something that a Christian is not supposed to have. *Love your enemies*, Jesus says. Edmond is my enemy and I hate, rather than love, him. Somehow, though, this contradiction feels OK with me: for finally, all the pain and anger that has been underground is now being brought into the light. I am deeply relieved, although I know that there will be many difficult days ahead if I do, in fact, testify against Edmond.

In my counseling and in my discussion with my siblings, I realize in a more intense way than ever before how profoundly Edmond has affected my relationships with other men—especially my two ex-husbands, Joel and Louie. As with Edmond, I had a certain feeling of powerlessness with them, even with all of my education and my good reputation. In subtle ways, Joel's addiction to books and Louie's to alcohol were a shadow of Edmond's addiction to sex.

I also come to understand the shame that I have lived with most of my life: the shame that was born when I was abused by the hired man at age 6. I recall how he had made me stand by him as he sat in the living room; how he touched my vagina; how filthy and shameful I felt.

The shame was intensified by the guilt of my childhood religious upbringing. As a child, I had repeatedly sought repentance for guilt—whether it was guilt for getting angry at my sister or for sneaking a sweet from the pantry. I lived in fear of being abandoned by God and doomed to an eternal hell.

I discuss some of this with my siblings. I do not tell them the depth of my feelings of shame and guilt: that seems too private. But I talk with them about the attraction I have had to men who are somewhat abusive and who have had addictive behaviors. I am surprised to find that they agree with me and that they have believed, for some time, that all of this is part of the dynamics of my mental illness.

I also come to realize in a stronger way than ever before, how the lack of protection from my parents has impacted me throughout my entire life. I felt profoundly abandoned by them when I told them about Edmond and they prayed with me, but never again mentioned it. For me, a fear of abandonment is always close at hand.

Related to this abandonment is the wish to find approval and protection from a father figure. On an unconscious level I was seeking this in my husbands—both of whom were seminary professors. Perhaps the determination to be a minister myself was also related to my need for protection from a religious figure, even myself. While it now is clear that none of this really worked, I at least have come to understand the dynamics of it all.

All of this adds to my determination to testify against Edmond—and in fact, after I make the final decision to testify, I can hardly wait. Before, I had told my siblings about the abuse. *Now I am going to tell the entire world!* I know I will be changed—transformed—in some ways. I know that light will penetrate my deepest inner darkness. And I know I will be free.

II

Baring My Soul

Yes, yes! I will testify! I will tell the truth! I will bare my soul! I will finally tell the world the secret that has burdened my heart and soul for 50 years. I can hardly wait!

Yet—yet, there is a very, very big dilemma in all of this: Do I tell Ruth what I am doing? Do I tell her that I am testifying against her husband? How can I do this to my beloved sister—the sister who calls me every week; who cries with me; who visits me; who is always bringing maple syrup from her farm, and bringing syrup for Nathan, also? We love her maple syrup, and we love her for bringing it to us.

I must tell her. I must prepare her. But how and where should I do this? Do I talk to her by phone? Do I email her? Do I write a letter and send it in the mail? Do I go to Canada and tell her in person? If I tell her face-to-face, do I ask my other sister, Rachel, to be with me? Where would I do this? Would it be at Ruth's house? At Rachel's house?

I talk to Rachel, Peter, Benny and Nathan. It is Benny who comes up with the perfect solution. As soon as he says it, I know it is right. "How about bringing Ruth to Binghamton, to your house? Joy should come also. We will lovingly tell Ruth the truth about Edmond, and then you can tell her about testifying." I realize immediately that if we do it together, we will have the courage we need; we will have the strength to hold Ruth, emotionally, as she hears the truth. I decide that I will tell Ruth what

Edmond did to me. Joy will tell Ruth what her father did to her. Benny adds, "And I will tell what Edmond did to my daughters. How he touched them." At first, I'm shocked when I hear this. Then I have the sickening realization that Edmond has spared no one—absolutely no one. And I know, beyond any shadow of doubt, that I will tell the truth to Ruth and that I will testify against Edmond.

We decide to gather the third weekend of October. Benny calls Ruth and asks if she will come to Binghamton to talk over the situation about Edmond. She agrees. Joy will drive her. Benny and Laura will drive on their own and, after telling Ruth the horrible truth about Edmond, they will go to Pennsylvania and visit their daughters.

It is now five weeks from the time Edmond was arrested. As I prepare my house for my dear guests, I try to prepare my soul. Yet I cannot. I try to sing the chant Luke and I composed years ago: *Let it come, let it go; let it come, let it flow. All is well.* It simply doesn't work this time. All is not well. In fact, it feels like all is hell!

That Friday night, when Ruth and Joy arrive at my house, I am almost sick with fear—fear of devastating my beloved sister. Benny and Laura arrive soon after, though, and they have a calming presence, so I am able to settle myself a little. We have decided ahead of time that we will all have dinner together, and then we will tell Ruth. I have carefully prepared a good meal that I know Ruth will like: sausage and beef meatloaf, baked in the oven with carrots, potatoes and onions. We will also have a simple garden salad with cherry tomatoes, cucumbers and red and green peppers. Breyers chocolate ice cream will be dessert.

The conversation around the table is tense, but everyone is making nice—commenting on the weather, and on the flowers that I have brought in for the winter. Ruth and Joy tell me how beautiful my home looks, and I try to be responsive and enthusiastic. PJ, my cat, provides relief when he crawls onto Ruth's lap; perhaps he senses her dismay. The meal seems to drag on forever, and I am very anxious. What, exactly, should we say to Ruth? How will she respond? Will she collapse? Will she deny what we are saying? Will she hate me when I tell her that I'm testifying?

We had decided ahead of time that Benny will reside over this gathering, as he has a bit more objectivity than Joy or me. Furthermore, I know that his calming presence will enable us to speak the truth. After we eat the chocolate ice cream, I'm quite anxious and I try to indicate to Benny that we should move ahead. Finally, *finally* he says, "We need to go to the living room and talk about the situation with Edmond."

We seem to know where to sit. Joy and I sit together on the sofa that faces the fireplace. Ruth sits on the rocking chair facing us, to the right of the fireplace. Benny sits on the rocking chair to the left of the fireplace. Laura sits on the cedar chest bench, which is on the right side of the room just in front of the windows. It feels, on one hand, like a warm, intimate circle; on the other hand, it feels like we are at the execution of my beloved sister.

Benny begins: "Ruth, we're here to tell you the truth about Edmond. We feel so badly about the pain this will cause you, but we know you need to hear the truth. We've been protecting you all these years and it's time that you hear the truth." He then turns to me. At least, I think he does. I somehow feel ready to speak, and by now I have a certain calm; the former agitation has almost completely receded. Afterward, I realize that I had been waiting for years to tell the truth, and when the opportunity arose, I was ready—relieved, and at ease.

I say it very simply. "Edmond abused me when I was 15 years old. It was in your house, when I came to help you paint. You were pregnant—eight months pregnant. I awoke at two in the morning with Edmond fondling my breasts and telling me he loved me. I was terrified. I fought him off. Finally, he stopped and went back to your bedroom. I lay awake the rest of the night, terrified he would return. He did not."

I do not tell Ruth about the way Edmond has stalked me over the years and how I have always dreaded being in his presence. But I do tell her that when I left her house and told mother and dad, they did not say anything; they just prayed.

Ruth appears stricken by what I have said to her, but she in no way protests. She only says, "Mother and dad chose me over you." I do not respond outwardly to this. I am relieved that she does not appear to be angry with me, but I am shocked that she states, so clearly and crisply, "Mother and dad chose me over you." I suddenly realize, in a way that I never had before, that they indeed did choose her comfort over mine. In the future I will agonize over this time and again. Why did they choose her comfort over mine? Did they fear Edmond? Did they fear Ruth's despair if she knew about Edmond? Did they believe that what he had done was not horrendous—that things like this just happen? Did they believe that I would "forget" what had happened? These are questions that will never get answered. In a way, they are wounds that never totally heal.

After I tell my sister about Edmond, Joy turns to Ruth and says, "Mother, dad also abused me—when I was 13 years old. He took me to a bedroom and touched me sexually." Joy does not give details. Ruth does not respond verbally. She just looks ashen.

Benny then talks. "And Edmond was inappropriate with two of my daughters, touching their legs when driving in a car with them." Again, Ruth in no way protests. She is simply stricken. I have never in my life seen such despair on anyone's face. She quietly says one thing, however. "That would explain some things." We do not ask her what that would explain, but we know that, on some level, she knows about Edmond. We realize that on a conscious level she has kept this knowledge from penetrating deeply, and that she has been persuaded by Edmond that his recent advances toward the little girl, Katie, were not as offensive as they truly are.

At this time, Joy, Ruth and I are in tears. Through the tears I hug Ruth, saying, "I'm so sorry about all the suffering this will bring to you. I love you from the bottom of my heart and I wish that you would not have to face all of this." Again, Ruth is in no way angry with me or with Joy. She just bends forward in agony. Then she gathers herself and says, "I need to tell the truth to Ed and Roy." These are her sons. Both have been very supportive of her and Edmond; Ed and his wife had even helped Edmond secure a lawyer for his defense. Benny tells Ruth that he will help with those calls, if she wishes. As it unfolds, Benny makes the calls for her. She is simply too stricken to talk with her sons.

After the calls are made, the next situation arises: will Ruth return home to live with Edmond? The answer seems to come easily: she will not return to live with him. She will ask Sherry, a dear friend and wife of Edmond's nephew, if she can live with her and her husband on a temporary basis. Ruth calls Sherry, and Sherry agrees without hesitation, happy to help Ruth.

Next, we all wonder: how will Ruth confront Edmond in all of this? Will she try to do it by herself? With someone else? At this point, Ruth decides to seek advice from a female pastor whom she knows well, Rev. Lily.

Rev. Lily's husband, Ned, was a former police officer who is now working with sex offenders. Rev. Lily promptly agrees to meet with her and to have her husband, Ned, meet separately with Edmond. After those individual meetings, the four of them will meet and Ruth will tell Edmond that she knows the truth about him. Ruth is terrified about telling him, and she even comments, "I hope he won't kill himself."

Benny, sensing Ruth's extreme distress, says, "I think you will need some counseling to handle all of this, and I would be happy to pay for that counseling." She hesitates for a moment. I add, "I agree with Benny, that you need counseling, and I hope you accept his offer to pay for it." Without any further hesitation she accepts his offer, and we are all relieved.

The next day, on Saturday, Benny and Laura leave for Pennsylvania. I'm anxious about their leaving—their presence was so comforting. But Joy and I had anticipated this, and we had discussed it earlier in the week. Joy had said, "What project can we do for you, Aunt Lucille? We need a project." I responded quickly. "And I have one for us! I need to make curtains for my dining room. I need them to match the ones that are in the living room." Joy had instantly replied, "Dandy. That sounds like a plan, Aunt Lucille. You get the fabric and we'll make your curtains."

Benny and Laura are barely out the door when we start our project. Joy has brought her own sewing machine and is clearly intending to do the sewing, which is fine with me. I'm not at all sure I'd have the ability, at this point, to sew a straight seam. We need relief from all of the pain, and working together not only provides relief but it brings a certain bonding that always comes when we women work together, whether it is canning pickles, shopping for Christmas or sewing curtains.

I bring my bolt of fabric from the front closet. It is a muslin, off-white, and it matches the curtains in the living room that came with the house. It is 12 yards of material and it is 4 feet wide. It's bulky, handling that much material, and it's complicated to figure out how to cut it. It takes all three of us almost a half-hour to figure it all out, and for that brief time, we almost forget the pain we are holding inside.

With the material cut, we need to decide the size of the seams for the bottom, top and sides of the curtain. We check out the curtains that are in the living room, as we know that we want to match the seams on them. Joy takes the lead in all of this. After we figure out the seams, Joy starts sewing. It takes about 40 minutes to sew the first curtain. It's Ruth's job to iron, and Ruth deftly irons each seam so that it lies on its side, with minimum bulk. I just stand by, watching the two of them work. PJ comes up to me, looking for attention, so I gently pet him. He provides the perfect distraction from the pain of it all. For almost two hours, we're lost in the sewing and ironing.

Then it is time to hang the curtains and examine our handiwork. Round, wooden curtain rods have been left in the dining room, and I had just purchased wooden clips on which to hang the curtains. Everything is ready to go. Joy and I crawl up on chairs to reach the top of the windows, and Ruth hands the curtains to us. It takes a lot of fussing to get them gathered and hung just right, but finally, Joy and I are able to climb down. We all stand back and admire our work; we are very pleased. They match the living room curtains perfectly, and the two rooms flow together in perfect harmony.

But now that our project is complete, what will we do? I am in agony because I know I must tell Ruth that I will testify against Edmond. I also know that I am not ready to tell her now. I simply can't do it yet. It is 6 p.m. on Saturday evening, and Joy and Ruth plan to go home on Sunday morning, but we have four hours until bedtime. We are all uneasy. I suggest we eat—always a good escape. So we go to the kitchen. Joy and Ruth sit at the island while I turn to preparing food for supper. It's pretty simple, because I pull out leftovers from the night before—meatloaf, carrots, potatoes and onions. I heat them in the microwave, and they are ready in 10 minutes. I ask if they'd like to prepare some salad, so this provides a little activity for them. In 15 minutes we're ready to eat. As always, we pause for prayer. I ask Joy to pray. Her prayer is simple: "Oh Lord, we need your help. Please guide us through this terrible time. Give us all wisdom and courage. Especially be with Mom. And now, oh Lord, we thank you for this food. Amen."

After the meal, we pick up the dishes and wipe the counters, as mother had taught us to do. I ask if I can take a picture. They agree, and they sit at the island. I see that Ruth tries to smile, but a smile does not come. Instead, there comes on her face a haunting look of despair and shame. She does not look into the camera, but seems to be staring off to the side, instead.

My heart breaks for her. I am also aware of the fact that I am about to give her another big blow: I will tell her I am testifying against Edmond.

I suggest we go into the living room and sit down. After a few minutes of silence, I begin. "Ruth, I want you to know that I am considering testifying against Edmond. I hate to do this, for your sake, but I need to heal. Will you be mad at me if I do?" She pauses, then responds, "I'm not saying that it won't upset me, but I know you have to do whatever you need to do to heal." That's all she says. I'm tremendously relieved, because she seems to understand. I see her pain, but I also see her care for me. I hug her. I hug her tightly through my tears, saying, "Thank you, *thank you*, Ruth—we all need to heal, and that is the most important thing in all of this." Joy joins in the hug and she implies but does not say directly that she will testify against Edmond. I am sure that she will.

The next morning, Ruth and Joy leave to return home. Ruth will be living with Sherry, as we had discussed the night before—at least, this is what Joy and I believe. With big hugs and lots of tears, I send them on their way.

After they leave, I lie on the sofa and stare into space. Then I remember that it is Sunday. I'm relieved, for I need church. I'm agitated while I'm driving, but am subdued as I enter the sanctuary. I sit where I have always sat—on the left middle isle, four rows from the front. My good friend Kate sits by me, as always, and she has no idea what I'm going through. Yet her presence is calming, and the whole worship experience provides tremendous relief. The song that the congregation sings every Sunday penetrates my soul and heals it—at least temporarily. *Surely the presence of the Lord is in this place. I can feel his mighty power and his grace. I can feel the touch of angel wings; I see glory on each face. Surely the presence of the Lord is in this place.*

On Tuesday, I see my counselor, Donna. I tell her everything that happened. She seems so proud of me, and she provides me with the strength to take my next step: calling Detective Gilbert and telling him that I will testify. I go straight home after the counseling session. I have carefully kept his telephone number, and I know what I must do.

Detective Gilbert answers the phone. I am so relieved that I did not get a secretary, as I do not want to explain anything to anyone else. Detective Gilbert seems to recognize my voice, and I say, very simply, "Detective

Gilbert, this is Lucille Sider. I have decided I will testify against my brother-in-law, Edmond Galter. What is the procedure for this?" Although we had discussed this briefly when I told him I could not come to Canada, he now tells me in greater detail. He says that there are two steps. The first is that a police officer will come to my house and will talk to me about the nature of the questioning I will receive in giving my testimony. He will come at a time we set for this meeting. He will be wearing a plain suit, and not a police uniform. He will be driving a plain car, rather than a police car.

Detective Gilbert then explains, "The second step is that you will go to the police station, and a different man—a detective—will ask the questions you have been given." Detective Gilbert gently asks if this is clear and if I am prepared to move forward. I say that I am. I am feeling two emotions at the same time: fear and excitement. I do not mention this to the detective.

Two days later, at 10 a.m., I see a plain car pull up in front of my house. I know it is the police officer. When he gets out of his car, I see that he is about 40 years old, of medium height and good-looking, wearing a grey suit. He knocks on my door; I open it. In a very soothing and rather quiet voice, he introduces himself. I invite him in and he sits on the sofa, with me on a rocking chair that faces him, about 8 feet away. He says, "I am here to prepare you for the interview you will have with the detective at the police department. I have a list of questions you will be asked. They are written out on this paper, and I would like to review them with you. Is that acceptable to you?" I respond, "This is totally acceptable and I know it will help me."

He then goes down the list of questions. They are all straightforward. He in no way asks me to answer the questions; he just wants to make sure that I understand them. These are the questions: "What is your name? Who is the person you will testify against? What is his relationship with you? When did the incident occur? Where did it occur? What, exactly, happened? How did you feel after the incident? What did you do after the incident? Did you tell anyone about it? If so, how did they respond? How did this incident affect your relationship with the offender and with other family members? Has this incident affected you in later times in your life? If so, how would you describe that?"

The officer asks me if I understand the questions, and I assure him that

I do. He asks if I would come to the police station in a week to answer the questions; I say that I will. When he leaves, I feel considerable relief. I know I will be able to answer these questions—and, in fact, I am eager to do so.

I immediately call my friend, Andrea, and ask her if she will go with me to the police station. Without hesitation, she says, "I will gladly go with you." I then call my sister, Rachel, and tell her all about the questions. As usual, she is supportive, saying, "I'm so proud of you for having the courage to do this, Lucille. I know it is the right thing. And I will pray for you the whole time you are testifying."

The next day I call my counselor, Donna, and set up an extra session. I want all the support I can get as I prepare, emotionally, to give my testimony. I later marvel at the fact that during all of this I am not feeling depressed and am not needing ECT. At this time, receiving counseling and taking medication is all that I need.

The following Wednesday is the day set for my testimony. I decide to wear a simple tweed jacket with black pants and a white turtleneck: I know the interview will be video-recorded, and I want to leave the impression of professionalism. At 9 a.m., Andrea picks me up and drives me to the police station. The waiting room is small, with white, painted walls and only a small window. I do not like the closed-in feeling. An officer greets us almost as soon as we arrive, and says, "The detective, Mr. Gray, will be ready for the interview in five minutes." The next five minutes are interminable, and I get very fidgety. Andrea tries a little small talk about the weather, and I barely hear her. The officer then comes out, saying, "Mr. Gray is ready to see you." He ushers me into a small room—12 feet by 15 feet. There is a rectangular table in the middle of it, with the detective standing behind it. He introduces himself. "I am Detective Gray. I will be interviewing you." He shakes my hand and asks me to sit down at the table, across from him. He then sits down. He is about 40 years old and dressed in a grey suit, with a half-smile on his face and restrained warmth. I sense that he is a kind man, but he clearly keeps a professional distance from me.

The walls are bare and white, and the room feels very sterile. In the upper left corner is a camera, and Detective Gray points to it, explaining, "This is a video camera. Your testimony will be videoed and this will be sent to Canada to be viewed by the detectives there." I respond, "I understand this." He then proceeds with the questions. These are the exact questions I had been given previously, and there are no surprises.

I am quite nervous at first. My voice is quiet and quivers considerably. The first question is, "What is your full name?" My response, of course, is, "Lucille Faith Sider." The second question is, "Who is the person you will testify against?" My answer, of course, is "Edmond Galter." "What is his relationship with you?" I say, "He is my brother-in-law, who is married to my sister, Ruth." Mr. Gray then asks, "When did the incident occur?" My answer is, "When I was 15 years old." The next question is, "Where did it occur?" My answer is, "It occurred at their home."

Until this point in the interview I am very tense, my voice is weak and I am quivering. I am having trouble recalling what I had prepared to say. Then Detective Gray asks, "What, exactly, happened?" As soon as I start to describe what had happened, there is a shift in me. While I proceed to answer the remaining questions, I am not frightened or anxious; I tell in detail what Edmond had done to me at age 15, how my parents had responded by praying, how Edmond has stalked me my entire life and how this has affected me for many years. My answers are straightforward and clear. My voice is strong. I am totally confident. While talking here, in the police station, I also feel that there is a part of me that has been transported elsewhere.

That part of me that is elsewhere is with Katie, the girl Edmond had just abused. I have a deep sense of solidarity with her. In my mind, I wrap my arms around her, I hold her and I tell her, "You are so brave. Thank you, *thank you* for what you have done. You are helping to bring healing not only for yourself, but for all of us. Now, together, we will be able to stop Edmond from abusing other girls. Together, we will bring justice. He will be in jail and he will pay for what he has done."

I then see in my mind's eye the other women Edmond has abused: faces that are unfamiliar. I become acutely aware that we are fighting for justice. We are banding together. We are fighting for all women everywhere who have been sexually abused. I see in my mind's eye that we women are standing in a circle, holding hands and singing. The picture reminds me of my feminist days in the '70s, when we banded together and fought for women's rights. I am aware that this fight is perhaps more pernicious than the other. The scars of sexual abuse run deeper than scars from women's inequality. I am delighted and determined to join in this battle for justice. I am energized and ready. I feel strong. I even feel radiant.

I had never before had an experience like this. It is as though I was in two places at the same time, having two different emotions. One emotion is trepidation; the other is exhilaration—confidence and excitement about the future. I later realize that this is a mystical experience akin to what others have had. It is, on one hand, being in a dreadful situation, but on the other it is being relieved and experiencing deep peace and joy.

Andrea later tells me that I emerged from the interview looking happy, even radiant. She was totally surprised, as she had expected me to look gaunt and drained. I tell her what had transpired inside of me during the interview, and I can tell that she is happy for me. We go to lunch and I tell her every detail. She is such a pillar for me; so wise. I am incredibly grateful for her.

With the testimony behind me I am acutely aware that I need to focus my mind elsewhere. My psyche cannot handle thinking about Edmond anymore, and so I need something else—something that requires creativity. I also need something that I can do with a friend. What might this be? I come up with the perfect project: decorating my bathroom. The person to help me with it is Andrea. I ask her to help, and she gladly agrees, "Yes, let's get to it."

The bathroom is a decorating nightmare. The bathtub is a rusty pink. The toilet is a dirty beige. The sink is off-white. Fortunately, the wall tile is also off-white. The countertop has an indistinguishable design of beige and pink. The floor is grey linoleum.

When I actually bring Andrea to the bathroom and ask her to help me pull all of this together in some tranquil, pretty way, she just shakes her head. Trying not to be too negative, she says, "Let's go shopping and see what we can find. Surely there must be a shower curtain, towels and a floor mat that will bring it all together."

We start off at Kohl's—a department store that is modestly priced and yet has high-quality merchandise. We find some plain, taupe-colored towels. Then we head to Boscov's, where we are delighted with the possibilities. There is a set of taupe towels with a row of pink crocheted flowers at the end, and a set of pink towels with mauve strips at the end. There are countless shower curtains: striped pink and purple; flowered; brown and beige; purple and pink polka-dot. We stand there, trying to choose, and then Andrea says, "Let's just get it all. Take them home, and try them." They cash out at $300.

Our arms are weighed down as we lug everything to the car, into my house and up the stairs, into the bathroom. We start with the shower curtains, and shake our heads. None of them will work. We try the towels and immediately see that the taupe ones with the pink flowers will be perfect as hand towels. But they won't work as bath towels. They simply do not provide enough color.

By this time Andrea is exhausted, so she goes home and we decide to continue our search another day. I still have some energy left, so I head to Wal-Mart. I first come upon mauve towels that feel perfect. Then I find a shower curtain, in a slightly darker mauve—almost purple. I find a bathmat that matches the towels. I buy it all and can't wait for Andrea to return the next day and check it out.

When she arrives, I have hung the shower curtain; I have laid the towels on the counter and the mat on the floor. "We're making progress now," she says. "But—there is too much mauve. Let's mix the taupe towels with the mauve." We both know immediately that we have the perfect combination. We are elated. We burst into laughter. We have solved our decorating nightmare. Most of all, we have forgotten about Edmond and Ruth. The bond between us is stronger than ever, and in the months ahead—when disaster hits my beautiful house—that bond becomes stronger than superglue.

In the following weeks I am in frequent conversation with both Joy and Rachel. Several people have come to them and told them about Edmond having stalked them. He had gone to one woman's house repeatedly when her husband was gone. He had grabbed a woman who was working on their farm—and she was so traumatized that she had stopped work because of it, but she never reported it. At the current time this woman still does not have the stamina to go through the pain of reporting.

Also during this time we find out that Edmond's lawyer is meeting with a female prosecuting lawyer from the local provincial government. In Canada, this lawyer is called the "crown lawyer." We are encouraged by the fact that there is a female prosecutor. While no one is privy to these meetings, we know that the lawyers are gathering evidence and that, if Edmond is found guilty, he will be arrested and will likely go to jail. But we also know that he may get out on bail.

We all assume that Ruth is convinced of Edmond's crimes and that she will leave him; divorce him. We will surround her with love, lighten her burden and lessen her shame. We will help her build a new life apart from the man who has been deceiving her for almost 50 years.

Yet in just two months, we will learn that we are wrong. She will choose Edmond. She will coldly turn her back on us!

12

Fifty Years

The day of the court hearing finally arrives. It has been three months since Edmond was first arrested. This is the day he will be arrested again, if the charges are found to be true. It is not an open court, so family members are not there—but the press is. The report in the major local newspaper states that police arrested Edmond Galter, a 72-year-old Wilmot Township man, in connection with an ongoing investigation into alleged sex offences of females known to him. These offences are believed to have occurred over the past 50 years, and Edmond Galter is charged with sexual assault, sexual exploitation and two counts of indecent assault on females. He will attend court for a bail hearing the next day.

Edmond is in jail for the night. If he is suffering, I have to admit that I am glad!

I learn that Edmond being arrested, at this time, is only the second step of the legal process; the first step occurred when he was originally arrested, due to the report of the 15-year-old girl whom he accosted on his farm. This arrest, now, is the second step, and it is based on reports from three additional victims: Joy, his daughter; Lucinda, who lived in a trailer on his farm; and myself.

The third step in the legal process is the trial, which I now learn could go on for a year. This seems like an eternity for those of us who are waiting to have him locked away and out of reach, never able to exploit a girl again. The final step in the legal process is the sentencing itself, in which the judge pronounces the exact punishment.

The night that Edmond is in jail, I'm restless. One way I handle this is by going online and looking up the definitions of the charges for which Edmond has been arrested: sexual assault, sexual exploitation and indecent assault. I learn that all three are lesser charges than that of rape. They are, rather, about forced and unsolicited touching, fondling and kissing. What this clearly means is that the sentence will be less severe than the sentence for rape. But, that is for the future. For now we must focus on the arrest.

I talk with Joy, and we're both relieved that Edmond is in jail for the night. Yet we expect that he'll soon be out on bail. Being out on bail, however, is not that easy, since Edmond is now known to be a sexual predator. As such, the court requires that there be a person who will be with him at all times—who will watch him, and make sure he does not exploit another girl or woman. The technical name for that person is a "surety." The pounding question, then, is who will be the surety? Usually such a person is a family member. We all hold are breath because we know that the only family member who might do this is Ruth. Surely she won't take on this demeaning role! But she does. She does not talk with any family members about this. She just moves back home, to live with Edmond and to guard him until he is sentenced.

The whole family is stunned. How can she return to that pervert? How can she turn her back on me, her sister—and on Joy, her daughter—whom her husband sexually abused? How can she? How *can* she?

I talk with Rachel and Joy. We thrash over and over why Ruth would go back to him. We heard that Edmond had repented of his crimes and begged Ruth to return to him, but we don't really know if this is true. What we do know is that Ruth, like Edmond, is receiving individual counseling—and that Ruth's counseling is being paid for by Benny, who had offered this on the night we had brought Ruth to Binghamton to tell her that Edmond was guilty. We also know that Ruth and Edmond have met with a pastor, Rev. Lily, and her husband, Ned, who is now a counselor for sex offenders.

Joy reminds me that Ruth seemed absolutely bereft after we told her the truth about Edmond. She also seemed very distant, emotionally. This emotional distance has only increased in the past two months. Ruth's son, Ed, and his wife have tried to reach out to her, even suggesting that she live with them. We had all assumed that she would never return to that "pervert," but we had all been dead wrong. Joy has visited Ruth at least once a week, bringing her food and company. Sherry, whom Ruth had been living with, is nothing but kind and compassionate. I have called Ruth several times during this period, only to find her extremely evasive, insisting on talking about the weather or recipes.

Our family does not know what to think about Edmond. Was he just repenting because he was caught? How can we know? We cannot. We now understand that Edmond should be considered a sex addict. We all know that with addictions, one never completely recovers. AA has taught us that while a person may stop drinking, he or she is an alcoholic for life. The only question real question is this: Will Edmond be restrained in some way?

At this point, I am truly enraged with Ruth. I feel completely betrayed by her. This is a much bigger betrayal than the betrayal by my ex-husband, Louie. It is one thing to have my husband run off with another woman and leave me behind, but to have my sister turn her back on me and fall into the arms, once again, of a husband who had abused both me and her daughter—well, this is totally heartless.

I am also enraged because Ruth in no way seems to recognize that for 50 years I had spared her from disgrace by protecting her from the truth about Edmond. I endured his assaults—his hugs, his stares at my breasts—and I had endured his visits, all for her sake. I had wanted to see Ruth through these years, and yet I knew that she would not come to see me without Edmond. They were always together—well, except for the times when he was sneaking away to exploit some child or woman. I had endured the recent incident in which he had grabbed me in my trailer in Pennsylvania. I had done all of this for her sake, and now she is turning her back on me!

After Ruth returns to Edmond, I have very, very little contact with her. I do not want to call her house because I fear that Edmond will answer. At one point she calls me, however, and after some superficial talk, I say, "Please help me understand why you went back to Edmond." Her response is terse: "I always knew I would go back to him." I then ask, "Are you angry at me for testifying against Edmond?" She does not respond, so I say, "We all have to do what we have to do to heal." The conversation ends there.

I am enraged, but at the same time, I mourn. I truly miss my sister. For several years now, Ruth had been in the habit of calling me every Tuesday night. We would chat away about this and that. I would tell her the ups and downs of my depression. When I cried, she always cried with me. We joked that I could always count on her to cry with me. I loved her for this.

In these conversations, Ruth would, on occasion, allude to the fact that things were difficult at home. I wanted to ask but was afraid to, and she certainly did not offer to tell me. So I lived with the secret, protecting her because I wanted a relationship with her. But now that relationship is gone. It is not only gone, but she has totally turned her back on me.

I regularly talk to Rachel, and we grasp at straws to try to understand Ruth's behavior. We remember that Edmond and Ruth had started to date when she was just 14 years old. Edmond was 18. Edmond, we think, was her only boyfriend. I ask Rachel, "Do you think that, in some ways, he was abusive with her? After all, she was only 14, and he was 18." Rachel replies, "I think it is very likely. But perhaps Ruth did not see it as abuse. Perhaps she just saw it as his affection for her." Perhaps … perhaps. We also wonder why my parents allowed their teenage daughter to date a man four years older than her. Did they try to stop the relationship, with Ruth being so young? We have no way of knowing.

Joy and I also talk about all of this. We analyze Ruth—and then analyze her again. Our questions are endless. Is she now, in unconscious ways, identifying with the abuser? Is she identifying with him to the extent that she, in some ways, sees his accusers as her own? Does she feel that her family is all against her, personally? Is she so enmeshed with Edmond that she cannot see the magnitude of the damage he has done to others? Is she, herself, diminishing it? Does she think we're all exaggerating? Or does she think you should "stand by your man," no matter what? Is it not a fact that, by standing by Edmond, she makes herself guilty of the crime, too—"guilt by association"?

Joy and I have no clear answers to most of our questions, but we are a comfort to each other. We know the path of being abused by Edmond. We know what it is like to keep secrets: the utter loneliness; the inner darkness; the depression, and the underlying anger and fear that causes it.

Yet with all this knowledge and all of the unanswered questions, the bottom line for Joy is that she misses her mother—terribly. They did everything together: gardening, sewing, baking and shopping. They undertook house projects, whether they be painting walls or building decks. Now her mother has left her. When Joy tries to talk with Ruth, she is cold and not responsive. I ache for Joy. I wish she were not so far away. Then I could hold her and we could cry together.

In the conversations with Joy, I remember the beautiful quilted hanging that she and Ruth had made for me. Those tiny squares—half an inch or less—and all of those delicate patterns made a stunning design. I once again feel the love that went into each of those tiny squares. I reflect on all of those hours of labor. I remember the moment that Joy and Ruth gave me the hanging. Both were radiant. With tears of awe and of gratitude, I hugged and hugged them. But now that hanging symbolizes betrayal. I consider taking it down, but then decide to leave it up. It gives me an ounce of hope that I will get my sister back.

During all of this, I have conversations with my brothers, Benny and Peter. When I talk to Benny, I sense that he is very angry with Ruth. He does not say this directly, but I know it is true and I feel very much supported by him. When I talk to Peter, however, I get mixed messages. He tells me he agrees with Ruth about returning to Edmond; he thinks she should forgive him, if Edmond is truly repentant. I am stunned when I hear Peter's support of Ruth. He assures me, however, that he is also supportive of me and he agrees that I should have testified against Edmond. Yet, he implies that I need to find a way to forgive Edmond as long as Edmond repents of his sin. I am in no way in a frame of mind to forgive! Still, I remember the words of Jesus: *Love your enemies.* I remember his prayer on the cross about those who had crucified him: *Father, forgive them, for they know not what they do.*

As I later look back on this, I realize that I was in no frame of mind to face the issue of forgiveness that Peter had posed. So I try to dismiss Peter, and I continue to turn to Joy and Rachel for ongoing support. I greatly need them .

I ask Rachel: "Is Ruth staying with Edmond because of her wedding vows to live with him "til death do us part'—no matter how he has treated her or others? Does the marriage vow taken 54 years ago override all other commitments—commitments to her daughter and her sister?"

Rachel and I even entertain the idea that perhaps Ruth's reason for staying with Edmond is that she truly loves him. He always gives her beautiful, loving cards on her birthday and at Christmas. He buys her beautiful gifts—most recently, diamond earrings. In many ways he has been kind to her. Edmond has been a good companion to her in their work, and they team up together, whether it be in the barn, in the garden or in chores around the house. They clearly enjoy working side-by-side. They have successfully owned two different farms over the years, and are now settled into retirement.

Edmond's passionate hobby has always been Belgium draft horses. He has raised them, trained them and often harnessed them, pulling a sleigh or a wagon. In the winter, he has given sleigh rides to children; in the summer, he has given wagon rides at the local fair. He has had a good reputation for generosity, and the children loved him. Now we can't help but wonder if he abused any of these children.

Edmond was also a devout churchgoer. He was on church committees—the most recent being the board of trustees. He was always a good worker and could be depended on. But apparently, at the same time, he'd had his eye on little Katie. He acted like a grandfather to her, doting over her and teasing her. After church she ran to him for affection, and no one thought anything about it except that it was sweet. But Edmond must have had other motives, because when she and other youth from the church came to his farm for a sleepover, he approached her, grabbed her, and kissed her. She was stunned and terrified. One of her best friends saw it all. Katie, in tears, called her mother, and her mother immediately came and got her. They went to the police station and reported it all. The next morning, Edmond was arrested. It was all over the news and local papers. That's how the case against Edmond had been launched.

During this time, when Ruth has little contact with the rest of the family, Peter and Eunice, visit her and Edmond. Peter asks Ruth and Edmond how they are doing and they obliquely reply that they are doing okay, given the circumstances. They admit that Edmond was wrong and they say he is truly repentant. Ruth and Edmond then close the door to any further discussion.

Benny has no contact with Ruth and Edmond. Rachel has a few brief and superficial telephone conversations with Ruth. Rachel feels shame about being part of a family in which there is a sex abuser. Rachel tells me that Edmond has little contact with his 11 siblings, with the possible exception of two sisters. But Ruth and Edmond remain friends with four couples they have been friends with over many years. One couple is from the church Edmond and Ruth attended before his arrest; the second couple is distant cousins. The other two couples are from business relationships in the cattle or horse industry. Rachel believes that when all of these people are with Ruth and Edmond they just don't talk about his arrest, his abuse and the pain of it all. They go on chopping wood, making maple syrup and eating cherry pie, just like they always have done. The elephant in the room is not addressed.

I later come to understand that this is like an inner iron-clad circle: that when a family member or close friend is arrested for any reason, an inner circle is often formed—a circle that tacitly agrees to not talk about the crime. Any people who wish to talk about it are essentially cut off.

I am very glad at this point that I do not live in Canada, where all of this is happening. I am glad I am in Binghamton, where no one knows that I am part of a family in which there is a sexual perpetrator. So I focus on my life here. Christmas, for me, is pure relief. Nathan and Erin come. My house is a perfect Christmas house, with its dark red accent walls behind the Christmas tree, which is twinkling with white lights. I just add a few red candles and Christmas angels here and there, and it is set for the holiday. Stockings are hung, wood crackles in the fireplace and Nathan and I make the pumpkin pie we have made for 30 years. PJ crawls onto Erin's lap as she works at the computer. We are all radiant and I forget about Edmond.

Three weeks after Christmas, I have an open house. My house is still decorated from the holidays, and I serve the shortbread and fruitcake Christmas cookies that I have made for many years. My shortbread is light and fluffy, always bringing a whole string of compliments. I have big bowls of grapes, chips and dip. Girlfriends bring crab dip, hummus, cheese, guacamole and plenty of wine. Other friends come bearing gifts—candles, stained glass, soap, trivets and more. They adore my house as much as I do, and I am very happy. PJ is in the center of it all, being carried around the house, petted and adored by all.

During all of this, I am diligent in visiting my seniors. For me, they are a beautiful relief. I adore hearing the love story of Jim and Alice, as they tenderly relay it to me every time I visit: how Jim was an American soldier in Germany during World War II; how he fell in love with a German beauty, Alice; how they secretly dated and married; and how he brought his bride to America. Even though Alice is having serious memory problems overall, she is crystal clear in her tales of love with Jim. When it is time for me to leave, I ask if they would like to sing *Amazing Grace*. They both sing at the top of their lungs and Alice remembers every word. They are just so inspiring!

I also love to visit Nelly, one of my many favorite seniors. Even though she has the beginnings of Alzheimer's, she never fails to show me pictures of herself skiing in the Alps and her awards for being the top senior skier at the local ski resort. Nelly was married to a handsome World War II vet who died recently, but she is doing pretty well on her own. I tell her on each visit how proud I am of her, and in my parting prayer, I ask God to give her strength to carry on. We both have tears in our eyes as I hug her goodbye. In my work with my seniors, it is true that I nurture them; but on some deep soul level, they also nurture me.

There are also many other ways in which I am being nurtured and supported. My friend Andrea and I love to indulge in minor clothing shopping sprees. Getting a $30 sweater for $10 is the perfect balm for an otherwise blue day. My friend Gloria, from Chicago, calls often, and we chatter away about the old days, when we lived in the same apartment building. My Sunday morning group of women listens lovingly to my pain about Edmond and they support me unequivocally in my testimony against him. Luke calls me every Monday morning at 9 a.m., and when I tear up with pain about the betrayal by my sister, he sings the chant we composed two years ago: *Let it come, let it go; let it come, let it flow. All is well.* That little chant, week after week, gives me faith that I will, indeed, recover from the ravages of sexual abuse.

I delight in my cat, PJ, who is always ready to be snuggled. I love waking up in the middle of the night and having him tucked against my leg.

I love taking a nap on the sofa in the afternoon, with him fast asleep on my stomach.

These days, as never before, I also find myself being held by my relationship with God. I feel only love and acceptance from God. The fear and judgment I grew up with seems to mainly be gone—at least for now. I feel that relationship most intimately when I play my keyboard and sing hymns. The hymn I sing most often is the one I learned at Yale Divinity School long ago: *God of our life, through all the circling years, we trust in Thee. In all the past, through all our hopes and fears, Thy hand we see. With each new day, when morning lifts the veil, we own Thy mercies, Lord, which never fail.* I almost surprise myself that my faith is so strong. But then I realize that even though I have been broken in some major ways throughout my life, light has always come through. The light of faith somehow finds its way through the darkness.

There is one other song that I find rolling around in my head. It is one that I learned recently, at a women's retreat: *How could anyone ever tell you, you are anything less than beautiful? How could anyone ever tell you, you are less than whole? How could anyone fail to notice that your loving is a miracle? How deeply you're connected to my soul.* At times I still feel shame about the sexual abuse: It's almost as if it has left a stain on the core of my being. Yet this song about wholeness not only sustains me, but seems to cleanse me in an deep, deep way. Again, the light seeps through the darkness.

A new sense of wholeness is coming to me also through my individual counseling. I am currently seeing just one therapist, Donna. For about a year I was also seeing Will, and while he is very competent, at this time I only need to see a woman. At some deep level, I find a woman to be safer and more trustworthy. Furthermore, I have a hunch that Donna herself has been abused in some way—if not sexually, certainly emotionally. We never discuss this, but all I know is that she is absolutely attuned to my struggles about abuse—and especially the feelings of abandonment by Ruth. Donna helps me to accept Ruth as she is and to let go of my desperation to try to win her back. As I later look back on this, I will see that some of my desperation about Ruth is akin to what I felt when Louie left me. At the root of all that fear of abandonment, is the childhood fear of being left behind, should the Lord return.

Donna and I also discuss whether or not I should resume ECT. We decide that I don't need it at the present time. We also agree that if signs of depression appear, I will begin ECT right away. It surprises me that, in the midst of all of the pain about the abuse, I am not having depressive symptoms. This shows me that the pain is bringing healing to me, and not devastation.

I become aware that when I was trained as a therapist, 30 years ago—and when I was in therapy myself, 35 years ago—there was little understanding of sexual abuse. Years ago, therapists were not taught to ask questions about sex abuse, and so these secrets often remained hidden. When I look back, I wonder about some of the women I counseled. Perhaps they were sexually abused. I deeply, deeply regret that I was not attuned to their pain.

Most of the time I go on, happy in my life. Yet, the sexual abuse is always in the back of my mind. I continue to talk with Rachel and Joy, and they keep me apprised of what is happening in Canada. Most importantly, the police are calling for women who have been abused by Edmond to come forward and report. No other woman comes forward, but the community is abuzz with stories of other women Edmond has abused—at his farm, on his route as a delivery man or at his church. I learn that two women left his church because of his abuse. Joy later tells me that she personally knows—or has been told about—30 women whom Edmond abused over the years. Another relative of Edmond later tells me she believes that Edmond has abused 60 to 70 women over the course of at least 50 years. I am simply aghast!

At this time there are monthly meetings with lawyers, but it will not be until the fall of 2011 that the case is actually tried in court—about one year since the first arrest. What will the judge finally decide? Will Edmond go to jail? If so, for how long?

It is around this time that Rachel tells me about the mental state of Katie, the 15-year-old girl whom Edmond abused. She is still very traumatized. She is withdrawn and unable to attend her youth group at church, even though Edmond is no longer allowed to go to her church. She is refusing to go to therapy, as she cannot bear to talk about the pain of it all. I feel great pain for her. I think I understand some of what she is going through, and I wonder if there is any way that I can reach out to her.

I talk with Rachel about this and we decide that I should contact Katie's mother, Carla. Rachel gives me Carla's email address, so I email her and ask if she thinks it would be appropriate for me to write a short letter to Katie. I would tell Katie that I admire her, and that I support and pray for her. Carla quickly replies, "Please do write a letter to Katie." It is now early June of 2011, which is eight months after Katie reported Edmond's abuse. This is what I write:

Hi Katie,

I have been thinking of you a lot lately and wanted to write to you and give you whatever support I can.

I am Lucille Sider—the sister-in-law of Edmond Galter. Edmond abused me 50 years ago—when I was 15 years old. And now, because you had the courage to report, it gave me the courage to report. But I waited 50 years. You are so wise to report immediately. I support you and am grateful to you.

I want you to know that when I was giving my testimony to the detective, I had a deep sense of connection with you. I knew I was reporting for myself but I was also reporting for you. I wanted to do whatever I could do to make sure your situation is heard and believed.

I was also reporting on behalf of all the other women Edmond has abused and who have not reported. I feel great solidarity with all of us. And I believe that in our reporting, we have encouraged and supported those many women he has also abused—even if they have not reported.

While we have never met, you are in my heart and prayers.

We are sisters who are working to stop Edmond from abusing others. In doing this we will also continue to heal the wounds we have and will help others heal their wounds.

Blessings, love and prayers,

Lucille Sider

Carla emails me later, saying, "Katie has just read your letter. She was quiet after she read it. And then she put it in a little wooden box where she keeps her special papers."

I hope I have done the right thing by writing to Katie. I hope that I have been an encouragement to her and that I have not re-traumatized her by writing. I know how delicate all of this is and I pray that I have helped her.

When emailing Katie's mother, I was acutely aware of how supportive and loving she is toward her daughter. How, when Katie telephoned about her abuse, Carla immediately came to get her. How they went, without delay, to the police station to report the abuse. And now, how Carla is being so attentive to Katie.

All of this is in stark contrast to my parents and how they treated me when I told them about Edmond's abuse. They were silent, with the exception of a brief prayer. How, I wonder, could a parent ever ignore their daughter like this? Where were their instincts for protection? Why did my father not go to Edmond with a baseball bat in hand? Why did my mother not go herself, even if my father did not go? Is it that they truly cared for my sister, Ruth, more than for me? Or is it that they did not want to stir up "trouble" in a church where Edmond's father was a deacon? Did they think I would forget about the abuse? My questions go on and on. My anger toward my parents builds in a way that I had not been aware of in the past. I know that in the future I am going to have to address all of this. I know that if I am ever going to forgive my parents, I will need to do considerable healing. I wonder if this can ever happen.

It is around this time that I have two different experiences that trigger some of my fears about Edmond. The first occurs when I am at Rehoboth Beach, in New Jersey. I am boarding a ship to go to Cape May when I see a man, about 40 years old, stalking a teenager. She is racing ahead of him, staying out of his reach. This sends a chill through me, painfully reminding me of Edmond's advances to me over the years.

The second incident occurs when I am driving down the street in Binghamton. I see a man walking on the sidewalk who looks like Edmond from the back—he is fairly big, with wide shoulders. For a second my stomach lunges in fear, and then I realize that this could not be Edmond because he cannot even enter the U.S., due to his arrest.

These two incidents show me that while I am handling all of the activity around Edmond's arrest very well, his abuse is still with me and those feelings can get triggered easily. It is this realization that influences my decision to respond positively to a new opportunity regarding Edmond.

Two months after I write the letter to Katie, a detective from Canada contacts me again. It is Detective Ann Brown—apparently, the male detective who had asked me about reporting to the police is no longer on the case. Ann asks me to write an "impact statement." She explains, "This is a statement that will be read in court after all the evidence is presented by the lawyers. It will be read especially to the judge so he can hear directly from the victims about how they feel the abuse has affected their lives." I am at first unsure about how to respond to the detective, so I tell her that I will think about it. I talk to Joy, and she says that she is writing an impact statement. We do not discuss what she is writing, but she encourages me to write one, also.

I talk to my siblings, and they think I should write it. I am soon convinced that this is the right thing for me to do. I call the detective and ask for guidelines in writing it. She emails these to me: "To state who you are in regards to Edmond Galter. To describe the emotional impact the abuse has had on you. To describe the financial impact."

When I sit down to write my impact statement, it comes pretty easily. In the next couple of days I revise it slightly, making it a more forceful statement. I read it to Rachel and Benny, and they encourage me to spell out, in greater detail, the impact Edmond had on my failed marriages and my mental illness. They also point out that I have understated the financial impact the abuse has had on me. Benny actually calculates the money I have lost in not practicing my profession as a psychologist: this adds up to more than $1 million. I feel very grateful to have siblings like this, who support me and help me find my way in a time when I am so vulnerable. I feel protected and listened to—unlike in my childhood.

This is what I write and submit on August 25, 2011:

IMPACT STATEMENT

I am Lucille Sider, the sister-in-law of Edmond Galter.

Emotional Impact

The crime affected my feelings about my personal safety in any situation in which Edmond was present. I felt fear and disgust whenever I saw him. At family gatherings I would make sure I would never sit by him. I would fear being hugged by him so would go out of my way to avoid this. When I was at his house I would never go to any room he was in unless someone else was there. I feared staying at his house overnight in case he would come in my bedroom and assault me. Yet, I did this at times because I was trying to protect my sister from knowing about him. I wanted to protect her from the pain and disgrace of this all. In fact, it was extremely difficult to report Edmond's abuse for this reason and also because I feared I would lose my relationship with my sister. Living this deceitfulness was very difficult and harmful.

The crime has affected how I relate to other men. I lived with a sense of powerlessness regarding Edmond and this feeling of powerlessness spilled over to other men. When other abusive situations arose, I was much more passive than what was healthy emotionally. I believe this stems back to the abuse I experienced with Edmond as a teenager and to the ongoing threat of abuse that was there for me until his arrest.

The abuse by Edmond initially, then throughout the years of trying to avoid him, has affected my general emotional well-being. I believe it contributed to my unhealthy choices of men and thus subsequent divorces. Upon my second divorce, I had an emotional breakdown with severe depression and multiple psychiatric hospitalizations. At that time I had to stop work as a clinical psychologist. I have not been able to return to full-time work since then, which is now 15 years. I lost my profession and the early abuse by Edmond was a big contributor to all of this.

The abuse by Edmond affects my current work as a visitor to the elderly. (I now am able to work 12 hours a week.) I am still affected by Edmond in that I fear older men who are sexually suggestive or aggressive in any way. This leads to loss of sleep, anxiety and depression. I then have to seek counseling to be able to cope and carry on with my work.

I never want to have any physical contact with Edmond—not a hug, not even a handshake. At family gatherings in the future, I do not want to sit next to him.

Financial Impact

The crime has led me to seek counseling and psychiatric treatment over a period of many years. The out of pocket costs well exceed $50,000. The crime has been a major contributor to my loss of work. The financial impact here is well over $1,000,000.

After I write this statement and email it to the detective, a heavy weight is lifted. It feels so good to have all of this written out—so crisp, clean and clear. It's as if I can let it all go in a way that I never could before. In fact, the little chant that Luke and I wrote comes to my mind repeatedly: *Let it come, let it go; let it come, let it flow. All is well.* I know that the impact statement is already bringing healing to me. It is bringing light into my darkness.

Furthermore, it feels simply wonderful to know that this will be read in court. I can imagine Edmond sitting there and hearing every word. I imagine him wincing. I also imagine the judge listening to it and looking surprised when I describe the sexual abuse as contributing significantly to my mental illness. I imagine that the judge is stunned when he hears that all of this has cost me $1 million in loss of salary over the years.

When I write my impact statement, I have no idea if it will have an effect on Edmond's sentence. Later, I learn that it will—significantly.

When I write my impact statement, I have no idea that in 13 days, I will face another crisis—but this time, it will be a natural disaster: a flood. I will have to flee from water racing into my neighborhood, which will essentially destroy my beloved house.

13

Floating in Sewer Water

Horrified, we cover our noses, but the stench floats through our fingers and into our nostrils. The floodwater stench is worse than any animal dung I've ever inhaled. It's Sunday afternoon, and the waters have receded. We're allowed to see our homes for the first time since the evacuation on Wednesday. We can bear to approach our homes only because we're doing it together … together with neighbors.

Four days before, on September 7, 2011, we were evacuated. The Susquehanna River roared into our neighborhood and into parts of southeast New York and northeast Pennsylvania. In Binghamton alone, 20,000 people were evacuated. Rain from record downpours in August—and recently, from Hurricane Irene and Tropical Storm Lee—destroyed hundreds of homes. In Broome County and in Tioga County, just west of Broome, there had already been $1 billion in damages. President Obama declared the flood a national disaster, FEMA was coming and countless other disaster teams were on their way.

Will the terror of that evacuation night, that horrifying Wednesday night, ever leave me?

It had started out like any normal day. But suddenly, as I was driving home from church, I was stopped by a police officer barking, "Take another road. This one's flooded. The river is rising fast."

Despite what he says, the message that the flood is truly serious is not getting through to me. Floods happen to other people in other places—not to me, in Binghamton, New York. At home, I listen to the message on my answering machine: *This is New York State Police. You must evacuate immediately. The river is rapidly rising and your house is in grave danger. Move quickly. Take your medicine and pets. Housing is provided in the college gym at Binghamton University.* I'm in shock. Can this really be true? I listen to the message again. Yes, I heard it right. My heart starts to race and my hands start to shake. I'm paralyzed at first—but only for a few minutes. I call Andrea, my friend and former landlady, who has become a pillar for me. With a quivering voice, I get the words out about the message. "I don't even know where the gymnasium at Binghamton University is." She quickly and firmly replies, "Don't go there. Come here. Move fast. You can use the apartment below me. It is empty."

I remember that part of the message was "Take your medicine and pets." I blurt out to Andrea that the message says to bring pets. At this point I am quietly crying, but I manage to get out the words, "May I bring PJ?" Andrea is terrified of cats, and I hold my breath—but only for two seconds, and then I hear her say, "Of course, of course, bring PJ. Now come."

Then I remember Danielle and her children, Ella and Justin, down the street. They don't have a car. Danielle is Cherry's daughter, and the children are the little darlings of my life. I had moved here one year ago to be near them. So I race across lawns to get to them, only to find Danielle saying, "No, we're not going. We can't leave the pets." They have two cats, one dog, five birds and four fish, with one fish being a 2-foot shark. "Well, I'm not going without you," I snap. Danielle digs in her heels, as she's wont to do, and I return home angry and frightened. I scurry around, assembling what I will take. Before I carry my things to the car, I run back to protest Danielle's decision to stay. By now she has called her friend, Tim, and has decided to take the children to his house, where they can all bunk in his living room. But she has to leave her pets behind: Tim's family is not pet-friendly. Knowing they are safe for now, I rush back to my house. I pack PJ, my meds, a change of clothes and my laptop. My hands are shaking so hard that I can barely hold the steering wheel. As I start backing out of my driveway, a police officer appears and shouts, "Is everyone out of your house? Are there pets still there?" In tears I answer, "I'm the only one who lives here and I have my pet with me." He then curtly directs me as I back out.

I get onto the road toward Andrea's house, but I'm soon stopped, for the road is flooded. I panic and my mind goes blank. There is no police officer around to help. I feel utterly alone. I sit in my car for a few minutes. Rain continues to pour down so hard that I can barely see out, even with the windshield wipers on high speed. I am frozen in fear. Then I remember that there is another route—a longer route—to Andrea's house. Maybe it is not flooded. So I turn my car around by backing into a driveway. My hands are still trembling. PJ is in the back, crying. I try to soothe him, but he just keeps on. I know he has some sense of my terror.

After retracing the road for about one mile, I then find my way to Andrea's house. It is on higher ground and is not flooded. None of the water is deep enough to keep me from driving through it, and I find myself saying as I drive, "Thank you, Lord, thank you, Lord." I'm still shaking as I pull into her driveway. I see Andrea at her door; she's been waiting for me. We say very little to each other. She quickly takes my bag of clothes and computer, and I bring PJ in his carrying case. He's quiet and I'm relieved.

Andrea guides me to the apartment, which she originally decorated for her mother, who now lives in a retirement home. It is simply charming, with two gliders, a soft sofa, pretty green, flowered rugs and all kinds of cute knick-knacks. She shows me the bedroom, with a wonderful quilt and sheets on the bed. I can breathe again. I'm safe and I have landed in this lovely place that Andrea is giving me.

That's Wednesday night—evacuation night. Thursday, Friday and Saturday, Andrea and I hover around her TV, watching, watching. Seeing aerial shots, we strain to catch a glimpse of my house. We cannot see it. Is it submerged? We cannot tell. I then go to the park near my house, straining, straining to see into my neighborhood. All I see is water and my hope is dashed.

I go back to Andrea's house. Then I see on TV what is happening to those dear people who have no place to go except the college gym: they're sleeping on narrow cots, packed in like sardines. The American Red Cross and local churches have brought food and water, but everyone is petrified of what might be happening to their homes. They're also panicked about their pets: some have left them behind, and others have brought them, but the pets cannot stay in the gym. They have to stay in cars. I do hear that food is provided for the pets.

On Saturday, we learn that there will be a meeting on Sunday afternoon at 3 o'clock. The purpose of the meeting is to inform us about the condition of our homes and to let us know when we can return to them. The meeting is to be at Vestal High School. I arrive by 2:15, wanting to secure a front seat, but many others have done the same. We stand in a long line and the crowds are restless. Some are angry, accusing the authorities for not acting sooner; some are crying, already knowing their homes have been destroyed. I am subdued outwardly, but am panicked on the inside. Is my house destroyed? For a second, the rooms in my house flash before my eyes: the sunny kitchen, the stone fireplace, the big dining room that opens up to the deck, which I have filled with big pots of impatience flowers—red, white, pink and purple. For a moment, I smile as I remember them.

But then I remember what has happened. My precious house—the one that I've had for just one year—is flooded. This is where I have been stable, emotionally. I have not needed ECT while I've been there. I cry inwardly, asking, "Can I remain stable with the flood? Will I collapse?" Yet I somehow find some inner strength. I find myself saying, "I must, I *must* stay stable. I will, I *will*."

My mind comes back to the gymnasium, and the meeting finally starts. I see three men on the stage. While they apparently introduce themselves, I do not recognize any of their names or faces. One of the men is from FEMA; he brings us only bad news. He says that part of the reason for the flooding is climate change and that part of it is because the ground will no longer hold water, due to all the cement that covers the surface. Although he doesn't say it directly, he implies that our neighborhood will be declared a flood plain in the future. That means that it is at high risk for further floods and that flood insurance premiums will skyrocket.

Then another man speaks. He explains why the water is contaminated— because the sewer facility upstream has been destroyed by the force of the water. He bellows, "Do not drink the water. Do not bathe in it. Do not flush your toilets."

Finally, the third man speaks. He makes a cursory mention of regret for the fact that many homes are destroyed, but what I mainly hear, shouted from the stage, are these words: "Some homes are permanently damaged. If there is an orange zero with a slash, this means that you may not enter your home—the foundation has been damaged by the force of the water and it is unsafe to enter. Do not enter if your house has a zero with a slash. But if your house has a 'K', an orange 'K' painted on it, you may enter briefly this afternoon. Take out items you may need. There is no electrical power and the water is contaminated, for the sewer station collapsed under the pressure of the rising river. Enter your homes carefully. The floors are slippery with sewer mud. Wear boots, masks and gloves, for mold is already setting in."

Only later do I come to understand the dangers of mold. It can cause swelling eyes, headaches, coughs, low-grade fevers and discoloration of the tongue. Touching mold can cause infections and create allergic reactions like sneezing and itching eyes. As it turns out, coughing is the only reaction I will have to it.

I do not have boots, masks or gloves, but I decide to enter my house anyway. I must, I *must* see it. At the meeting I had run into Pam and Tim, neighbors whose houses were also flooded. We decide to go together to see our houses. I take my camera because we have been informed that we must submit photos to our insurance company to get reimbursed. We head to my house first. "Is it marked with a zero and a slash?" I ask, holding my breath. "No—no zero, no slash. Just an orange 'K'." We may enter. Banded together, we enter my side door and start down the stairs to the basement. We're stopped halfway down—stopped by the stench of the water and stopped by the water itself, for it is 3 feet deep. We barely see the tops of my washer and dryer. Floating clothes, floating books, floating tables—all are drowned in the sewer water. We are almost frozen—by the stench—but we have to press on. Cautiously, we turn around and enter the first floor. The floor is slippery, the rugs are swishy and the water marks two feet up on the walls tell the tale. My new sofa is drenched, my mother's rocker is slimy with mud and her cedar chest is already warped.

Oh, no! Not my sewing machine! How can I live without her—without my dear sewing machine? I love my Singer Featherweight—a gift from Nathan and my dear friend Gloria. Now she is dripping with sewer water!

I turn toward the door to leave my house, with all its sadness, but I'm stopped. Something inside me says "Go back, go back. Get your keyboard and your hymn book." That voice inside me knows I'll need those hymns in coming days. I'll need them to calm my soul and to face the future. So I climb the stairs. My keyboard is safe on the second floor. I take the keyboard to my apartment, where I need it that very night. I play the hymn I learned 41 years ago; the hymn I sang over and over again with my Korean friend, Lauh, at Yale Divinity School. We sang it in our dorm rooms at the top of our lungs—she, a high soprano, and me, a strong alto—blending together across cultures. She was later to become my maid of honor.

The hymn we sang over and over is *God of Our Life*. We needed that hymn then; I did not know I'd need it in years to come. But now I must—I *must*—have it to survive the flood. As it unfolds, many nights before going to bed I play this hymn on my keyboard and sing the words softly. They soothe me, lulling me to sleep, and soon I am resting, trusting in God. *God of our life, through all the circling years, we trust in thee; In all the past, through all our hopes and fears, thy hand we see. With each new day as morning lifts the veil, we own thy mercies, Lord, which never fail.*

Many months later, a friend asks me: "Aren't you angry with God? Look at what's happened to you! Sexual abuse, religious rigidity and now a flood that's almost destroyed your beloved home." I'm taken back by her question. I realize that many people would be angry with God in circumstances like this, but for me—somehow, my faith has barely waned.

My faith has clearly changed over the years, though. I grew up in a church where fear of God's wrath hounded me daily. I had little sense of God's love. But I have found God's love and grace in more liberal denominations, which is where I am now firmly rooted.

Furthermore, I have found a contemplative faith where mediation has become part of my heart and soul. I came to this long ago, when I started to pray and meditate with Luke and Christa. I am now in constant contact with Luke and he has become my spiritual companion. It was in meditating with him and his friends that Luke and I composed the chant, *Let it come, let go; let it come, let it flow. All is well.* That chant has become an anchor for my spirituality. It has helped me dare to believe that if I do not hold on to all the pain that comes my way, I will be well.

Right now that anchor helps me stand firm in the way I relate to Danielle, Justin and Ella. I'm in close touch with them, and have been since the day of the flood. Danielle tells me that her children have no toys to play with. All of them were lost in the flood. So I take them to the Dollar Store, where we buy the basics—crayons, construction paper, glue, pipe cleaners, two small dolls and two race cars. We also buy underwear. When evacuated, Danielle had not thought to bring underwear for herself or for her children. They were simply fleeing from the flood.

I know that Danielle is suffering from the loss of her beloved pets. She doesn't say much, but I know that she is quietly desperate. Her dog is safe, as he was rescued three days after the flood. The pet rescue team had paddled around the neighborhood, picking up animals that had been left behind.

But all of her other pets are dead. Her cat, Pucca, had drowned in the basement. Her fish are dead, also: without electricity, they could not survive. Silently, Danielle has buried them in her backyard. Danielle is very quiet for the next few days. Justin and Ella tell me over and over again that Pucca and their shark are dead and that Mommy buried them in the backyard. They don't cry out loud, but I hold them, stroking their cheeks and wiping away their silent tears.

On the Sunday evening following the flood—after we were allowed to see our houses—I go to Wal-Mart to buy masks, rubber gloves and boots. I am able to purchase 30 masks, thinking that it will be an adequate supply. I also buy five pairs of rubber gloves. By this time, though, boots are sold out. I try not to get frantic. How can I walk on the sewer-drenched floors with only running shoes? All of my boots lay on the closet floor, filled with sewer water.

Late on Sunday evening, Diane—the deacon from the Presbyterian church, who accompanies me on my visits to difficult seniors—calls me and asks, "What do you need?" I respond immediately, "Please, can you find me some boots ... somewhere ... I'm afraid they're all sold out." The next day Diane arrives with black, heavy winter boots. She had scoured the whole area to find lighter ones, but only the heavy winter boots were left. That's fine. At least they're boots.

On Monday morning, friends arrive to help with my house. "What can we do?" they ask. While I know nothing about flood cleanup, it is clear that everything that is wet must either be carried out to the curb, to be thrown away, or washed and saved. My friends brought large, extra-heavy garbage bags for hauling things to the curb. Most things are carried out there.

Jeannie and Jan begin in the kitchen. They open my spice drawer. Of course, my precious spices are drenched. All are thrown into trash bags. The flour, sugar, cornstarch and rice—all are far gone. The pots and pans can be saved, but they are covered with sewer mud. What are we to do? We decide to wash them in bleach water. Jan brought two gallons of bleach. Even though the tap water is contaminated, it is better to use it than to leave the pots and pans in sewer mud—after all, the bleach will kill at least some of the germs. Then my friends dry the pots and pans with paper towels that Jan had brought. Jan had heard on the news that paper towels, like bleach, were at a premium, and I thank her profusely for bringing those paper towels. The washed and dried pots and pans are set on the countertops that the mud has not reached. We have no boxes to put them in, though, as my own boxes have been drenched and stores have sold out of them.

As we wash those pots and pans, my mind flashes to the food I have made in them: the African peanut soup that I took to a church supper; the chicken noodle soup I made for Andrea; the curry lentil stew that I made for my friends from church. For now, we just leave the pots and pans on the counter.

I work with the women only a brief time because I know that I need to turn to another matter: taking pictures that will be used for insurance claims. I ask Jeannie to join me and to take notes about each photo. We first go to the front closet. We take pictures of boots and purses floating in water, my sewing machine, my black suede coat, scarves and gloves. We take pictures of my sofa, rocking chairs and Lay-Z-Boy, the cedar chest, cases of books, desk, china cabinet, dining room table and chairs. The list goes on and on. I am at the verge of tears, but am determined not to cry.

Jeannie and I then return to the kitchen. We open the refrigerator and take pictures of the food, which is now fetid. We gasp in horror and look at each other, wondering if we have the courage to empty the contents and carry everything to the curb. I say, "We must." So we stop the photo-taking. We find fresh masks and heavy rubber gloves. We start with the freezer. The smell of rotten meat almost takes our breath away. We work very quickly. We then pull out the squishy vegetables—the ones that were once frozen. We turn to the lower part of the refrigerator and take out the lettuce, which is now mush, and the milk, which is now sour. We work furiously. We finish in 10 minutes.

Then I turn to the beautiful hand-woven rugs in my dining room and living room. They are my Mediterranean rugs, both 6 feet by 8 feet and each with a different design. They are the precious rugs that I bought a year ago, just before I moved into the house. I had painted my walls taupe and red to pick up the colors in the rugs. As I look at the rugs, I am crying inside. I cannot bear to have them destroyed, so I determine that, somehow, I will save them.

The next day, I call a rug dealer. In a quivering voice, I ask, "Can my rugs be saved? My house was flooded." He hesitates for a moment, then responds in a quiet voice: "No, ma'am, I'm very sorry, but the sewer and mud in those rugs would never come completely out. And the mold that would remain would contaminate your entire house." I am in tears when I hang up the phone, but then I catch myself—after all, they're only rugs. Just rugs. Perhaps they can be replaced. The next day I silently haul the rugs to the deck and hang them over the railing. I cannot bear to drag them to the curb yet. In fact, it is a full week before I find the fortitude to drag them to the curb.

During the first few days of flood cleanup, Ed and Martha arrive. I do not know them, although they're members of my church. When they arrive, they don't need my guidance—they just seem to know what to do. Not that I really know how to guide a flood cleanup, but I'm somehow making my way.

Ed and Martha begin with my mother's cedar chest, which is already warping. They open the lid, finding my precious woolen blankets—the blankets you can barely buy anymore—sopping wet. They carry them out to the curb. Ed and Martha gently scrub and spray the cedar chest with bleach water—bleach water, the destroyer of mold.

Then Ed stands still, examining my front door—my round, wooden front door that's already warping. The door that welcomes my visitors, blessing them with its sheer beauty. Mild-mannered Ed turns to me and says, "We can save your door. I can stop the warping by adding a board and a gold plate across the bottom. I can stain it with new finish." I cry with relief and joy. My precious door will be saved. *Saved!*

Another friend goes to the deck and hoses off the furniture. Since it is not wood, it can be saved: the round, glass tables; the green, plastic chairs; the black glider. As soon as the glider is washed, I rush to it. I sit down, and gently glide. I glide and glide. At first, I glide with gratitude—I am so thankful for all of the help and so happy that my front door is saved. As I rock, I see, for the first time, that my big pots of impatience flowers have survived the flood. There they sit, smiling at me: their red faces, white faces, red-and-white, pink and purple. They don't even seem to know that there's been a flood because the big pots have held them safely above the flood water.

Then my gliding speeds up, and I burst into tears. There are no words—there is just sobbing. My body buckles forward in pain, fear and exhaustion. I don't know how long this lasts, but what I do know is that Jeannie appears behind me and rubs my back. "Cry," she says. "Cry as long as the tears keep coming." That glider becomes my place of comfort and gratitude; of sobbing and despair. It is not a despair from depression, for I am not feeling depressed; it is despair over the loss of my house and the feeling of being overwhelmed by all the work that is ahead to restore it.

One problem that I have not tackled in the flood cleanup is the water in the basement. When I was first allowed into the house, four days after the flood, the water was at the top of the washer and dryer. While it has receded about a foot, it is still 2 feet deep. By this time, pumping water has become a lucrative business and there seems to be no alternative to having it done. The cost of this is $1,000. Yet before I move forward on this, Seth—my neighbor from across the street—tells me that his church has bought a pump and he will come and pump my basement. I'm over-joyed—at least, on one hand.

On the other hand, I know I will have to face the pain of all that has been destroyed there. Most of all, it is my photographs. Sofas and sewing machines can be replaced, but photos of a lifetime cannot be saved—at least, that is what I believe. I'll never, *never* forget that day my photo albums were rescued. With the water pumped out, I beg Seth, "Please, *please*—search for my photo albums." With only one flashlight, he rum-mages and searches through all the debris. He finds 10 albums, "Are there more?" he asks, hoping that he has them all. "Four more," I cry. "Please search more." He searches again, and he finds them—all four of them. They are black with sewer mud, but he carries them, one by one, up the stairs.

In tears, I carefully lug all 14 albums around the side of the house to the deck, hoping—hoping against hope—that I might save them. I fearfully and lovingly take a few of my favorite photos from under their plastic covers. With soft paper towels I start gently wiping off the mud and setting them in the sun to dry. Right then, my pastor, Stan, appears. "The church will do this, Lucille—we'd gladly do this for you," he says. "You don't have to do this." I can't believe my good fortune, that my pastor had arrived just at that moment. We carefully place the dripping-wet, sewer-drenched photo albums in black plastic bags and Jeannie delivers them to the church.

Two weeks later I will I learn that my church friends lovingly wiped each photo—about 3,000 in all. They spread them on tables to dry. They bought new albums and placed each photo in those albums. Three weeks later, they present them to me. Opening each album, I cry tears of joy. I see my life with fresh and grateful eyes. There are baby pictures: my son, 2 days old, wrinkled and red—beautiful. There are his wedding pictures: his bride walking down the aisle, the two of them in each other's arms, dancing. There are skiing pictures: me jumping the waves, showing off. There are grandparent pictures, with children at the zoo … birthday parties … a whole lifetime of memories—saved. *Saved.*

While saving my photos is exhilarating, I feel myself wearing down. I am thoroughly drained and exhausted. I have never, *ever* felt this tired. I begin to lose hope. I talk to my family every day, and somehow they help guide me. Even from miles away, they hear my fatigue. Nine days after the flood, they say, "We're coming! We're coming in just two days." Hope returns and I find the strength to press on. My family is coming. Nathan and Erin are coming from Washington, D.C. Peter and Eunice are coming from Philadelphia. Benny and Laura are coming from Canada. Rachel and her husband are not coming, but they are in their 70s and do not have the strength for a disaster of this kind.

For a moment, I remember Edmond and Ruth. They are not coming, of course. I later realize that I had barely given them a thought since the flooding began. How freeing that has been! I realize that, yes—the flood is disastrous. Yet it does not come close to the disaster and pain of sexual abuse; of testifying against Edmond and waiting for his sentencing and enduring the pain of Ruth turning her back on me. Somehow, remembering all of this makes handling the flood a little easier.

Two days later, I'm working in my kitchen. I stop: do I hear car doors? Yes. Is it family? Yes. I relax when they walk in. My body melts in their arms. I can breathe again. They'll take charge for now. I'm exhausted from flood cleanup. I joke, "There's no book called *Floods for Dummies*. You take charge for now."

My family assures me they'll shovel me out. And I mean *literally* "shovel out." They shovel the mud in the basement and clean up the mud in the kitchen. We divide into two crews: the basement crew and the kitchen crew. I'm in the kitchen crew with Laura and Eunice, my two sisters-in-law. We finish what my friends had started five days ago: washing pots and pans, utensils and dishes in bleach water.

The basement crew—Peter, Benny, Nathan and Erin—attack the basement with vengeance. With heavy boots, plastic gloves and masks, they start hauling. They haul everything, because it is all drenched in mud: skates, rollerblades, a helmet and old blankets. They haul out things just there for storage—a Christmas tree, olive wood crèche, Christmas angels and Christmas tree ornaments. They haul out the hammock, hung in my basement to cradle and rock Ella—and, sometimes, to rock myself. They haul out my ironing board, my iron, and precious fabric—purple velvet, from my niece—and on and on and on. They take out my white satin sheets that were waiting to be washed.

Then they haul out the keepsakes—my mother's lace tablecloth, my son's kindergarten certificate for good penmanship, my high school yearbook (with pictures of my high school sweetheart), CDs, feminist papers—all carried, sopping wet, out to the curb; all waiting to be picked up by the big claws that heartlessly drop them into gigantic garbage trucks and carry them off to hell.

Then they scoop up the remaining mud on the floor—slippery mud that is almost an inch thick. Some organization had come by and donated shovels, so they shovel and carry the mud up the stairs and into the yard. Through it all, they cope with the power outage. With no electricity, they work by the light from four small windows and two industrial-size flashlights that they had brought.

By this time, the whole neighborhood is lined with heaps of garbage in front of each house. In some cases, the garbage heap is almost level with the first story of the house. As I drive down the street, I half-close my eyes: it is too painful to see, and yet I do see. Sofas, tables, clothes, endless garbage bags and rugs, all ready to be carried away. I talk briefly with my neighbors next door, and they have lost everything—and they have no flood insurance. They do not seem to have the support that I have and they are overwhelmed, crying as we talk.

At the corner of my property is a blue portable toilet; because of the contamination of the water, toilets cannot be used. At the end of the street and around the corner is an outdoor barbeque that seemed to magically appear. Hamburgers and hot dogs are served, along with potato chips, sodas and Dunkin' Donuts coffee.

Other food and water is delivered directly to our homes. Sandwiches—lots of ham and cheese and ham and turkey—are delivered, as are chips, apples and large supplies of water. The American Red Cross brings cleaning supplies—Pine-Sol and bleach, shampoo, hand soap and more. The kindness is endless.

My gratitude is endless too, as I now turn to another matter: flood insurance. Yes, I have flood insurance. But, tragically, most of my neighbors do not. We do not live in a flood plain, so insurance is not required. One year ago, though—when I bought my house—my daughter-in-law, Erin, insisted—or, shall I say, she *badgered me* until I got it. It cost me $300. That $300 is now going to pay for at least $70,000 in flood damages. I am spared the financial disaster that most of my neighbors face. I hug Erin, secretly promising myself to obey her for the rest of my life.

The procedure for collecting insurance is extremely tedious and time-consuming, though. When the Allstate insurance adjustor, Charles, arrives on Saturday afternoon, we have no idea what this will entail in future days. Charles is a pleasant and kind man. He says to me, "I'm so sorry for all the damage. We'll do our best to help you." He then carefully measures the size of each room, to calculate replacement costs of both floors and walls. He goes to the kitchen and basement and makes notes of the appliances, cupboards and everything else that has been destroyed.

Charles then kindly instructs us to record the model and serial numbers of the appliances that have been carried out to the side yard—the washer, dryer, water softener, dishwasher, stove and refrigerator. Erin sits on the ground, deciphering these tiny numbers on each appliance. Nathan takes pictures of each one, for insurance claims.

When Charles leaves, my family returns to work. The basement crew continues to shovel mud. The kitchen crew continues to wash mud off of dishes, pots and pans. My friends had done some of this, but there is more. By now we have mold, too. It has been 10 days since the flood, and mold is rampant—it invades the entire house. Some of the mold is white and some is green, but all of it leaves a powerful, musty odor that adds to the stench of the sewer. With masks, gloves and boots, we try to keep the mold from invading our bodies, but some of it still creeps into our lungs. Already I've had fits of coughing that have kept me awake long into the night. It's one thing to see doctors wearing masks in hospitals: it's quite another to see crews of people wearing masks in your own beloved house. I actually pause for a moment to try to remember my house when there was bread baking in the oven or wood crackling in the fireplace. Somehow, I cannot remember. The sewer mud and mold have totally overpowered those memories.

I am not fully aware at the time of the premium of those masks. The next day I go to Wal-Mart to get flood pictures developed, and the woman helping me tells me that she and her husband have run out of masks—and there are none left in any stores in the whole area. I realize again how fortunate I am, because I had asked my brother from Canada to bring masks. He had brought a box of 50. So I tell the woman, "I'll give you some masks." Later that day, her husband comes by my house and I give him 10 masks. "Thank you, thank you, thank you," he says, with tears in his eyes. This also brings tears to my eyes.

I return to the kitchen to help the kitchen crew. Working with my sisters-in-law reminds me of my childhood days of picking strawberries or canning pickles with my sisters. While part of me is focused on the job, the other part is just so aware of the sweet and comforting presence of my sisters. We're now packing everything in boxes and carrying them upstairs. I am blessed with boxes: Binghamton has sold out, but I had asked Peter to bring some from Philadelphia, so I have plenty.

In one of these boxes that we are packing is my mother's set of silverware—the set that I had been fortunate enough to inherit. I love that silverware, with its delicate flowers gracing the handles of the spoons, knives and forks. The silverware had been safely stowed away in the wooden chest that had come with it, years ago, when my mother received it for a wedding gift. As is typical, the knives were safely stowed in the lid, held individually with soft cloth. What I do not realize until one year after the flood, is that the knives were mistakenly thrown out with that lid. Those knives, in the future, become quite the conversation piece!

Now that the boxes are packed, we start carrying them up the stairs to store them in the bedrooms. It's easy enough—quite straightforward. Sisters working together. But at one point, on my way down the stairs, the evacuation night flashes before me—rushing to my car, with PJ crying, grabbing for my computer at the last moment ... finding my way to Andrea's through the flooded streets. Then my mind floats to the good memories. I remember guests who had slept at my house before the flood. I remember Luke—my dear friend from Chicago—as we sang Christmas carols, composed new tunes and sat silently by the fire, with wood crackling and candles flickering.

I remember Nathan and Erin opening Christmas gifts—slippers and sweaters. I remember Nathan helping me bake our special pumpkin pie: chiffon-like, made light with whipped egg whites.

I remember my open house—just eight months earlier—with its champagne blessing. The gifts from the open house—pine-scented candles, roses, copper trivets and stained glass hangings. Were they destroyed? I don't know. There's so much I don't know. Yes, it's only a year that I've lived in the house, but it already holds so much joy—and now, also so much pain. Will that joy ever return? Will I ever again feel safe in my house? Or will I panic at every drop of rain?

But then something kicks me in the stomach as I walk down the stairs. I bend over in pain—for I have caught a glimpse of a photo on my fireplace: my photo of the waterfalls in Pennsylvania, where my precious trailer sits. In the chaos of coping with the flood in Binghamton, I have pushed into the back of my mind the fact that my trailer has been destroyed. My sweet trailer that overlooks the beautiful waterfalls. The trailer where Luke had visited and where I read to him the first story I had ever written; where, together, we sang the chant we had composed: *Let it come, let it go; let it come, let it flow. All is well.* But now my trailer is destroyed, victimized by the flood. It is not reparable and not replaceable, because I had purchased no flood insurance.

I linger silently by the photograph of the waterfalls—the photograph that was my first real attempt at photography. I see the sun, shining toward the top of the waterfalls and reflected at the same time in the pool below; the big, grey rock dividing the sunlight, making the rays even brighter. On Monday I will go to Pennsylvania with Benny and Laura and haul the debris out of the trailer. The trailer itself will then be hauled to the dump. The thought of that makes my stomach lunge, and I almost fall forward in pain. But I catch myself. I will face that on Monday. Today is Saturday, and my family is here. I return to carrying the boxes up the stairs with Laura and Eunice.

After eight hours of hard labor, my family drives to the apartment that Andrea had provided the night I had to evacuate. I am proud to show them my apartment: my home away from home. This sweet apartment is my haven, decorated so warmly with cushy rugs, charming lamps, ticking clocks and lots of cute knick-knacks. I do not realize until much later how Andrea had already become a pillar for me. If I'm feeling at all discouraged, I simply walk up the stairs to her apartment. The caramel candies she provides, in combination with her listening ear and wise advice, drives away despair and any hints of depression.

I do not realize until much later that Andrea is a pillar for others coping with the flood, too. She has another friend whose home has flooded, just like mine. Her daughter and son-in-law have lost the building where their painting business was located. They have no flood insurance. Andrea herself is coping with a flooded basement in one of her apartment buildings. Yet through all of this, she has time for me.

Now, 10 days after the flood, I bring my family into Andrea's lovely, clean apartment. We all reek of sewer stench: it clings to our bodies, invading our hair and skin. But we have a shower, plenty of hot water, Ivory soap and Dove shampoo—unlike many neighbors, who are bunked at the college gym. We have a washer and dryer, while many have to go to laundromats. Soon our clothes will be clean, with that slight fragrance of Tide.

My family obliquely and tenderly asks, "Are you OK? Is depression and despair setting in with all the loss—all the cleanup?" I tell them that since the flood, I often feel overwhelmed from the losses and fear about the future—especially about rebuilding my house. But at the current time, this does not feel like depression. It is not that place in myself where there is no hope for the future or a deep sense of isolation. Since the flood, in fact, I have been surrounded by people coming in, day after day, to help me. Furthermore, I tell my family that a flood is not abuse—especially not sexual abuse—and it is not betrayal. This, I can handle. At least for now.

I tell my family about my counselor, whom I'm faithfully seeing; about Andrea, upstairs; and about the hymn that sings within me: *God of my life through all the circling, I trust in Thee.* I show them my keyboard and my hymnbook, both carried to the apartment on the night we were first allowed back into our houses. I feel so encircled by my family and by their love. Each one of them ... so committed to me. They are here to help me reassemble my life.

As my family moves into the apartment, they carry their sleeping bags and pillows. Then they decide who will sleep where. They insist I stay in the bedroom; Benny and Laura will sleep in the TV room; Peter and Eunice will be in the entrance room; Nathan and Erin will sleep in a corner of the dining room. My cat, PJ, goes from room to room and lap to lap, taking in all the extra love he can get. PJ seems to have adjusted well to his temporary home.

My family gathers around the dining room table, eyeing the food. We're starving. Early in the day the Red Cross had come by, handing out water, chips and ham-and-cheese sandwiches, but that did not stretch very far into eight hours of hard labor. Lucky for us, Laura had brought her Crock-Pot full of big chunks of beef, onions, potatoes and carrots. Eunice had brought brownies—double-chocolate brownies.

As always, we pause to pray before our meal. With hands joined, I pray: "Thank you, O Lord, for my family; for a place to stay. Be close to all those bunked in the college gym. Be with their pets, trapped in their cars, not allowed in the gym. Thank you, O Lord, for flood insurance. Thank you, Lord, for this food and the loving hands that prepared it. Thank you, Lord, for all the love, thick in this room. Amen."

14

Hickory and Cherry Cupboards

The next day is mainly filled with pain and sorrow. At noon, it's time to say goodbye to Peter, Eunice, Nathan and Erin. As I hug Nathan I softly cry into his shoulder, but I try to not let others see. He whispers, "I'll be back soon, mother. I'll be back."

Benny and Laura are staying to help a little bit more—to bring electricity back into the house, and then to travel to Pennsylvania and help me face the tragedy of my precious trailer. Yes, my *precious* trailer. This is the shadow I've been primarily ignoring for 11 days, and now it's time to face it.

Before we leave for Pennsylvania, Benny is working on getting electricity into the house. Laura—with big, sparkly eyes—says, "Let's go to Lowe's and look at kitchens. This is the fun part." At first I'm slightly taken aback. Then, for the first time, it dawns on me that I really will have a brand-new kitchen, that my insurance will cover it. That life-saving insurance that Erin insisted I purchase when I bought the house.

At Lowe's, Laura and I first look at cupboards—beautiful hickory and cherry wood cupboards. I can get rid of my cheap oak cupboards! Then we look at appliances. I can get beautiful, stainless steel appliances and get rid of my dirty yellow ones. I can even get a garbage disposal and ice maker— luxuries I would never before have dreamed of. I'm lost in all the beauty and possibilities when Laura gently remarks, "We need to get back to the house soon so we can head to Pennsylvania."

I've been in touch with Cherry and Gabe only briefly since the flood, and they've told me that my trailer has been severely damaged. I have not allowed the full reality to penetrate me, as my focus has solely been on the house in Binghamton, but now it is time to face my trailer in Pennsylvania. Thankfully, I am not facing it alone: Benny and Laura are by my side. The two of them are just so even-keeled; so wise; so grounding for me.

Laura rides with me in my car. The ride is 80 minutes, but it seems like 180. When we pull the car up to my trailer, I do not get a real glimpse of the damage. I have to walk inside to get the full impact. Inside, my sofa is totally soaked; my books, sopping wet, are strewn all over the floor; my bed is drenched; my knick-knacks are spread across the muddy floor, having floated around in water.

We talk about whether or not the trailer can be saved. The inner walls are made of cheap clapboard, which is now drenched and warping. The water had come up almost 4 feet. It becomes apparent very quickly that the trailer cannot be saved. I quietly cry to myself, but I try to be brave. I decide then and there that in time I will replace my trailer, even though I don't have insurance money for it. I had not bought flood insurance because the trailer was sitting high on a cliff, where flood water had never before reached. The chance of the trailer being flooded was miniscule and the insurance man had told me that flood insurance would be a waste of money, even though it was in his best interest to sell it to me.

We have brought two boxes of industrial-strength garbage bags to be filled with debris from the trailer—or with anything we might salvage. All of the books—with the exception of a few on a top shelf—go into the bags, and we carry them solemnly to the huge dumpster that Gabe rented. While I can cope with losing most of these books, the one that quietly rips my heart is my doctoral dissertation—my precious research on mothering. The research that had been inspired by Baby Nathan.

There are a few things we save: books that were on an upper shelf; life vests that were hung high in the closet; and two pieces of art that depict scenes from my childhood, one of ladies playing baseball, their skirts flying in the air, and the other of little girls in bonnets playing croquet. These are among the sweetest memories of my childhood. I carefully wrap them in plastic and place them in a bag. As it turns out, I have only six garbage bags of various things that have been spared from the flood and that I will take back to Binghamton.

After about three hours—with the trailer emptied—it is time for Laura and Benny to leave. It's a very hard moment, as they have been my pillars. Yet, I am determined to stand strong without them. "We'll stay in close contact," they assure me. As it turns out, they will call me every day.

After they are gone, I have a brief conversation with Gabe. I tell him that I would like to replace my trailer when I can afford it and I ask him to save the space it is on. He readily agrees. I have hope.

Then I head over to the senior center, which Cherry runs. She is busy at her desk, but I ask if we can talk for a minute. She is brisk—unlike her usual, affable self—but her losses have been tremendous and I know that she is suffering. She has had two houses severely damaged by the flood: the one here, in Pennsylvania, and the one in Binghamton, where her daughter and grandchildren live. She has no flood insurance on the Bing-hamton house and very little on the one in Pennsylvania. I'm not sure I should talk with her, but I proceed because this may be the only opportu-nity I have in the foreseeable future. I feel desperate to keep my spot on her property, so I can once again have a trailer in the midst of its paradise. I ask, "Would it be OK with you if I keep the spot my trailer is on and then replace the trailer as soon as I can afford it?" Cherry snaps back, "No, I want to save that spot for my children and grandchildren. We may need to set them up here." I am shocked, and quiet for some time. I had assumed that Cherry would agree with Gabe that I could keep the space. There is nothing for me to do but back down, and I curtly reply, "Well, if that's your wish, there is nothing I can do." I leave quickly but I am deeply confused and hurt. This is the first time Cherry and I have exchanged harsh words. I sense that a big rift will grow between us.

In my travel back to Binghamton, I cry almost uncontrollably. Not only have I lost my precious trailer, but I have lost the rights to the spot it was on, with its amazing view of the waterfalls. Most of all, I fear I have lost the life-giving relationship with Cherry that has sustained me for six years.

As soon as I arrive home, I call Andrea and ask if I can store my six bags in her basement. She agrees without hesitation. She then invites me to her apartment and asks me about the trailer. I not only tell her about the trailer, but also about the conversation with Cherry. She hears my hurt, and in her quiet, calm way, she responds, "In times like this, harsh things can be said. Everyone is under pressure. Cherry has lost many things in both of her homes. Perhaps she is holding on to anything she can grasp." She adds, "I believe that, over time, your relationship with Cherry will heal. You will find a way to work out the problem of a spot for a new trailer, if that's what you want. But for now, why don't you focus on your house here and on getting it rebuilt?"

Andrea then offers me food, and I am calmed down for a while. I am so grateful for her. The next day I see my counselor, Donna, and she helps me to stay stable. Her house was not flooded, but her church was and, being the minister's wife, she has been steeped in that cleanup and possible new construction. She tells me that research conveys that a solid two years is what is necessary to recover, psychologically, from a disaster of this nature. She encourages me to take the time necessary to grieve over the losses of it all, to take plenty of time in rebuilding.

I talk also with Donna about Ruth and Edmond. In the midst of the flood, the situation with them has been on the back burner. Yet, it is always there—always a gnawing pain. I have been in conversation with my sister, Rachel, and my niece, Joy, and they inform me that the trial for Edmond will begin at the end of September—one week from now. I am aware that the evidence I have reported will be discussed in court. I am so very thankful that I had the courage to testify. I am also grateful that I was able to do it from Binghamton, as traveling to Canada now would be impossible. Now, more than ever, I realize that I had made the right decision.

On the evening of the first court date, Joy calls me. I ask her for every single detail. She tells me about the courtroom itself: rather dark, with wood panels. She tells me that the front wall had a big portrait of Queen Elizabeth in the middle and a Canadian flag on the right; the judge, Judge Reynolds, sat behind a big desk in the front of the courtroom. The desk sat high, she explains, and all others were on levels below. On the level directly below and in front of the judge were two court clerks. On the right sat Edmond's lawyer, John Baker. Edmond sat beside him. The crown attorney, Jan Williams, was on the left. (It is the crown attorney who is defending the victims.) Edmond appeared to be without emotion, Joy said, but he sat with his head down and shoulders slouched. There were about 30 spectators in the courtroom, with about half supporting Edmond and the other half supporting the victims. Edmond's supporters sat on the right side of the courtroom and the victims and their supporters sat on the left.

On the left, then, was Katie, the 15-year-old girl who had reported Edmond. With Katie were her two parents, the friend who had witnessed the assault and her friend's mother. Joy was there, but the other victim, Betty, was not there. Betty had come forward to the police and reported to them but, like me, could not face Edmond in a courtroom. Her report was presented in the court, however, as was mine.

Supporting Joy was her husband, one of her brothers, a female cousin and my sister and brother-in-law, Rachel and Don. Supporting Edmond were several couples Ruth and Edmond had known from either their church or associations on their farm.

After Judge Reynolds brought the court to order, the crown attorney, Jan Williams, described the reports from the victims that had been given to the police. The first was that of Katie, the 15-year-old girl Edmond had assaulted one year ago. The second was Betty—a young woman, approximately 20 years old—whom Edmond had also assaulted on their farm about four years ago. The third was Joy, whom he had assaulted 35 years ago, when she was 14 years old. I was the fourth victim presented, whom Edmond had assaulted 50 years ago.

Edmond's defense attorney, John Baker, then spoke. He said that Edmond was pleading guilty, had sought counseling and was truly repentant. He said that Edmond had told him, "I hated myself," after each incident.

Edmond's lawyer then brought in statements of Edmond's good character that had been submitted to the police. The statements described his lifelong service to his church and community. He was a trustee at church at the time of his arrest and he had been a prominent person in his community, offering sleigh rides and wagon rides behind his prized Belgium draft horses.

Several local newspapers reported the events of the day. The newspaper article that my family sent to me stated that a Wilmot man admitted to sexual abuse that spanned almost 50 years; that Edmond Galter, age 72, pleaded guilty to sexual assault, sexual interference and two counts of indecent assault for crimes going back to 1961.

When I receive the newspaper article, I immediately search Google to gain a better understanding of the meaning of the charges. I had done a little research on these at the time of Edmond's second arrest, but now I'm driven to learn more. I'm desperate to better understand the meaning of the charges. I find that "indecent assault" refers to intentional sexual contact without the consent of the victim that is without the intent of rape. "Sexual assault," on the other hand, can include rape, but there is no evidence that Edmond raped any of his victims. "Sexual interference" refers to a perpetrator who, for sexual purposes, touches the body of a person under the age of 16. In a way, I feel relieved. This all makes perfect sense. Now—finally—there will be legal consequences. *Finally.*

For about two days, I am preoccupied with the reports of the trial. I am relieved that at last, the secrets I have carried for years have been revealed and that Edmond is being brought to justice. Yet I am burdened by the shame this is bringing to my sister, Ruth. I am also aware of the pain that my other sister, Rachel, is carrying. Rachel feels torn between Ruth and me: she wants to support us both, but she cannot really support Ruth. Her heart is deeply divided. Rachel later reports that when in the parking lot of the court, Ruth came rushing to her, assuming that she was there to support her. Rachel, in pain, said, "No, I am here to support Joy and Lucille."

In a couple of days, my spirits are somewhat lifted. I reach out to my beloved friends, Luke and Gloria. Gloria prays for me over the phone and Luke sings our chant: *Let it come, let it go; let it come, let it flow. All is well.* I play my keyboard and sing, *God of my life through all the circling years, I trust in Thee.*

I also find myself soothed by my darling cat, PJ. It becomes routine that a couple of times a day, I lie on the sofa; he comes and crawls on my stomach, and immediately starts purring; at the same time, the clock on the wall keeps ticking. It all happens so faithfully! PJ and the clock are so predictable, unlike the flood and Edmond's trial. It's almost a ritual, really, as stable as saying the Lord's Prayer in church.

But the reprieve does not last long. It is time for me to work with my insurance company and prepare the report of my losses. I am stunned by the detail that is required. For each item declared, there must be a photograph, a statement of the room in which the item was located, the brand or manufacturer of the item, the model and serial numbers, a description of the item (in years or months), the original cost of the item and the cost to replace it. I am overwhelmed at first—at the thought of trying to gather all of this information. Yet, I press on, assuming that I will be able to retrieve my losses. It does not even occur to me that there may be a problem collecting the insurance money.

Thankfully, my family and I had taken countless photos. Thankfully, also, Erin had recorded model and serial numbers wherever she could find them. For several days, I focus on assembling all of this information. It is very tedious. Furthermore, I had lost some of that information in the flood: my "product" file had been drenched and taken to the dump. For some of the purchases I had made recently, however, I am able to go to the stores and retrieve the information. Such is the case with my sofa, for which I go to Olum's Furniture and retrieve a printed copy of my invoice. They are very sympathetic, and I realize that they are doing this for many of their customers who have lost furniture in the flood.

I stop in my tracks when it comes time to report my sewing machine. I've lost the information, and I realize that to get it will require considerable research and guesswork. My sewing machine was a gift in 2001 and had been purchased in Chicago. I remember that the original cost was approximately $1,100, but I have no records of this. I ask Nathan if he remembers where he purchased it. He does not. He talks to Erin about the problem and she sets out to research what she might find. I marvel both at her skill and her willingness to help in all of these tiny details. Together, the two of us make an educated guess that my sewing machine was purchased from Singer Factory Distributor on Irving Park Road in Chicago.

I then go to the local fabric store and try to find this same sewing machine. There isn't one, but with the help of a saleswoman, we find a Singer sewing machine that is comparable to mine. The cost for the new one is $899, and so this is the information we give to the insurance company.

By this time, Erin and Nathan have volunteered to research the items I have no information on. They integrate this information with the photos we had taken and they submit it to the insurance company. There are 177 items in all. They have taken over a job that I was simply incapable of doing on my own, and for this I am profoundly grateful.

At the end of September, Benny and Laura return for a weekend. Our first priority is securing a contractor to rebuild my house—and this is where Laura's genius comes in. When she realized that my house would be rebuilt, Laura went online and researched local general contractors. One of these contractors was Bill, and she had had him come to the house the weekend the whole family had been there. He had seemed trustworthy, with good recommendations, and he assured us that he knew how to work with the insurance company and how to keep his costs within the limits of what would be covered. So when Benny and Laura return, we meet him again. We think he is the right contractor for the job and he assures us that he is already beginning to work out the details of a bid.

The weekend Benny and Laura are visiting, we tear—and I mean *tear*—into the work of demolishing the walls. With crowbars and heavy hammers, we literally rip apart the plaster on the walls and the slats of thin wood that hold the plaster. Although we wear masks and gloves, the dust from it penetrates our bodies. I have never worked this hard in my entire life. I had never before used a crowbar or a heavy hammer, but I like it. I like the sweat of it all. It's grounding, in a certain sort of way.

I am stunned by the speed with which both Laura and Benny work. I try very hard to keep up, but I cannot. They seem not to notice, though. It is a real joy to work with them, and somehow, tearing out walls together creates bonding in a very deep way. Back when they helped me paint my house, right after I had bought it, I had come to know them in a way I never had before. Now—in this crisis, and with their help and direction—I come to love and appreciate them even more.

After they leave, however, I become overwhelmed. I'm not sure what to do next. Should I be working at more demolition? Should I visit my seniors? I want to be careful to not fall behind in my ministry. I talk to Rev. Louise, the senior pastor, and she is very gracious, saying, "Focus mainly on the flood. Perhaps you can see a few seniors, but for the most part, others will fill in."

In the midst of my confusion, my brother, Peter, and his wife, Eunice, call. They sense my uncertainty as well as my fatigue. In response, Eunice offers to come and be with me for the weekend. I cannot believe my good fortune. On Friday morning, Eunice arrives with a car filled with groceries. On Friday afternoon, she travels with me when I see two seniors. I am eager to see them, even though Rev. Louise had said I could take more time off. I realize later that I need them to help me briefly forget about the flood and about Edmond. Having Eunice in the car when I visit, too, is just the right amount of support.

Eunice also goes with me to see my doctor. By this time I have developed a nasty cough that I think may be caused by the mold in my house. My doctor agrees, but assures me that it is treatable. He gives me a prescription and tells me to continue wearing a mask when working in my house.

Eunice takes my telephone calls. For two days she acts as my personal secretary, whether it be the insurance man or a colleague on the other end of the phone line. She goes with me to Wal-Mart to develop photos for insurance. She is such a warm and protecting presence.

Then, on Sunday, she declares that we need a day of rest. She drives me to Watkins Glen, a beautiful gorge 70 miles west of Binghamton. This is my first break in 20 days. I would have never thought of my need for such a break, but as soon as we start to climb the hills of the gorge and take in the beauty of the waterfalls, my worries fade. The purple and yellow flowers growing miraculously out of the rock seem to take me into a world of utter beauty and peace. I am in awe of it all. I am deeply grateful to Eunice. For four hours, I forget about the flood and I forget about Edmond.

In the next few days I am in contact with Bill, the contactor whom I hope to hire. He assures me that he has almost completed the bid. On October 2, it arrives—just 25 days after the flood. It is six pages long, very detailed and looks to be totally authentic. It includes an estimate of $9,440 for demolition, with a total cost of $79,087.

When talking with Benny and Laura, we realize that, overall, the bid seems reasonable, but we wish to reduce the cost of the demolition because the three of us had done considerable demolition ourselves. We also would like to do additional work ourselves, and thus further decrease the cost of the bid. So I call Bill, asking to reduce the costs in light of the work we had done and for work we would like to do in the future. Bill does not immediately get back to me on the proposal, and I get quite concerned. Maybe he is not as personable as we had thought.

Before we have time to pursue the problems with the contract, though, another tragedy strikes. This time it is about PJ, my darling cat. He runs away. I arrive home from seeing seniors on Thursday afternoon and PJ does not greet me at the door. At first, I think, "Maybe he's snoozing," even though this is the first time he has not greeted me. I go into the living room to see if he is sleeping on his favorite rocking chair. He is not there. I start calling for him, and he does not respond. Usually, if I call, he saunters out from one of his comfy abodes. I look under the bed. He is not there. I look behind the sofas and in the bathroom. He is not there. By now, I'm starting to panic. I step outside to see if, by some chance, he slipped out the door. Maybe he would be hovering around the back door or in the bushes. Yet this frightens me, because PJ is not an outdoor cat. I check for him near the garage and at the back entrance to the house. Now I'm really panicked. What should I do? Whom should I call?

The answer comes quickly: I'll call Diane. Diane is the deacon who goes with me to visit seniors who are too difficult to visit alone. She has a calming presence—plus, Diane is a cat lover. She has a sign at her house that reads, "Cats Welcome Here." She has taken in many strays. Diane has met PJ, and in fact, she came by my house once just to meet him. He took to her immediately.

When I pick up the phone to call her, I am literally shaking. Thankfully, she answers right away. I can hardly get the words out because I'm crying. "I can't find PJ! I've looked everywhere." She instantly responds, "I'll be right over." In 10 minutes she arrives. She immediately starts looking everywhere: under the bed, and behind the sofas; in the dresser drawers, in case he might have crawled in one of them; in the closet. Together, we rummage through my laundry basket and through other clothes strewn on the floor.

Finally, Diane says, "We need to make a poster. We'll take it to the printer and get copies to put up around the neighborhood." We work quickly and soon have a simple poster. It states "LOST CAT" in big letters, and it includes a picture of PJ playing on my lap. It gives PJ's name, size and color. It ends with, "Call Lucille at 221-5686. Reward Offered."

Diane and I rush to the print shop to make 50 posters. We then scurry around the neighborhood, frantically fastening the posters on every telephone poll in sight. We also ask every person we meet if they have seen PJ. No one has. We go into an apartment building and I start knocking on doors. Diane is very hesitant at this point, as the apartment building has a reputation for possible drug activity. But I insist. People are very friendly and assure me they'll watch for him. But no one has seen PJ.

By this time, we are absolutely exhausted and we return to my apartment. We both cry for a while. She gives me a big, long, tight hug. I say, "It's OK if you go now. I'll call Nathan and a couple of other people. You've been just wonderful. Thank you, *thank you* for coming." We give each other another big, long, tight hug before she leaves.

I call Nathan first. He answers immediately. "PJ is lost," I cry. "He is nowhere. We've put up 50 posters in the neighborhood. What shall I do?" At first, Nathan just listens. Then he says, in faltering, tender words, "Oh, mother, I'm so sorry. I'm sure I can help. Let me go online and see what I can do." An hour later, he calls back and says, "I contacted and purchased a service that will automatically put a message about PJ on 250 telephones in your neighborhood." This gives me hope.

I start calling other people. I call a friend from my Methodist church, and—unbeknownst to me—she posts a message about PJ on the prayer list. Also unbeknownst to me, Diane goes to the Presbyterian church where I work and posts a message on that prayer list. Now PJ is on two prayer lists, and tender, kind people are praying for his safe return home.

I then call my sister, Rachel, in Canada. I sob, saying, "I cannot bear to lose my cat. I can handle losing my house; I cannot handle losing my cat." She lovingly responds, "I believe you will find your cat. And I believe that you can handle this. I believe you're strong enough. And I will pray that PJ will be found."

I call Cherry in Pennsylvania. She immediately says, "Lucille, I will come to you tomorrow night after work and we will search the neighborhood for PJ. And if we cannot find him, I will help you find another cat. I will, in fact, give you our cat, Lucky. He would be a good cat for you." While I do not want Lucky, it dawns on me for the first time that I could get another cat. This is a small comfort, though it feels like it would be disloyal to PJ. Yet, it is good to hear. I am aware also that the conflict Cherry and I had a couple of weeks ago is in no way harming our deep and long relationship. Another blessing! I am also aware that in the midst of handling the flood in her two homes, Cherry is stopping it all to come and help me.

Late Thursday night, Andrea brings a message of hope. Her tenant, Ben, saw PJ this afternoon. PJ was on the third floor, outside the door of Ben's apartment. Ben had shooed him away, thinking he was just a stray, but after he saw the posters of PJ, he called Andrea.

That night I barely sleep. I take an extra sleeping pill, but it doesn't help. I go to the door and call for PJ, but he does not come. The next day I decide that I must try to get my mind off of PJ, so I visit two seniors. I go through the motions—listening to them, asking questions, singing *Amazing Grace* and saying a short prayer. I briefly mention my missing cat, but I in no way reveal to them the agony I'm in.

After I see my retirees, I call Nathan again. He tells me that last night, he and Erin both cried about PJ. They love him, too. They hurt so much for me. It is very touching to me that they, sitting in their Washington, D.C. apartment, had cried for me and for PJ. They are just so wonderful!

When Cherry arrives Friday evening, we begin our search. We systematically begin to scour the neighborhood, shining our flashlights in the bushes of the various houses. Then we actually begin to go into garages and search for him. Cherry is hesitant about doing this, but I insist. We see an occasional person on the street and tell them about PJ. Everyone says they have not seen him.

The next day, I get two calls. Two kind people have seen a big, beige cat in the neighborhood. But PJ is small. Then, on Saturday night, Ben—the neighbor who had seen PJ on Thursday afternoon—calls and says, "PJ is in my basement. He was hovering inside the stairwell and I simply opened the door to the basement and PJ ran in."

I race over to Ben's house, with PJ's crate in hand. Ben carefully opens the door to the basement, and there—in a closet—is PJ. I reach to him and he comes easily into my arms. He is clearly happy to see me. After holding him a few minutes, I put him safely in his crate and carry him home. I almost can't believe it's PJ, but it clearly is. I give him water and food. He is very hungry. Then I go to the living room to see if he follows me, as he has done so many times. He does. I go to the sofa and lay down. He comes, as always, to lie on my lap. He immediately begins to purr. But this time, he does something else—something he has never before done: he puts his little paw on my cheek. I know he is telling me that he is happy to see me. I pet; he purrs. The clock is ticking. All is well.

We snuggle for a good hour. Afterward, I get up and start calling and emailing all of the people I had called two days ago. I joke with my friends about the prayer lists that PJ was on. Was it the Presbyterian prayers, the Methodist prayers or the Canadian prayers that brought PJ home? Or was it the combined prayers—an ecumenical effort—that helped bring him home? All we know is that we are deeply grateful that he is back. The next day at church, I announce that PJ is back—and the whole congregation claps! I feel strongly held and supported, whether it is about my cat, the flood or the ongoing trial of Edmond. Only later, as the support continues, day after day, do I really grasp the enormity of it.

The next day—with PJ safely asleep on the rocking chair beside me—I return to working on flood damage. I need to talk with our potential contractor, Bill, and his wife, Janet, about the contract. I find myself confused, however, and not quite able to understand the details of it. I discuss this confusion with Benny and Laura, and we decide that they need to talk directly with Janet. I call her and tell her this. At this point Janet becomes caustic and says they cannot deal with more than one family member. I respond by designating Laura and Benny, rather than me, to be the spokespeople in the negotiations. In this, a huge burden rolls off my back.

Two days later, I receive a call from the insurance company. It is bad news. I am told that I have misunderstood what it means to be covered by insurance, and that while the structure of the house is covered, all of its contents are not. The items from the deck and the basement are not covered, with the only exceptions being the washer, the dryer, the furnace and the water heater. I'm enraged. I learn that, in the fine print of my insurance contract, this fact is stated. I had not noticed this and no insurance agent had pointed it out to me. All that time that we put into assembling information for 177 items—wasted! The entire experience leaves me feeling very leery.

While the emotional impact of this insurance fiasco is receding, we return to the bid for the work on the house. We had asked that the bid be revised to reflect the work we will do ourselves—and this is where it all stops. The contractor says he will not revise the bid. He says, "If we revised the bid, you would then have to resubmit the new bid to the insurance company and wait to see whether they approve it or not, starting the process all over again. To do otherwise would be tantamount to insurance fraud."

I call the insurance company to verify the statement about "insurance fraud." I learn that it is incorrect. I call Laura and Benny. We realize that we cannot trust the contractor. We feel betrayed by his dishonesty and we are so glad that we had not moved ahead and accepted the bid.

But what do we do now? I once again turn to Andrea for help. She gives me the name of a neighborhood contractor, and I contact him. He seems reasonable. Yet before I sign the contract, I hesitate: I've already been burned once. By now, Benny and Laura are calling every evening, and one night, Benny says, "There is something I want to discuss. If you're interested, Laura and I could come and oversee the rebuilding. We could come about one week per month. We could hire subcontractors for the big jobs. Then Laura and I, along with you and perhaps other family members, could do the small jobs."

I can hardly believe what I'm hearing. I'm silent for a moment as I digest it. Is he truly offering to come and oversee the rebuilding of my house? I know that he is. Through tears of joy, I answer, "I would love that. I would love to have you come and oversee the work. And I would gladly work alongside you. And I know Nathan and Erin would sometimes come. I can hardly believe that you are offering this, but I know you are and this makes me very, very happy." Benny and Laura have built or remodeled four of their homes, and they are pros. I can hardly believe how fortunate I am. They say they could come in early November. It is now late October.

We then discuss the fact that, in the meantime, I need to find subcontractors and schedule them to meet with us. I need to find nine contractors: three each for furnace, electrical and windows. Benny says that he and Laura, along with me, will interview each contractor and that together we will decide whom to hire. I chuckle. "Yes, I'll know exactly how to interview contractors. No different than clients, right?"

With Andrea's help, I find nine contractors. On November 8, when Benny and Laura arrive, I am ready. Over the next two days, we interview the contractors. We hire Jack Mills Electric to replace the whole electrical system. We hire TJ Heating to replace the furnace and heating ducts. We hire Best Windows to replace the windows.

At the end of these interviews, I'm elated. I have never learned so much in a short time as I have during these two days of interviewing. It is stunning, really: a whole new world has opened up to me— opened up in a way that is safe, because Benny and Laura will come every month to oversee the whole endeavor. They will also do a great deal of work themselves, and I will be their assistant. I'm delighted. I'm eager to learn. I also know that I can carry on my part-time ministry with seniors while working on the house. Benny and Laura make it clear that they absolutely support this.

For two days, Benny, Laura and I throw ourselves into more demolition of the house. We continue what we had started four weeks ago: tearing down the plaster in the walls that were underwater. We throw the plaster pieces into industrial-size garbage bags and lug them out to the street. By this time, garbage collectors come by every few days to pick up mounds of building materials and other garbage. Street after street, the neighborhoods are lined with huge heaps of garbage. Sometimes you almost have to close your eyes when you drive; it's too painful to see. Monstrous trucks come with gigantic forks, lifting the garbage into trucks and carrying it to some unknown dump. Treasures, gone forever.

In the midst of all of this, big things are happening in Canada. On the morning of the day that Laura and Benny leave, Edmond is in court once again. I can hardly think of anything else all day. It's like I'm holding my breath. Finally, at 7 p.m., Joy calls.

"Oh, Aunt Lucille, this was a very big day in court. So much happened," she says. "Tell me everything," I say. "I want to know it all." Joy explains: "Well, first of all there was the apology letters." "Whatever are they?" I ask. Joy explains that apology letters are letters that Edmond prepared for his victims. His lawyer, John Baker, presented them to the judge as evidence of Edmond's remorse for hurting his victims. Joy says Baker argued that Edmond knows he has sinned, that he has repented and that he wants to make things right. He has been in counseling since his arrest and now he truly understands what he has done.

Joy received her apology letter in court. She tells me that it was very short and very general. She assumes mine is the same. She does not read it to me and I do not ask. I'm not ready for it. I do not want to hear from Edmond; I don't trust a word he would say. Joy, also, is extremely skeptical. She believes it is just a ploy to get a light sentence.

Joy rather quickly moves on to what happened next in court—that is, the reading of the victim impact statements. These are the statements that the victims were invited to write concerning how Edmond's abuse had impacted them.

The first impact statement was that of Katie. Katie's mother, Carla, read it for her. Not only was there emphasis on broken trust, but also on the fact that Katie has withdrawn from many friends, refuses to go to church and refuses counseling. Carla then read her own impact statement, which emphasized broken trust and tremendous upheaval for her family.

Joy informs me, "Next was my impact statement. But I could not read it. I knew I would cry, so I had my cousin, Anne, read it." While I knew that Joy had written an impact statement, as I had, we had not discussed what was in them. She now tells me—just briefly—what she had written. "I talked about the trust that was broken since the day he abused me. I talked about the fear I had for my father. And the fear I have had for other men." Joy says me she knows that all of this is at the root of the depression that she has struggled with for years. Joy and I had talked about our depression many times, but she had not told me that the abuse by her father had triggered the beginning of it. It all makes sense.

My impact statement was not read. Joy says that there seemed to be confusion about whether or not I wanted it read. It was decided that I would be consulted about this and then have it read at a future time, if this was my wish. I cannot believe my impact statement was not read! I had poured over that statement. I had agonized about what to say. I had talked it over with my son and with my siblings. And it was not read? I'm enraged.

After I calm down, Joy goes on to report that after the reading of the impact statements, the judge asked the two lawyers to speak—to make their case about the sentencing and to argue how Edmond would pay for his lifetime of abuse. Joy reports that these were very tense moments in the courtroom. The room was silent.

Edmond's lawyer spoke first. He argued that Edmond should get some jail time, but that it should be less than six months. After jail, Edmond should have at least six months of house arrest. This means that Edmond would not be able to go anywhere where there are children without a family member accompanying him. When Joy tells me this, I'm furious. "Only six months! Only six months in prison? Where is justice?"

Joy joins me in the rage, but then she continues. She says the crown attorney, Jan Williams, argued for a sentence of two years less a day. I snap back, "Why just two years? And whatever is this 'less a day' about?" Joy rather calmly explains that it is about whether or not Edmond would be in a federal prison or a provincial one. Federal prisons are for hardened criminals—for more severe criminals. If a person is sentenced for two years or more, he or she must go to a federal prison. If the sentence is "two years less a day," the person goes to a provincial prison. Williams argued that a sentence of two years less a day would be long enough to give the victims a sense of justice. It would give victims the sense that Edmond had paid for his crimes.

Joy reports that the judge listened intently to these arguments before saying that he would consider all of it in his sentencing. He was matter-of-fact about it all, saying that the sentencing would occur at the next court hearing, at the end of November. He then dismissed the court.

I still can't believe my impact statement was not read! Why did they ask me to write it if they were not going to read it? Did I need to be there to read it myself? Joy does not know how this happened, and when I call my sister, Rachel, she says the same. But I am at least relieved that it will be read at the next court hearing, which is to be the time of the sentencing.

After hearing about that day in court, I decide that I must calm down and simply wait for my apology letter. Yes, that mysterious apology letter. What could it possibly say? This is constantly on my mind, even though I return to see a few seniors and work on flood issues. The letter arrives in five long days. I open it, my hands shaking slightly. It is very short: five lines long.

> *To: Lucille Sider*
>
> *I am truly sorry for the broken trust and the hurts and the pain and suffering I have caused you. I want you to know I have received much help from my counselor Bret Smith. I have come to realize with Bret's help how deeply I have hurt you. I want to give you as much space as you need to heal. I hope one day you might come to the place you can forgive me.*
>
> *Edmond Galter*

What a joke. What a jerk! So his lawyer talked him into writing an apology! I have no illusions about whether or not Edmond came to this on his own. I don't believe for a second that he said to his counselor one day, "I believe I should write to my victims and tell them how sorry I am." I believe his lawyer and his counselor planted this in his head—in that thick head of his, where he somehow has justified abusing girls for the past 50 years. I truly believe that he would be abusing girls today—and for the rest of his life—if he hadn't been caught. He hadn't stopped at age 72. Why would he stop at 82, or 92, or 102?

Yet there is that last line in Edmond's letter—that line that starts to haunt me. It's like I catch it in my peripheral vision and it is picking up momentum. It keeps coming back, more and more. It simply won't stay away! The line is "I hope one day you might come to the place you can forgive me."

My Christian belief teaches me that I am to love my enemies. Yes, Edmond is my enemy. Has been for 50 years! But how could I ever love him?

Then the scene of Jesus on the cross flashes before me. For the people who were driving nails through his hands, Jesus cried, *Father, forgive them, for they know not what they do.* While I am not Jesus, I am a follower of Jesus.

It remains a raw and open question whether I will ever be able to forgive Edmond. I know that at the moment, I cannot forgive. But the future is open. I do know that time heals—and I wonder. I can't help but wonder.

15

Just Here. Just Now.

I call Luke and tell him about the apology letter. As soon I get the words out of my mouth, he replies—all in one breath—"You need to come to Chicago. You need some time away from it all. We'll go to Second City. We'll go for a retreat at a great convent. Two days of prayer and meditation is just what the doctor ordered."

I know immediately that Luke is right. I get off the phone and book a trip to Chicago, arriving in the city a week later. After getting settled, Luke takes me to a Mediterranean restaurant, where I order baba ganoush, hummus and tabbouleh. Then we head to Second City and laugh our sides out.

The next day we go to Wisconsin, to the Siena Retreat Center—a convent located along Lake Michigan. It's lunchtime when we arrive, so we begin by joining the sisters in the dining hall for a simple meal: hearty vegetable soup and spring mix salad. What I like most about the meal, however, is that it is eaten in silence. Somehow, eating in silence has a way of settling my entire being—both the inner and the outer. It also helps me to eat slowly rather than gobble down my food, which is what I tend to do, especially lately.

After the meal, Luke takes me downstairs to the labyrinth. The labyrinth is a space for a walking meditation that helps enable one, in the midst of the busyness of life, to slow down and be present in the moment.

It is a time for listening to the still, small voice of divine inner wisdom. To aid in meditation, the labyrinth has a winding path that leads to the center.

Labyrinths can be found in cathedrals and gardens throughout the world; those in cathedrals are usually built into the pattern of the floor. In recent years, cloth labyrinths have been designed in order to accommodate spaces that were not part of the original design of a building. Such is the case with the labyrinth at the Siena Retreat Center.

This labyrinth is made of a thick canvas, with a beige background and black lines that mark the path. It is round, about 30 feet in diameter and is divided into four quadrants, with each quadrant flowing into the next. The path flows into the center of the circle, which is about 8 feet across.

The meditative practice of walking the labyrinth involves walking slowly on the path; stopping in the center, to wait for any leadings of the inner spirit; and then walking again through the path and out to the perimeter.

As I enter the path of the labyrinth, I relax almost immediately. My body and soul are calm and open. Within 20 feet of the entrance, a phrase comes into my awareness: *This step, each step, just here, just now.* The phrase stays with me throughout the walk, totally calming me. The whole experience melts away the anxiety and fatigue that I brought with me. By the end of the walk, I am aware of nothing but the sweetness of the phrase and the next step: *This step, each step, just here, just now.*

After Luke and I have walked the labyrinth, we share our experiences. When I tell him about mine, he says, "This phrase is not only exactly what you need now, but it is exactly what you need for the future, especially as you return home. As you rebuild your house and cope with the situation with Edmond." When I leave Chicago, I feel at peace and confident that I can handle whatever is waiting for me.

What I do not realize at the time is that walking meditation will become a spiritual practice that I will continue for the rest of my life. I will find myself drawn to walking slowly and meditatively in all kinds of settings: in my house, in my garden, in parks and in churches. And, of course, I will always seek out labyrinths. In fact, in the future I will help design and create a labyrinth in my church and will lead a walking meditation group there.

As soon as I return home, I am thrown into the chaos of trying to rebuild my house. I learn that the check from my insurance company will be written to both me and my mortgage company, which means that I will not have the money immediately: I will have to sign the check and send it to the mortgage company, and then they will distribute the money to me in three segments. The first check will come soon, thus enabling me to begin the rebuilding process; the second installment will come when the rebuilding is halfway finished and inspected; the final installment will come when the house is complete and has, once again, passed inspection.

When I absorb all of this, I am somewhat overwhelmed—but not totally. I don't know if I will be able to follow all of the stipulations involved in rebuilding my house, so I turn to another option: selling it as-is. I call my realtor—the one who had helped me buy the house—and she compassionately walks through it. Her news is very discouraging, though: she says that, given the condition of my house and the likelihood of my community being declared a flood plain (and a very risky place to live), the house would not sell for more than $40,000. I am truly disheartened. Before the flood, my house was evaluated at $118,000; I still owe $70,000 on it. I love my house, and I cannot bear to sell it at that price.

After the conversation with my realtor, I try to forget about everything by taking a trip to Wal-Mart for groceries. I'm hungry. My diversion works somewhat, but on the way home, I notice that my purse is not on the seat beside me—where I always put it. I panic at first, but then try to calm myself. I pull over to the side of the road and search my car; perhaps I have put it in the trunk or on the back seat. It is nowhere. Panic seizes me again, but then I remember the phrase I had received at the retreat: *This step, each step, just here, just now.* I sit back and repeat it over and over again, for several minutes. *This step, each step, just here, just now.* I realize that it will not be disastrous if my purse is lost. Although my cell phone is in it, containing all of my contact telephone numbers—contractors, insurance company, friends and family—I realize that, with time and research, I will be able to retrieve all of these numbers again.

I calmly turn my car around and go back to Wal-Mart. My purse is at the customer relations desk, having been found in my shopping cart by an honest soul. When I open my purse, it is totally intact: nothing had been taken—not even the $100 in cash.

For the next couple of days, I turn to visiting seniors. While I have kept up fairly well with this work, I realize that I need a few days of giving myself to it completely—and, in doing so, hopefully forgetting about the house. It works.

I first visit Hazel. She is an upbeat person who has overcome many odds in her life, including that of caring for an ailing husband for 20 years. Hazel is getting up there in years and has many physical problems—neuropathy and scleroderma, to name two. She is considering moving into a retirement facility, and yet she is tossing around this decision in her mind. She also loves her house, which she has lived in for 50 years. Her house has beautifully sculpted wood in doorways and antique furniture throughout; it is perfectly polished. If she were to move, she would have to leave most of this beauty behind.

I listen to her for a while, then gently hold her hand and say that I believe there will be a way through the trials of a move. The two of us sing the song we've been singing since the first day I visited her: *One day at a time, sweet Jesus, that's all I'm asking from you. Just give me the strength to do every day what I have to do. Yesterday's gone, sweet Jesus, and tomorrow may never be mine. Lord help me today, show me the way, one day at a time.* I'm so aware that I need this song as much as Hazel does. It is simply a different version of the words I had been given on my labyrinth walk: *This step, each step, just here, just now.*

The visit with my next senior, Betsy, is very sobering. Her memory is slipping. She can barely do the puzzles she loves to do and has done for 60 years. Also she sometimes gets lost when she drives her car; her son is threatening to take away her keys. I also learn that, recently, she has been known to drive 50 miles per hour in a 30-miles-per-hour zone. It will not be long after this visit that she will have a minor car accident.

Yet, Betsy and I have a lovely time together. We work on her current puzzle for a bit, then we sing *What a Friend We Have in Jesus* and *Jesus Loves Me.* When I leave, she hugs me tightly, saying, "Now you'll come back, won't you?" Giving her a squeeze, I respond, "I'll always come back, Betsy—I'll always come back." As I get into my car, I am painfully aware that Betsy is rapidly developing Alzheimer's and that it will not be long before she has to move into a facility. She, like Hazel, has lived in her house for 50 years, and a move will be very hard. As I leave, I'm profoundly aware of the blessings my seniors give me: the joy of serving and helping them through hard times, as I am able to love them come what may. Furthermore, I'm aware that they invariably love me back. They think I do no wrong, and they just love singing with "Rev. Lucille." Visiting seniors is so much easier than rebuilding my house or worrying about the ongoing trial of Edmond up in Canada!

For the next couple of days, I continue to take things easy. I visit a few more seniors, then hang out with Andrea. She makes chicken noodle soup and gives me maple caramels and chocolate ice cream. We do a little shopping and I get a couple of sweaters on sale. She is just so easy to be with; so wise and so solid.

Benny and Laura arrive for a week of work at the end of November. It's such a joy to see them—and a tremendous relief. We waste no time getting to work. First, we walk into the kitchen and look at the ceiling. It's a cheap, T-bar ceiling with glaring fluorescent lights. I've always hated that ceiling, and I sheepishly ask, "Could it be replaced with a regular ceiling?" I'm aware that the costs of this are not covered by insurance and that it will entail considerable work, but Benny and Laura agree to it immediately. What I do not know at the moment is that this is only the beginning of their remodeling my kitchen in ways that are not covered by insurance. Yet I can afford to do it because they are giving me thousands of dollars in free labor. Only in the future will I really, *fully* comprehend how much money they have saved me.

We begin demolishing the old ceiling, and we're done in three hours. We head to Lowe's once again, this time buying planks for the new ceiling. Then we're back, and Benny climbs up on a ladder to hammer planks into the ceiling. I watch in wonder.

The next job we turn to is much more tedious. It involves carefully prying the beautiful chestnut-wood trim from around the floors, doors and windows. We want to save this trim, as chestnut wood is now not replaceable since chestnut trees are nearly extinct. So we painstakingly unfasten each piece and wash off the dried sewer water. Next, we spray each piece with an expensive mold retardant. We mark each piece, indicating where it was located, and then we take it to the garage to dry and be stored until we can refinish it. When we later count the number of pieces we have saved, it is over 150.

With this done, we head, once again, to Lowe's. (It seems that we're there at least once a day.) This time we're looking for light fixtures for my new kitchen ceiling. Laura and I happily find the electrical section, and we chat as we wonder: should the new light fixtures be square or round? Should the rims be white, silver or antique brown? With Benny and Laura with me, all of this is fun and fascinating and in no way overwhelming. They know the ins and outs of it all.

In our meanderings we see a shop vacuum, and Laura says I should buy it. I ask, "Why would I ever need an industrial-size vacuum cleaner? Won't the contractors clean up after themselves?" She chuckles and replies, "But you *are* the general contractor, and you will be surprised at the amount of dust they leave behind." It has not occurred to me that I now am a "general contractor." My whole body smiles: I like this title. At the moment, I like it more than my other titles, "Rev." and "Dr." I am also happily aware that the only reason why I am a general contractor is because I have two assistants who mastermind it all—plus do most of the work. But it's fun. I buy the Shop-Vac. It turns out that over the next months, my Shop-Vac becomes almost a friend. After each contractor leaves, it magically sucks up the pile of dust and I chuckle as I empty it.

Yet with all of this good fortune—all of the support from my family and friends—I begin to feel touches of an inner despair. I gradually realize that depression is once again at my doorstop. There is a certain darkness inside: a fear of failure, even when succeeding perfectly well; a fear of being alone; a deep fear of the future. The depression is subtle but nevertheless present, and it catches me off-guard at times when I'm alone— especially at night. With the days getting shorter and the nights longer, the darkness of the night seems to settle inside me in an almost tangible way. My childhood fears of the dark have never totally disappeared.

I discuss all of this with my therapist, Donna, and we both realize that it is time to resume ECT. I had stopped ECT nine months ago because I was feeling great. I had also stopped because each ECT treatment is brutal. Perhaps most importantly, I stopped because ECT is still a stigma for me. I so badly want to never have to have it. Only a few people with a mental illness need ECT to stay well. But, the reality is that ECT is sometimes the only thing that carries me through dark times. When I stopped ECT nine months ago, I had promised both Nathan and my psychiatrist that I would resume if and when depression symptoms returned. The reality is that now, they're back—though not too severely. So I call my psychiatrist and begin a course of treatments. The treatments are two weeks apart for the first four, then four weeks apart for the remaining. The plan is to continue treatments monthly after that, with the likelihood of spacing them out even more over time. This is called "maintenance" ECT, and could go on indefinitely. I can't help but wonder: will I ever get over the stigma of ECT? Even if I do, will there ever be an extended time in my life when I won't need it? These questions never really go away.

The other thing that will not go away these days is the awareness that in Canada, the sentencing of Edmond is about to occur. On the one hand, I can't wait for it; on the other hand, I dread it because I just know Edmond will never get the punishment he truly deserves. This makes me very, very angry.

On the evening of the sentencing, Joy calls. I hear excitement in her voice as she reports, "Aunt Lucille, the sentencing did not happen today and it was your impact statement that delayed it. The judge was taken aback when he heard your statement. He found it to be powerful and persuasive. He said he could not pronounce the sentence without further thought."

I am now so grateful that I had taken such care in writing my impact statement. I had described all of the years I had lived in fear of Edmond but had not reported him because of the shame it would bring to my sister. I had described how the abuse by Edmond was a contributing factor to my mental illness and, most especially, to my debilitating depression. Edmond's abuse contributed to my low self-esteem, my distrust of men and my failed marriages. I described the years of therapy and rehabilitation I have had to endure, and how I lost my career as a psychologist—which resulted in a financial loss of over $1 million.

Before my statement was read, the judge had indicated that he was ready to pronounce the sentence. After it was read, he said that he had to rethink the sentence. So the judge dismissed the court and postponed the sentencing for two weeks.

When I hear all of this, I am thrilled; elated. I can hardly sit still. Then, after a few minutes, I calm down. A great peace comes over me. I am so thankful that I had had the courage to both testify against Edmond and to write a strong impact statement. I realize that all of this has helped to heal some of the pain that was inside of me. Yet, I am aware that there still is considerable pain and a damaged psyche that needs more healing. For now, though, I am at peace.

I return to the rebuilding of my house and the next two weeks pass quickly. But on the day of the sentencing, I am very edgy. What will the sentence be? What has the judge decided, now that he has had time to digest my impact statement? On the evening of the sentencing I receive phone calls from both Joy and Rachel, describing it all.

I learn that Judge Reynolds made detailed and long explanations of the verdict that he would give to Edmond. He said it was a hard case to balance. He pointed out that Edmond is not a violent predator. In most regards, he's an upstanding citizen who serves his church and community. Ninety-nine percent of his behavior is good. A local newspaper reported the judge as saying that the remaining one percent has compromised so much of what Edmond did in life: that he only occasionally gave in to a weakness—an Achilles heel—for inappropriate touching, which included breast fondling.

The judge went on to say that the consequences of Edmond's behavior, however, have had unbelievably devastating effects on his victims, resulting in anger, distrust and mental illness. He cited my impact statement, in which I had argued that Edmond's abuse led to mental illness, failed marriages and a loss of career. Judge Reynolds emphasized that he took all of this into consideration when deciding on a sentence.

Joy tells me that when he was ready to pronounce the sentence, the courtroom was silent—with the exception of a few tears, which were coming from Edmond's supporters. Ruth looked stricken. Edmond was ashen. Then the judge said, "I am giving a sentence of two years less a day." He went on to explain that a two-year sentence would put him in federal prison, but "less a day" would mean that he would only be in a provincial prison, which has a less cruel atmosphere. Edmond's age, lack of a record and the criminal nature did not warrant a federal offence. Judge Reynolds then reduced the sentence to 14 months, deducting six months because Edmond had pleaded guilty; two months for getting counseling; and two months for his otherwise good behavior, which included service to the community. So, 14 months in prison was the final sentencing.

In addition, Edmond would be on probation for 10 years after his release and would have to stay away from places where children gather unless he was with a family member. He would also not be allowed to see the victims for three years unless they had given written permission to the probation officer for him to do so.

Joy reports that when the judge finished his final statement, two uniformed offices came and ushered Edmond out. He was taken directly to jail. Upon hearing that Edmond is now in jail, a 100-pound weight rolls off my back. Still, I have many emotions: gladness that he is in jail and paying for his crimes but sadness that Ruth is alone at her house. I've thought that a lighter sentence might have brought her less pain. However, I am overjoyed that finally—*finally*—my story was heard and the secrets that I carried for so long were revealed. I am relieved that Edmond is now in a position where he cannot abuse one more girl—at least, not while he is in jail. I certainly don't think 14 months is enough time to pay for all his damages: four years would be better! *Much better!*

But the bottom line is that I am delighted—even exhilarated, at some level—knowing that Edmond is sitting in jail. My sister, Rachel, tells me that the jail he is in has inmates that are known to be cruel and hateful to sex abusers. While a little fearful that he will be seriously abused, I am also thrilled. I want him to be terrified, even hurt—the way he hurt others. At this moment any inclination to forgive him is nonexistent, although the truth is that I think about it. I just wonder if there is any truth at all in that apology letter. Does Edmond understand, at any level, what he has done? Does he really care whether or not we forgive him?

I am in close touch with Nathan during all of this, and I feel extremely supported by him. He talks about how proud he is that I testified against Edmond and how relieved he is that Edmond is in jail. At the same time, though, his heart goes out to Ruth.

Nathan also is interested in the details of the rebuilding of my house, though he has no clear understanding of what it entails. But that's fine. His listening is all I need. He repeatedly talks with me about all of the help our family is giving me, and he later writes a note to Benny and Laura: "I am so amazed by what a generous family I have. Thank you for everything you are doing for my mom."

A few days after Edmond's sentencing, I am back into the swing of things and returning to working on my house. It is time for the subcon-tractors to come—the subcontractors Benny, Laura and I had carefully chosen. As it turns out, we had made good decisions in two out of the three; the third caused considerable trouble before it was all worked out.

The first contractor, the furnace contractor, comes, and the work goes smoothly. The total cost is $4,000. Although I have not yet received money from my mortgage company, I am fortunate that I have sufficient savings to pay for it.

It is now Christmastime. I take a sweet break and spend four days with Nathan and Erin in Washington, D.C. We attend a Christmas Eve ser-vice with carols, scripture readings and candles. It is beautiful, as always. On Christmas Eve, we open our gifts: sweaters, towels, slippers and more. On Christmas morning, the three of us cook in their kitchen. I so love cooking with them. I'm the cook's helper, cutting up onions and mush-rooms, grating the lemons and washing the mixing bowls.

When I arrive home, the check from my mortgage company has arrived. It is for $22,326. This represents one-third of the insurance money I will receive. While relieved to get it, I'm also a bit anxious because the other two checks will arrive only after the mortgage company inspectors have come and approved the work that has been done. I can get myself into quite a tither about this, but I try to put it out of my mind. This mainly works because I have such trust in Benny and Laura's competence. After all, they build their own houses.

On January 2, three electricians arrive. Their work is finished in four days, and I give then a check for $4,987. I love the new light switches, sockets and fixtures; I love the white fixtures with bronze rims that we had chosen for the kitchen. It dawns on me that my house will be 100 times more beautiful than it was when I bought it 18 months ago.

Benny and Laura arrive on January 9 for six days of work. Again, I love to have them come. They are such good companions. I've just never been good at being alone, and I need companionship. I'm an extrovert, after all, and I need people around me. In the days ahead, Benny and Laura work in the kitchen. One day I am working in the dining room when I overhear a conversation they are having. Laura has had the idea that if a certain wall is moved about a foot, there would be room to include two small broom closets. This sounded wonderful to me. Then, as they are working at this, I overhear Laura say to Benny, "I have another idea." Benny wryly responds, "No more ideas." He says it without any anger or irritation; without any further explanation. Laura does not respond but is simply quiet, and I do not sense that she is upset or offended in any way.

I do not say a word about this conversation but just take it in, admiring their respect for each other. Laura is clearly a brilliant designer, filled with countless ideas. Benny is a skillful carpenter and can easily figure out how to bring her ideas to fruition. Laura helps Benny with the building, the figuring, the measuring and sawing the wood. I absolutely delight in the fact that she runs a power saw as well as she runs a sewing machine. Laura and Benny don't talk much about feminism, women's right or the equality of men and women, but they live it. They are such a joy to be with.

With a day of work at the house behind us, we head once more to Lowe's. This time we meet with the kitchen expert and look at options for the new kitchen. We choose several pull-out drawers, rather than traditional shelves, and in terms of the wood for the outside of the cupboards, we choose hickory. For the countertops, we go back and forth between a hundred choices, it seems. I realize later that decisions like this are quite intuitive, and I choose a countertop that is dark brown with flecks of light brown and black. It has a very rich look to it—almost marble-like. I am simply delighted in the beauty of it all and I can't wait to see my new kitchen in its entirety.

During this time, I am in close touch with Joy and Rachel. The world feels like a safer place when Edmond is in prison, but sadder, too: Ruth is at home, alone, trying to find her way in a world where almost everyone she meets knows her husband is a sex offender. I learn that Ruth and about 10 other people visit Edmond in prison, as they are on a list of people allowed to visit him. Rachel reports that no family members from either side are on the list. Rachel is somewhat offended and feels cut off by Ruth, as do the rest of us. Ruth has clearly turned to people who seem to be less judgmental of Edmond: who believe his crimes have been overstated and that he has repented of his crimes and is paying for them; that there is no good reason to dwell on it all.

Rachel tells me that Edmond has been moved to a new facility. While originally in a facility with a very hostile environment—where prisoners are known to torment sex offenders—the new facility focuses on rehabilitation. There, Edmond is receiving counseling and education about sex abuse, and a woman chaplain is compassionately working with him from a religious perspective. While I believe that this is a much better setting for Edmond, there is a small part of me that wants him to be in an environment of fear—the way I lived in fear of him for five decades. But, mainly, I forget about Edmond and focus on the house.

The next step in the process of rebuilding my house involves replacing the walls we had torn out. I soon learn that there are two parts to rebuilding walls, both of which need to be done by a contractor. In the first step, large panels of sheetrock are fastened to the studs in the walls. In the next step, plaster is placed over the seams of the sheetrock, thereby making the wall smooth. At this time, we have not interviewed sheetrock contractors, so I ask around and get a recommendation from my neighbor down the street. I call the company, and a very friendly man comes and gives me an overall estimate: $5,270. I email Benny and Laura and they tell me that this is a reasonable bid, and that I should go ahead with it.

I'm very excited and now am able to see that my house is truly going to be finished soon. While I had never really doubted this, to actually see it all unfolding—with the end product well in sight—leaves me absolutely delighted. By this time I have been in contact with Nathan and Erin about when they will come and help, and Benny and Laura tell me that they plan to bring some good friends with them in their next workweek.

I now have enough data for scheduling everything, so I sit at my computer and type out a schedule. It is an exhilarating experience, and I can see the end product. I am very much aware that this represents thousands of dollars in free labor—free labor by Benny and Laura and their friends, as well as by Nathan, who will come one weekend by himself and then another with Erin. Typing out my schedule, with all of the work to be done and the people who will be doing it, feels better to me than outlining the timeline for finishing my Ph.D. My precious schedule includes:

Installation of windows, Jan. 23-25
Installation of sheetrock/drywall, Jan. 26–Feb. 3
Installation of insulation of walls with Benny and Laura, Feb. 6-8
Plaster application to walls, Feb. 9-14
Plaster dries, Feb. 15-30
Painting kitchen with Nathan, March 2-4

Installation of kitchen floors with Benny and Laura, March 5-7
Installation of kitchen cupboards, countertops and appliances with Benny,
Laura and friends, March 11-17
Painting of living room and dining room with Laura and friend,
March 11-17
Installation of hardwood floors with Benny and friend, March 11-17;
later to be finished by Nathan, Erin and Benny

As I type, it's as if a miracle is happening before my eyes: I see my house being transformed into something more beautiful than I have ever imagined.

With all of this love and support, something very deep in me heals. I had always feared that I would be judged harshly by my siblings because of our religious differences—after all, I have left behind much of the theology we were raised with. But in all my hours working alongside Benny and Laura, I have never felt any judgment in regard to these differences. The differences are there: they are conservative evangelicals, and I'm a liberal. But I realize that they are in no way rigid and dogmatic, the way my parents were when I was growing up. They are softer, and I learn from them that the church I had grown up in—and to which they still belong—is now kinder and more flexible.

Furthermore, I feel greater love and protection from a Sider male than I have ever felt. While my older brother, Peter, has been an advocate and has walked alongside me throughout my years of mental illness, I feel protected in a whole new way by Benny.

I feel this most poignantly after my windows are installed. The contractor has made a mistake and has installed the wrong type of window. When I see these windows, I'm distraught and don't know what to do. I consult two friends, and ask them to come and look at the windows. Both say they look OK, but they understand my concern and they encourage me to call the window contractor and make a complaint.

This takes a lot of courage on my part. When I tell him that the wrong windows have been installed, he curtly responds that they have installed exactly what I had ordered—and that to change them would cost $60 per window. I insist that this is his mistake and not ours, and he gets caustic and ends the conversation abruptly. When he hangs up, I am shaken and don't know what to do. So I call Benny and Laura. Like me, they are certain that we ordered the correct windows. Benny says to me, "I'll call the contractor."

When Laura and Benny arrive two weeks later, we meet with the window contractor. Although he never admits his mistake, we agree that the windows must be replaced and that he will split the difference in doing this.

Later, Benny tells me what he said to the contractor: "I hear that you weren't nice to my sister." When I hear this, my hearts melts. Somehow, those simple words heal my heart. I have been defended and protected. I feel safe. On an innate level, Benny feels like my grandfather, who rocked and protected me when I was a little girl. Benny is unlike my father, who did not protect me when I was abused.

When Benny and Laura are here, we also schedule the first inspection of our work by my mortgage company. This is nerve-racking, and we worry that they will not approve of the way we have handled the mold problem. But a friendly young woman comes and does a 30-minute inspection. It passes. I will then be issued the second check, which will be for the same amount as the first one: $22,326. This means that I will have plenty of money to pay for upcoming expenses. In fact, it means that I will even have some extra. My brain gets geared up for some shopping sprees, and I think that a new corner China cabinet and a beautiful upright piano may be the fruit of that extra money.

Benny and Laura go home and I call the contractor that has done the sheetrock. His company will now return to do the plastering. In two days, they apply a thin coat of plaster on the walls, making it smooth and attractive. I'm impressed with their skill. They leave the plaster to dry for two weeks.

With this lull in the work, I have time to turn to some other things. For a few days, I am focused on looking at new appliances. I will need a refrigerator, a stove, a dishwasher and a microwave. So, of course, I go to Lowe's.

I have already discussed the first choice with Laura: the color of the appliances. We had decided on stainless steel. Stainless steel is certainly the prettiest, in my opinion, although I'm told it is harder to keep clean. But with me living alone, I can easily manage the cleanliness issue.

Of all the appliances, the one that is most complicated to choose is the stove. Do I want gas or electric? I finally decide on gas. Nathan and Erin truly dislike their electric stove and would much prefer gas, and with the two of them being gourmet cooks, I trust their opinion.

Then the question is, which gas stove should I choose? The one with four burners? The one with five? I decide that I would like five burners—plenty of space for holiday cooking. But the final decision about the stove really comes down to beauty. There is one stove that stands out from the others, in that the design of the grates on the top is truly beautiful. It makes me smile just looking at it. It seems like a true artist designed it, and I'm thrilled to have that kind of beauty in my stove.

Choosing the other appliances is then a no-brainer, because I will purchase the corresponding models to the stove. They all look very attractive, with matching handles. I ask if the refrigerator comes with an ice maker and I learn that it does not, but that one can be bought separately and installed easily. I realize that it is a job Benny can do when he installs the appliances. I don't really comprehend the kind of work it will take to do all of this, and while it is presumptuous, I just assume that Benny and Laura can do anything. I am right.

I drive home from Lowe's elated, almost in love with all of my appliances. I can't wait for Benny and Laura to take a look at them. In the next few days, I start to get anxious, however: I become obsessed about the possibility of another flood coming and destroying my beautiful new house. I simply cannot bear the thought of it happening again, and at times, I can almost hear the rain pouring down and see it seeping through my basement windows. I see it destroying my new furnace, creeping up into my kitchen and invading my new cupboards and appliances. Yet most of all, I'm afraid that I would have another mental breakdown if I ever got flooded again. I would collapse, and may even need hospitalization. For a few days, I am overwhelmed with fear.

I talk to Luke. He listens and listens, and then he gently reminds me of the chant we composed eight years ago: *Let it come, let it go; let it come, let it flow. All is well.* He reminds me that part of my mental illness came from believing I could not live without Louie: I just couldn't imagine a life without him. Now Luke gently asks, "Are you going to allow a house—a *house*—to imprison you? Are you going to need a particular house to keep yourself stable, mentally?"

I know that Luke is right. I talk to my counselor, Donna, and she totally agrees with Luke. I then remember the words I was given in Chicago in my walking meditation: *This step, each step, just here, just now.* I also turn to my keyboard and play the familiar hymn that has sustained me over the years: *God of our life, through all the circling years, we trust in thee … God of the coming years through paths unknown we follow thee …*

Over a period of several days I settle down, and out of my settling arises a poem. It seems to come out of nowhere, yet from that still, small voice from within. I know immediately that it comes from the deepest part of my soul, where God dwells. The poem itself emerges in one evening— on February 3. I edit it slightly over the next couple of days, and the main line that is repeated, over and over again, is, "Oh Lord, Please give me the grace …"

The idea underlying the poem is that asking for God's grace enables me to accept whatever comes my way, whether it be losing my house again, losing a person again or letting go of some cherished idea or theory. The last stanza of the poem asks God to give me the grace to open my heart to God's abounding love and abiding rest—and then, to be free.

This is the poem:

Bless My House

Oh Lord,
Please give me the grace
To delight in my house:
To cherish each stone,
To love its precious wood,
To swing in its trees
But not grasp them.

Oh Lord,
Please give me the grace
To know deep within
The flood may come again.
The call may come again
To evacuate, to take my pet
And leave all else behind.

Oh Lord,
Please give me the grace
To own my house
But not let it own me.
To love my house
But hold it loosely.

Oh Lord,
Please give me the grace
To hold lightly
Any place or person;
Any thought or feeling.

Oh Lord,
Please give me the grace
To open my heart
To your abounding love
And abiding rest
And be free!

And Lord,
Please bless my house.

16

A Soft, Warm Cotton Ball

After writing my poem, a deep peace settles over me. It's the kind of peace that is almost tangible: you feel it both on the inside and the outside of your body. On the inside, it's like a soft, warm cotton ball sitting gently in your stomach; that same place in the stomach where you feel a "pit" when you're scared. Yet for now, all fear is gone.

On the outside of the body you feel a gentle glow—a radiance, perhaps. It's as if your very skin is softened by this radiance. This energy holds no negativity, no confusion and no ambivalence. There is nothing to weigh or to wonder about; there is only surrender, at the core of your being. It is not a weak surrender, either; it is a very strong one. It is the surrender of letting go of all of the burdens that weigh you down.

In my poem—a prayer/poem—I ask God to give me the grace to let go. It's a letting go of all the things I think I have to have to be happy. It is a letting go of my new house, knowing that a flood may come again. My neighborhood has now been designated a floodplain, but somehow, I have been given the grace to know that I do not have to have my house. It really *is* okay if another flood were to come: should it happen, I would not rebuild; I'd move to a mountain. And that's okay.

In my poem, I ask for God's grace to help me hold lightly any person. This is a big one—far bigger than letting go of my house. I am letting go of the notion that I have to have another person to make me happy. My

whole life has been lived out of the assumption that I have to have a man
to make me happy, and thus, there was the endless string of boyfriends as
a child and teenager; there was my mental collapse at age 50, when I had
lost the man I'd planned to grow old with. I now realize that I had given
my soul away. I had lost myself.

In my poem, I also included the line, "give me the grace to hold lightly
... any thought or feeling." When I wrote this poem, I didn't know exactly
what I meant by it; I just knew that I had to include it. Now I am sensing
what that line means. It is about doggedly holding on to any opinion as
if my life depended on it; grasping for a belief that will never change. But
what this flood is teaching me is that everything can change. One's mind,
thoughts and even feelings can change. Nothing is solid, except for love—
divine love. And now I understand the last stanza of my poem:

Oh Lord,
Please give me the grace
To open my heart
to your abounding love
And abiding rest
And be free!

For a while after writing the poem, I am completely free. I grasp nothing: neither anything nor anyone. I hold no judgments of myself or of
anyone else—and that includes Edmond and Ruth. I am free of the burden of judging them, of feeling rejected by Ruth or victimized by Edmond.
For now, all of that is gone. Only loves resides in my heart, mind, body and
soul. It is a love that is within me and around me, above me and below me.
I am at peace, I am at rest and I am free. Those lines of my poem seem to
lodge in my very bones: *Open my heart to your abounding love and abiding*
rest and be free.

The next couple of days are nothing but sweetness. The peace and freedom from the poem exudes into all of areas of my life—most especially
the interactions with my seniors and with my friend Andrea. When I visit
my seniors—as I comfort them in whatever stress they may have—their
very presence brings a certain peace. As I sit by them, holding their hand
and saying a prayer, we all seem to be filled with love. We are free of the
worries of the changes in our lives.

This peace is also powerful in my relationship with Andrea, in whose apartment I am still living. My gratitude to her—for taking PJ and me in, when my house was flooded—settles into me in a new way. I read my poem to her and she listens in wonder at the surrender and freedom and love that flows out of it.

Andrea and I clearly delight in being together. The house we live in is designed in such a way that I can enter her apartment by simply walking up my living room stairs. There is no lock on the door to her apartment: she is so accessible. She is such a comfort to me, and she tells me I am a comfort to her. In chumming around with Andrea, I feel the peace that I have expressed in my poem. I feel free.

In all of this, I forget about Edmond—that is, most of the time. But when Edmond does flash across my mind I remember that he is in jail, and I have very mixed emotions. Part of the time I rest in my newfound freedom of holding no judgment of him; of letting others deal with him and resting in the fact that I have done my part in bringing about justice. Now, I am free.

At other times, my old hurt and anger returns. I love that Edmond is in jail. I delight in the fact that he is paying for the pain he has inflicted on so many people during the last 50 years. I am aware that what he is paying is miniscule, in terms of the damage he has done, but at least he is paying for some of it. When my old disgust and hatred returns, I justify it. Still, I am vaguely aware that it binds me up from the inside. When that happens, the inner freedom—the peace that I felt just days ago—is barely present.

During this time, I sometimes think of Ruth. I have no contact with her, and I feel so sorry for all of the shame she is enduring. Yet, I am still upset about and perplexed by the way she has turned her back on most of the rest of our family. I often talk to Joy and Rachel, and they relay having only superficial conversations with Ruth. Joy has tried repeatedly to talk in-depth with her mother, but Ruth briskly cuts her off.

As Edmond sits in jail, one question does, on occasion, cross my mind: how will he relate to our family when he gets out of jail and after his 10 years of probation? During the first three years of the probation he is allowed to be in the presence of victims *only* if we give written permission to the probation officer for him to do so. That feels right.

One weekend, something happens—it happens during a retreat with women from my church. The retreat is an annual event—about 20 women attend—and it takes place out in the country, near a beautiful lake and rolling hills. There is snow on the ground, as it is February, and the scenery is exquisite, especially as the snow falls lightly. I go for a quiet walk around the lake and feel profound peace: the kind of peace that I wrote about in my poem. That peace continues as we gather to sing hymns around the piano, as we sip wine in the evenings, share personal experiences, have Communion and read poetry.

Our pastor leads the retreat, and it is deeply satisfying—except the point when he introduced a hymn I had never heard before. The hymn is entitled *A Place at the Table*, and with five stanzas, the first line of each is, *For everyone born a place at the table.* (The composer is Shirley Erena Murray. Copyright is Hope Publishing Company, 1998.) The first stanza describes clean water, shelter and a safe place to live, and how everyone born deserves these. The second stanza details a place at the table for woman and man, envisioning new roles and sharing power. This is, of course, what the feminist movement was about, and I can't agree with it more. The third stanza is about old age—that elderly people must have a voice and a place at the table, along with the young and healthy. Again, I couldn't agree more.

But the next stanza shocks me; it almost takes my breath away. I can barely sing it. It states: *For just and unjust, a place at the table; abuser, abused, with need to forgive; in anger, in hurt, a mindset of mercy; for just and unjust, a new way to live. And God will delight when we are creators of justice and joy, compassion and peace: yes, God will delight when we are creators of justice, justice and joy!*

I try to cover my shock and I do not say a word to anyone about this hymn. On the way home from the retreat, I chatter away with the friend whom I drove with—about how much fun the retreat had been, and how meaningful. We talk about feeling closer to the women on the retreat than ever before, and how glad we are that our church has the tradition of a women's retreat.

When I get home, I try to forget this hymn. I go about my business: I see my seniors, work on my house and spend time with Andrea at the end of a hard day of work—watching a movie with her on her big-screen TV.

Sometimes I lay on my sofa, petting my cat as he purrs and listening to the clock tick away: this provides such a clear rhythm, and a certain stability. Yet these distractions do not work for very long, and the hymn keeps popping back into my head. The lines of that fourth stanza simply won't go away: *For just and unjust a place at the table; abuser, abused, with need to forgive; in anger, in hurt, a mindset of mercy; for just and unjust, a new way to live.*

I do not talk with anyone about this: not Luke, not Donna, not Andrea and certainly not anyone in my family. But an image keeps popping into my head: I see a family gathering, and there—around the family table—sits Edmond. I do not sit by him; I'm a couple of chairs away from him. I imagine myself acknowledging his presence, but not giving him a hug, as I had often felt obligated to do. I imagine myself not even giving him a handshake. I imagine myself avoiding looking at him, and even cringing at the thought of him looking at me. I shrink at the thought of him looking at my breasts, the way he had done for years.

As I lay on my sofa, with PJ purring and the clock ticking, I imagine that my family has been very sensitive about not pushing me to have Edmond at that family gathering. It would be my decision and I would be grateful for their support.

Yet the part of the hymn that I cannot endure states, *with need to forgive ... a mindset of mercy, for just and unjust ...* I am painfully aware that I have no feelings of forgiveness for Edmond; I have no peace. Just three weeks earlier I had written the poem about letting go of my house, and even letting go of any thought or feeling. But now I am not letting go of my anger and hatred toward Edmond. I have lost my inner freedom.

I remember that Edmond had written a letter to me, asking for forgiveness, and I had dismissed it. I'd assumed that it was just a legal ploy, used to argue his case for receiving a lighter sentence. In court, he had used this action as a way of showing that he understood the harm he had done, that he was repentant and thus asking for forgiveness. I root through my filing cabinet and find the file marked "Edmond." I read the letter again. In fact, I read it several times. It states: "I am truly sorry for the broken trust and the hurts and the pain and suffering I have caused you. I want you to know I have received much help from my counselor Bret Smith. I want to give you as much space as you need to heal. I hope one day you might come to the place you can forgive me. Edmond Galter."

I wonder—I wonder and I wonder—if Edmond understands what he has done: if the help from his counselor has penetrated deep into his own consciousness. I also wonder what led Edmond to abuse countless girls and women for a period of 50 years. Surely this is rooted in some deep wound in himself. Was he abused as a boy? Was he marginalized in his large family of 12 children? I can't help but wonder what led to this life-long addiction.

While almost memorizing Edmond's letter, two Bible verses that I learned as a child keep popping into my head, as they have various other times during Edmond's arrest, trial and incarceration. The first is Jesus's simple and revolutionary command: *Love your enemies*. The other verse contains the words of Jesus, as he was on the cross: *Father forgive them, for they know not what they do*. Jesus was referring to those who had crucified him, and I know that I am clearly far from this kind of forgiveness. I have had moments of forgiveness, but will I ever truly forgive Edmond—for once and for all? Will I ever be free of the pain in my own heart, from carrying all of this rage? Will I ever find an inner peace and freedom in regards to Edmond, or will I go to my deathbed angry and hating him?

I remember the poem I had written just three weeks ago: The poem about letting go of things or persons who have hurt you; of letting go of thoughts or feelings that at one time seemed so right—so valid. Then I remember the last part of the poem: "Oh Lord, please give me the grace to open my heart to your abounding love and abiding rest and be free!" I agonize: Will I ever—truly, over the long haul—be free?

In the next couple of weeks I am all over the map, emotionally. Part of the time I fear I will never forgive—I will never let go of my anger toward Edmond and Ruth. At these times the anger wells up within me, holding me captive. I am troubled by my own vacillation about this. I want to forgive, once and for all, and have the matter settled. Sometimes I even have the confidence that I will be able to do it—that I will be able to put this whole issue about the sex abuse at rest: put it behind me and move ahead with the life I have, as it is truly a good life. My life is filled with abundance on so many levels.

It seems that I'm enjoying visiting my seniors more than ever before. Without realizing it, they inspire me to embrace change—to let go of the past and lean into the future with hope and joy. I see that, in many ways, their lives are abundant—and my life is abundant, too.

I feel this abundance very strongly when I am in nature—especially now, in the coming of spring. The days are getting longer and the buds are about to burst. Crocuses have boldly pressed through the soil and chipmunks are ascending from the earth's darkness. The warmth of the coming summer seems to be reaching back into the spring, leaving me with both an inner and an outer glow. At times my mind flashes to Edmond, and I hold no malice.

Even better is the awareness that my depression is totally gone: the minor depression I had three months ago has been alleviated. Certainly the coming of spring is part of this, but another big part of it is ECT. I did not have any ECT for several months, but I had to resume it in December. I realize that I am now at a place of accepting that I am one of those people who will need ECT indefinitely.

A big factor that is related to the alleviation of my depression, as well as to the sense of abundance, is acutely connected to the fact that my beautiful house will be almost completely renovated within the next six weeks. The precious schedule I had made is completely on target, and family and friends are lined up to come and help finish the project.

The first person to come is Nathan, who arrives the first weekend in March. The two of us have the great pleasure of painting my kitchen. We paint the kitchen a deep gold—the same color as my old kitchen. I've always loved painting, as I watch a new color emerge magically with each stroke of a brush. And now, to be doing this with my son—what more could a mother want? The two of us chatter away about religion, politics, floods and family, but beneath it all is simply the pure joy of being together.

The next weekend, Laura and Benny return. First, they insulate the part of the kitchen floor that was never properly insulated when the house was renovated 20 years ago. It is almost miraculous the way Benny squeezes into the 2-foot crawl space below the floor and somehow tacks the insulation to the floor above. Then they turn to laying the tiles on the kitchen floor. While the tiles are not slate, they look like it, and we know that their brown and grey hues will blend perfectly with the hickory cupboards that will soon be delivered.

The next weekend, Benny and Laura's friends arrive. The men work in the kitchen, installing the beautiful hickory cupboards. We three women set about painting the living and dining rooms. I had started this project on my own, so we have only two accent walls left to do. They will both be dark red, the same as before the flood. With the three of us chatting away as we paint, I remember my childhood days: my sisters, mother and I canning peaches. There is simply a bonding that occurs in times like this that lasts a lifetime.

The next job is installing hardwood floors in the living room and dining room. I had purchased this wood without Laura and Benny's help, and I'm a little anxious about how it will look. This is also different from my old floor, which was a blonde oak with subtle lines. The new flooring is a red oak, slightly rusty in color and with distinctive designs. The knots in this wood seem to pop out, and I wonder if they will be overpowering. Yet my answer comes quickly, as soon as I see those first boards pounded into the floor: I love it.

The men work on the floors for two solid days, and then Nathan and Erin come to help. It is such a joy to have Nathan and Erin here once again. Erin, though petite, wields that electric hammer as firmly as the men. That hammer is like a miniature gun, shooting slender nails through the side of the boards and into the floors. I stand on the side and watch in awe and gratitude.

Meanwhile, the other women are in the garage, sanding, staining and shellacking the exquisite chestnut wood we had saved eight months ago. It's a tedious job, but doing it together—and chatting away while we are working—totally takes away the monotony.

When my family and friends leave to go home, I'm a little sad, though not much. I feel that they haven't totally left because their imprint is on the walls we painted, the floors they laid and the wood we refinished. I feel like I'm slightly glowing with their presence.

By this time, it is the middle of April. My house is almost finished. It's Easter, and I have planned to go to Washington, D.C. to be with Nathan and Erin. My time there is beautiful. Nathan and I see the cherry blossoms, and at the Easter service we heartily sing, *Christ the Lord is risen today! Hallelujah.*

On Easter Monday, my dear friend Luke flies in from Chicago. We eat at his favorite Mexican restaurant and worship at the Washington National Cathedral. And, as Luke and I always do when we're together, we meditate. We open our hearts and let go of whatever thoughts or feelings come to the surface. What surfaces in me is a vague feeling of resentment toward Edmond. I tell Luke about this at the end of the mediation, and he begins to quietly sing the chant we had composed eight years ago: *Let it come, let it go; let it come, let it flow. All is well.* We prayerfully sing it over and over again. Once again, I am free. Once again I am held in God's abounding love and abiding rest. I am free.

The next day we head to Ohio, and it is there that some truly extraordinary things occur. We arrive in Columbus, attending a retreat with Neil Douglas-Klotz, a Sufi mystic and scholar in Middle Eastern languages. The retreat is centered around the Beatitudes, and while Luke and I had studied these on our own—and even given three retreats on them—it is a real privilege to experience them with this scholar, who has brought them into focus in biblical studies.

The Beatitudes are part of the core teaching of Jesus, given to his 12 chosen disciples. As a child I had memorized the Beatitudes. I still know them. I still try to follow them. The first five, in particular, are forever implanted in my mind. They are found in the Bible, in Matthew 5:3-7. (New International Version) They are as follows:

Blessed are the poor in spirit, for theirs is the kingdom of heaven.
Blessed are those who mourn, for they will be comforted.
Blessed are the meek, for they will inherit the earth.
Blessed are those who hunger and thirst for righteousness, for they will be filled.
Blessed are the merciful, for they will be shown mercy.

The retreat was designed in such a way that we both study these words and experience them. Douglas-Klotz first reminds us that the language Jesus spoke was Aramaic. This was the language of the common people, so to understand Jesus's words most clearly is to understand the Beatitudes from the Aramaic language.

One of the first points he teaches is that the word "blessed"—the word used in most translations—can also mean "mature," or "ripe." So the Beatitudes can mean "mature are" or "ripe are" those who are meek or merciful.

It is clear from the beginning that our teacher not only has had personal experiences of maturity or ripeness as it relates to these Beatitudes; he has had experiences of Jesus himself. He loves Jesus, he knows Jesus at the core of his being and he engages us in a way so that we might do the same. He has us sing the Beatitudes in the Aramaic language. Somehow, just knowing that these are the very words of Jesus penetrates the core of my being. Then he has us dance the Beatitudes using tunes and steps that he composed but that are like those that date back to the first century. This is a powerful experience. There are 30 people in a big room, and we sing and dance the words of Jesus. We feel the words from the inside out and from deep within our souls.

Of all the Beatitudes, it is the one on mercy that penetrates into my innermost being. It states, *Blessed are the merciful, for they will be shown mercy*. One of Douglas-Klotz's renderings of this is "Blessed are those who, from their inner wombs, birth mercy; they shall feel its warm arms embrace them." The dance for this includes steps that symbolize feeling embraced by warm arms when one has given birth to mercy.

I later come to understand that the essence of the "mercy" beatitude is that same teaching that I learned back in high school, when studying Shakespeare's *The Merchant of Venice*. The lines that captured me then are still capturing and challenging me: *The quality of mercy is not strained. It droppeth as the gentle rain from heaven upon the place beneath. It is twice blest. It blesseth him who giveth and him who receiveth*. It's as if that "mercy" idea just won't go away.

At the end of the session on the "mercy" Beatitude, I sit by the small lake. The lake is a distance from the retreat house, and I want to be alone. It is there, at the lake, that I experience Jesus—the Jesus who totally embodies love and mercy. I have never had an experience of actually feeling the presence of Jesus, although I have often told Luke that I wish I would.

But now, as I sit by the lake, I have that experience. I don't know how long I was sitting there before it happened, but as I sit, it is as if I sense Jesus walking on the water toward me. As soon as I sense this, I remember the biblical story of Jesus walking on the water. I've always been a bit cynical about that story, although at the same time, I'm intrigued. It's a beautiful story, telling of the twelve apostles on a stormy lake. Jesus himself is not with them; he is up on a mountain, praying. The disciples are frightened by the storm, and the fright soon turns into terror. It is then that they see Jesus walking on the water toward them. They fear it's a ghost, but Jesus lovingly tells them, *Take courage! It is I. Don't be afraid.* (Matthew 15:27) Jesus then calms the storm and everyone is safe.

While I am sitting by the water, I sense Jesus walking on the water toward me. Then I sense him sitting beside me. While I am full of surprise, I am also full of peace. It is a peace that gives me confidence to ask Jesus a question. I challenge him. I ask, "Jesus, where have you been?" For the remainder of the time that I have with Jesus, he tells me where he is and has been. He says that he is in nature; he is in churches. He is in people who are good and people who are bad. And Jesus then tells me that he is in me.

All to soon, I realize that Jesus is gone—but I feel his love all over me. I feel myself glowing in love from the inside out. It is somewhat like the radiance I felt after writing my poem about the flood, but it is deeper, softer and warmer. It is a transforming mystical experience that will stay with me for the rest of my life.

I see Luke soon after this and tell him about my experience. He listens lovingly, because he knows that I have longed to know Jesus at a level that was beyond my mind alone. He in no way questions my experience.

After my experience with Jesus—and after telling Luke about it—I walk slowly back to the cottage where I am staying. It has six small rooms, one bathroom and a medium-size living room. I go to my bedroom and just lay on the bed, filled with love. I have no idea how long I am there. Perhaps it is an hour or more. As I lay there, the love and peace that fills me is indescribable. I immediately remember the verse in Scripture that states, *And the peace of God, which transcends all understanding, will guard your hearts and minds in Christ Jesus.* (Philippians 4:7)

Suddenly, it just feels right to get up from my bed. I walk to a chair beside the window, sit and pick up a book—but before I open it, I have another experience of love and peace. Again, I have never had a mystical experience like this but I have heard that others have had something akin to it.

I feel like a beam of light is emanating from the middle of my forehead: it is like a candle that, when you watch it attentively, seems to offer a beam that comes right toward you. I've always welcomed that beam and it is, in fact, one of the reasons why I love candles so much.

But now that light comes from my forehead, and it shines all the way to Edmond, who is sitting in prison. While the beam is coming through me, it seems to originate from a source beyond me—from a divine source. It is not a light that I could somehow manufacture on my own, but rather the light of God, shining through me. I later come to realize that this may be like the experience of seeing through the "third eye," which is considered to be a bridge into spiritual insight and intuition.

I don't know how long I feel that beam directed at Edmond. Perhaps it is not very long: perhaps it is just a few minutes. And then the beam moves, and it is directed at Ruth. She is at her farm in Canada. Like Edmond, she is by herself. But the beam travels all the way from Ohio to Canada.

After this experience I go back to my bed and lay on it, filled with profound joy and peace. Again, I don't know how long I am on my bed. I just know that I feel very light, very unburdened and almost in a cocoon of love. After a while, I notice the time—it is almost 7 p.m., which is the time Luke and I had decided to meet. He will meet me in the living room in my cottage. So I go into the living room, and he is sitting there on the sofa. I sit beside him—quite close, as I don't want anyone else to hear our conversation. I then very softly begin to cry. It is not a sad cry. It is joyful. It is the kind of cry that just happens when you meet a friend you haven't seen in years. It's the kind of cry I felt when I saw my son for the first time. Luke just listens, with those kind, receptive eyes. He smiles, affirming it all. He in no way seems surprised, and this expels the small amount of doubt that I am having about myself.

Ever since my mental breakdown, I have been on guard about any deeply-felt, happy experiences. I ask myself if this is my old mania kicking in—the mania that is part of my manic depression. While depression is what has usually plagued me, I have had those times of feeling so happy that I have attempted totally unrealistic behaviors—like skating wildly at Gould farm, when I competed with the young men in a game of hockey, fell on the ice and cracked my head open and ended up getting a concussion.

Yet as I sit on the sofa with Luke, that small doubt about my possible mania vanishes. Luke simply accepts what I am telling him. He in no way questions it, just as he had not questioned my experience of Jesus several hours before. During the remaining day of the retreat, the love and peace of these two experiences settles deep within me. I feel a profound inner freedom, even deeper than the freedom I felt when I wrote my poem about the flood.

On the drive from Ohio to Binghamton, Luke and I talk a bit about my experiences. Mainly, though, we chat about the retreat as a whole and how grateful we are for making the decision to attend it. We are aware that back in Binghamton, Benny and Laura are at my house, working. They had encouraged me to get away for a while, to spend the time with Luke and to go on a retreat. They had recently been on a retreat them- selves and had experienced deep healing, and they clearly wished the same for me.

When Luke and I arrive at my house on Sunday evening, I am abso- lutely overjoyed with what I see. The house is ready for me to move in. Benny and Laura have just finished the last job: installing the wooden trim around the windows, doors and floors. It is the precious chestnut trim we had saved nine months ago; the trim that a contractor would have carried to the curb. But Laura had said, "No, we can save it and refinish it. It will be beautiful." Each of those 150 pieces we had sanded, stained and shellacked three times. And now, I just shake my head in awe and gratitude.

The next day is one of the happiest days of my life. It's moving day. It has been almost seven and a half months since the flood, and this is the day when Luke, Laura, Benny and I will carry everything that we saved from the flood, down the stairs and into the first floor. We begin with the big items. First, we bring down the dining room table. The dark wood of the table looks absolutely gorgeous against the new red oak floors and chestnut trim. Then we carry down the slate-grey sofa and coffee tables. The grey slate both blends in and carries its own, distinctive pattern.

It's my two cherished rocking chairs that almost bring me to tears. Those chairs sat in 18 inches of sewer water and we had wondered if we could ever save them. But we did. We had washed them several times with water before spraying them with mold retardant. As I carry them down the stairs, I see that there is still a little bit of mud on them, but no mold. I just smile at the miracle of it all. That mud can be scrubbed off at a later time.

With all of the furniture settled in, it's time for the artwork. I love carrying down my artwork, which has been stored away all this time: I have missed it so. I have especially missed the Mary Cassatt 3-foot by 4-foot print of the mother with her little child. It feels that, during the flood and rebuilding, many other people—and God—have been protecting me. It feels also like I am that mother in the Mary Cassatt print, protecting myself from danger. Somehow, the whole experience of the flood has, in some new way, given me a new confidence. While not invincible, I do not feel as fragile as I did before. Luke helps me hang this precious piece of art.

Then we hang the 3-foot by 5-foot grave rubbing that I had created 40 years ago in a cathedral in England. The woman and man facing each other, with hands as if in prayer and reverently honoring each other, remind me of Laura and Benny. Perhaps this also reminds me of Luke and myself. I don't know. I just know that I love this piece of art and I am so grateful to have it in my life once again.

By this time, it is late afternoon. I suggest that we have a house blessing. I had mentioned this to Luke, and he had said that he'd love to lead us in this. It just feels like the right thing to do with the right people. I can tell that Laura and Benny think this may be a rather quaint thing to do, but they agree to it without hesitation. I gather us together in the kitchen, and Luke explains what we'll do. "We'll go to each room, and I'll give a blessing for each. Afterward, we will sing around the piano."

As always, Luke's prayers are moving and beautiful. We stay in the kitchen and begin there. He prays, "Bless the cooks who will prepare the food here in this beautiful place. We thank you for their skill and for all the culinary delights that will come from this room. Amen."

We then move to the dining room. Luke prays, "In this beautiful place may all who gather here have grateful hearts for all they receive. May they enjoy each other, grow in love and friendship and leave this place nourished in body and soul."

We then move to the living room. Luke prays, "For the guests who gather here, may they always know they are truly welcome. May the warmth of the fire bring joy into their hearts."

Finally we move to the entryway, and here he prays, "May those who enter here know they are coming into a place of peace and true fellowship. A place of respect for all. A place where love dwells."

We then gather around the piano—my new piano, the one that had arrived the day before I left for my retreat. This is the piano I was able to buy because I had extra money left over from the house renovation. And I had that money solely because Laura and Benny had become my contractors and had given me thousands of dollars in free labor. At this time I have not calculated the exact amount, but rough calculations are at least $32,000. I later calculate that it is at least $5,000 more—yes, $37,000 of free labor. A true labor of love!

As soon as we are gathered around the piano, Luke starts to play *Amazing Grace*. We sing at the top of our lungs, and this reminds me of my childhood—when our family, with mother at the piano, would sing gospel songs in four-part harmony. The first stanza of that great hymn moves me just as it has the hundreds of times that I have sung it before: *Amazing grace! How sweet the sound that saved a wretch like me. I once was lost, but now am found. 'Twas blind but now I see.* Yet it is the third verse that almost brings me to tears. *Through many dangers, toils and snares, I have already come. 'Tis grace that brought me safe thus far and grace will lead me home.*

The next day, when Benny, Laura and Luke return home, I feel absolutely nourished and loved. While I know that I will miss them, I do not feel lonely. I busy myself settling into my house and anticipating having Andrea come as my first guest. The first night I am there, I wonder how I will sleep. Will I fear that rain will begin, and my house will be flooded? Will an intruder come? I have been in a house with Andrea for more than seven months. Will I be safe alone? I fall asleep almost as soon as these questions run through my head. It is a sound and safe sleep.

Four days later, I am ready for Andrea to visit. I set my dining room table with blue linen placemats and white napkins. I lovingly unpack the exquisite blue-and-white dishes that I had carried from Israel years ago. I serve Andrea a meal I know she loves: homemade chicken noodle soup and chocolate ice cream. Andrea just *loves* chocolate ice cream—especially dark chocolate. We giggle and carry on like little girls with a new doll-house. I could not be happier.

I am not the only one loving to be back in the house. PJ, my cat, is also happy. He is back to his old fun, racing though the house and up and down the stairs, chasing his imaginary enemies. Sometimes he just sits at the top of the stairs, guarding the whole house like a lion guards his jungle.

What I love most is lying on my sofa with PJ on my lap, as he purrs happily. He purrs, and I hear the clock ticking. It's the way it was back in Andrea's apartment, on all those nights that I needed soothing. Now I don't need the soothing in the same way. I just delight in PJ's presence and in my new house.

I also delight in my new piano. I have time to savor its wonderful golden oak wood, which contrasts subtly with the red oak floors. I often sit at night, singing and playing favorite hymns and chants. It seems that whenever I play, I end with the hymn I learned in seminary: *God of our life, through all the circling years, we trust in thee.* In fact, I often find myself humming the hymn throughout the day. It's as if this hymn has pene-trated my very bones.

Yet in the midst of all this joy, I cannot help but think, at times, of Ruth and Edmond. Sometimes I feel some anger and hurt. My recurring dream about being stalked by some man shows me how severely the wounds left by the abuse have affected me. I later come to accept that these dreams may haunt me for life, and that I may always have triggers that bring me back to the pain of the abuse. I hope not, but I know that this is a possibility. I come to realize that the dreams and triggers are a form of PTSD—post-traumatic stress disorder. Maybe they can totally heal, but then again, maybe not.

Most of the time, the softness of mercy and forgiveness that I felt at the recent retreat seems to permeate me. It occurs to me that I might write a letter to Ruth and Edmond. I contemplate the idea for a day or two. If I write to them, will it help me forgive, once and for all? Will it help Edmond and Ruth? After all, Edmond had asked for forgiveness. Can I trust him? I realize that I'll never have the answer about Edmond's motives for asking forgiveness. That is between him and God.

I become acutely aware that the resentment I still sometimes hold for Edmond only hurts me. It hurts my heart. My heart is meant for love, and not for hate. My heart is meant for mercy and forgiveness. Only in living out of mercy and forgiveness will I be free. So I sit at my computer and I begin to write. I have learned by now that sometimes, if I just start writing, the right words will flow. This is what happens. The words come easily and the feelings flow, and in an hour, my letter is written.

The only part of the letter I wonder about is how to end it. Usually I end a letter with "Love, Lucille." But I pause. Do I want to say "love" to Edmond? Do I, in fact, feel any love? Not much, if any. But I do feel love for Ruth. So I decide to include it.

Then I realize that I want to include the words "blessings" and "grace." I realize that there is a place within me that wants them to be blessed no matter what they have done. There is a part of me that wants them to know and feel grace—the grace that I feel every time I sing that famous hymn, *Amazing Grace*. So I end the letter with "Blessings, Grace and Love."

The next day, May 14, I revise my letter. When I save it to my computer, I call it "The Forgiveness Letter." This is what it states:

Dear Ruth and Edmond,

You have both been on my mind lately and my heart is changing. I was at a retreat a few weeks ago, which had a big emphasis on healing. One night there, when I was in my room, I experienced a beam of light that went from me to each of you. It was like a light from a candle that, when you look at it, seems to come straight to you. In my experience the light beamed to each of you. It beamed first of all to you, Edmond, in jail, and then to Ruth on the farm. At that point I felt a deep forgiveness and freedom from hurts and wounds caused by you. Since that time, whenever I think of you, I beam that light of love to you. I believe this is not just my love but God's love, coming to you. And it is coming from God to me as well.

Then at another retreat, which was actually earlier, we sang a song that had several verses, but here are a few. The title of the song is A Place at the Table.

Verse 1: For everyone born, a place at the table. For everyone born, clean water and bread. A shelter, a space, a safe place for growing. For everyone born a star overhead.

Verse 2: For woman and man, a place at the table …

Verse 3: For young and for old, a place at the table …

Verse 4: For just and unjust, a place at the table, Abuser, abused with need to forgive. In anger and hurt, a mindset of mercy. For just and unjust, a new place to live.

Chorus: For God will delight when we are creators of justice and joy, compassion and peace. Yes, God will delight when we are creators of justice, justice and joy.

I am deeply grateful for these two experiences at these retreats. They have been liberating for me, for I was bound in resentment and anger towards you, Edmond. And I was bound in feelings of rejection from you, Ruth. I don't know exactly how this will impact our future. But I believe our relationships will unfold in healing ways for all of us. I believe God will guide us in all of this. I'm not saying I will never be wary of you, Edmond, and I'm not saying I will give you a hug when I see you. But as the song says, there is a place at the table for all of us. We have all been wounded in life and we are being healed with love as our hearts are open.

Blessings, Grace and Love,

Lucille

After I print out the letter, I read it once again. I am almost startled by the last line: *We have all been wounded in life and we are being healed with love as our hearts are open.* At that moment, what pops into my mind is the last full stanza of my "flood poem," as I now call it. I had written it two months ago, when I was desperately afraid of losing my house to another

flood. But now I realize that the last stanza speaks as much to my relationship with Ruth and Edmond as to the flood.

Oh Lord,
Please give me the grace
To open my heart
To your abounding love
And abiding rest
And be free!

Epilogue

It is now six years since I had the amazing mystical experiences that enabled me to write a forgiveness letter to Edmond and Ruth. While I have not heard from them about the letter, specifically, that is fine; it was more about my soul and psyche than about them. I often chat with Ruth over the phone, but we do not discuss the issue of Edmond's abuse. I have been told, however, that he regularly attends a support group for men who have been sex offenders. For that, I am deeply grateful.

In regard to my mental health, I am delighted to say that I am doing well. In fact, I have not needed ECT (electroconvulsive therapy) for the last three years. I still take psychiatric medication for depression, manic depression and sleep disorder, and I still see a counselor weekly. I also spend considerable time in nature, whether inside or outside of my house. (I always have many, many houseplants, and they help to keep me grounded in a primal type of way.) I am quite diligent in eating well and exercising, and I am blessed to have close friends and family members who uphold me during the times when I am shaky. A steady attendance at and involvement in my church also provides stability. Most of the time, I also have a project that I am working on, whether it be making rugs, knitting or photographing flowers. If I do not have projects, I can get very anxious and slip into a mild depression. I call all of these things my "mental health and spiritual practices," and I'm committed to following them diligently. I'm aware that other people have their own mental health and spiritual practices; each person has to find what works for them.

I still am very vulnerable in regard to triggers that remind me of my early abuse. I now know that this is a form of post-traumatic stress disorder

(PTSD). When this occurs, fears of abandonment loom large and dreams about a man chasing me are frequent. As time goes on, however, these triggers and dreams occur less often.

After living in my beautiful house in Binghamton for three years, I felt a strong desire to move back to Chicago, where I had lived for most of my adult life. (I am still a Canadian at heart, though.) Part of the pull to move back to Chicago was to be near my dearest friends, Luke and Gloria.

Luke and I meditate twice a day: first thing in the morning and right before bed, the times when I am most vulnerable to depression. Our times together do not just include silent meditation, but also the reciting of an Aramaic rendition of the Lord's Prayer. We embody each line of the prayer with yoga-like postures and supplement this with additional spiritual readings. In our morning prayer, we end by sharing and analyzing our dreams. This helps us to understand the unconscious mind and embrace and integrate whatever it has to teach us. In our evening prayer, we end our time by audibly praying for those in our life and in our world who are in need of special strength and guidance from God. These prayer and meditation times are a large part of the bedrock of my emotional and spiritual life, and for them I have exceeding gratitude. Again, I refer to all of these as my "mental health and spiritual practices."

I have a great sense of forgiveness toward Edmond and Ruth. I still struggle, on occasion, with anger toward my parents—especially my father. During these times, my friend Gloria reminds me of what Jesus said in regards to how many times one needs to forgive: He said *70 times seven,* which means an infinite number of times. This sounds just right to me. When I find this forgiveness in myself, I feel a great deal of inner freedom. Always, when I am struggling with any heavy emotion—whether it be anger, fear, despair or loneliness—I sing the chant that Luke and I composed years ago: *Let it come, let it go; let it come, let it flow. All is well.*

Acknowledgments

Writing this book was not my idea. Six years ago, my dear friend Alyce Claerbaut asked for my permission to feature my story in a one-woman show she would produce. I agreed to this. Then we sought advice from Dr. Arlene Malinowski, who writes and performs one-woman shows, and she said, "First, you must tell your story in a book." So that is how this book came to be.

Along the way, there have been a myriad of wonderful people giving me advice and cheering me on.

The person who accompanied me more than any other, however, is my beloved son, Soren Dayton. In a real sense, my story is his story. When I asked his opinion about writing the book, he said, "Yes, go for it. It will help you heal." He was right.

My friend, Rev. Frank Showers, was with me every step of the way, giving me courage and advice and reading many of the drafts over the years. But the person who read them all was my good friend, Anita Clubb. She seemed to never grow weary of reading yet one more draft. Her advice was invaluable.

During the years of writing my story, I've had two psychiatrists: Dr. Arun Shah and Dr. Morris Goldman. I've had three therapists: Diane Sawyer, Rev. William Orr and Dr. Barbara Friedman. They are the very best. All of them gently guided me as I worked my way through the vicissitudes of my life that were then penned on these pages.

Three of my siblings were extremely supportive, each in their own way. My sister, Muriel Albrecht, remembered many details that I had forgotten, which I then incorporated into the book. My brother, Tennyson Sider, and his wife, Marsha Sider, were simply there when I needed to talk. My brother, Dr. Ron Sider, and his wife, Arbutus Sider, were the first family members to read the entire manuscript. They said the book was powerful, relevant and needed to be published. They have advised me all along the way.

Then, of course, is my beloved writing teacher, Dr. Arlene Malinowski. Arlene is one of those rare individuals who glows inside and out and her radiance penetrates you, whether you realize it or not. Arlene is brilliant and tough. She lets you know when you have a paragraph that falls flat and she cheers you on when an image lights up the page.

After I completed the book, I asked my friend, Dr. Elinar Lowry, to read it. She said, "I couldn't put the book down." She gave me unqualified support as I began to seek a publisher.

Of course, it was my editor, David Crumm at Read The Spirit Books, who, after reading my manuscript, made it absolutely clear he wanted to publish it. He said, "Your book is authoritative, authentic and timely." David, the editor, Dmitri Barvinok, the production manager, and Susan Stitt, the marketing director, were not only efficient and wise, but they were also very, very kind and respectful of me. They made the publishing of the book a real joy.

And finally, I am grateful to God. I want to end these acknowledgments with a hymn that I started singing 50 years ago at Yale Divinity School. It expresses the bedrock of my faith. I, of course, sang it though all the years of writing and producing this book. And I will sing it for the rest of my life. The title is *God of Our Life*.

God of Our Life

God of our life, through all the circling years, We trust in Thee.
In all the past, through all our hopes and fears, Thy hand we see.
With each new day, when morning lifts the veil,
We own thy mercies, Lord, which never fail.

God of the past, our times are in Thy hand; With us abide.
Lead us by faith to hope's true Promised Land; Be Thou our guide.
With Thee to bless, the darkness shines as light,
And faith's fair vision changes into sight.

God of the coming years, through paths unknown, we follow Thee.
When we are strong, Lord, leave us not alone; Our refuge be.
Be Thou for us in life our Daily Bread,
Our heart's true Home when all our years have sped.
Amen.

Study Guide

The following are suggestions for reflection and discussion. Discussions could occur in any number of venues, ranging from individual reflection to group discussion. I have divided the suggestions into four parts.

Before you move into reflection or discussion, however, I wish to offer some important statistics about mental illness and sexual abuse and about resources that are available regarding these issues.

- Approximately 1 in 5 adults in the U.S.—43.8 million, or 18.5%—experiences mental illness in a given year.

- Approximately 1 in 25 adults in the U.S.—9.8 million, or 4.0%—experiences a serious mental illness in a given year that substantially interferes with or limits one or more major life activities.

- Approximately 1 in 5 youth aged 13–18 (21.4%) experiences a severe mental disorder at some point during their life. For children aged 8–15, the estimate is 13%.

- Every 98 seconds, an American is sexually assaulted. And every 8 minutes, that victim is a child. Meanwhile, only 6 out of every 1,000 perpetrators will end up in prison.

Help is Available

NAMI (National Alliance on Mental Illness) is the nation's largest grassroots mental health organization dedicated to building better lives for the millions of Americans affected by mental illness. Their website is: www.nami.org. Call the NAMI HOTLINE: 800-950-NAMI or text NAMI to 741741.

RAINN (Rape, Abuse & Incest National Network) is the nation's largest anti-sexual violence organization. RAINN created and operates the National Sexual Assault Hotline 800-656-HOPE, www.rainn.org in partnership with more than 1,000 local sexual assault service providers across the country and operates the DoD Safe Helpline for the Department of Defense. RAINN also carries out programs to prevent sexual violence, help survivors, and ensure that perpetrators are brought to justice.

Citations

1. Any Mental Illness (AMI) Among Adults. (n.d.). Retrieved October 23, 2015, from http://www.nimh.nih.gov/health/statistics/prevalence/any-mental-illness-ami-among-adults.shtml
2. Serious Mental Illness (SMI) Among Adults. (n.d.). Retrieved October 23, 2015, from http://www.nimh.nih.gov/health/statistics/prevalence/serious-mental-illness-smi-among-us-adults.shtml
3. Any Disorder Among Children. (n.d.) Retrieved January 16, 2015, from http://www.nimh.nih.gov/health/statistics/prevalence/any-disorder-among-children.shtml
4. Department of Justice, Office of Justice Programs, Bureau of Justice Statistics, National Crime Victimization Survey, 2010-2014 (2015).

Part One

Regarding mental illness:

Mental illness is not easily defined. Thus, a good way to think about it is that of watching for symptoms. The Mayo Clinic provides a list of symptoms of mental illness:

feeling sad or down
confused thinking and reduced ability to concentrate
excessive fears or worries or extreme feelings of guilt
extreme mood changes of highs and lows
withdrawal from friends and activities
significant tiredness, low energy or problems with sleeping
detachment from reality (delusions or paranoia)
inability to cope with daily problems or stress
trouble understanding and relating to situations and people
alcohol or drug abuse
major changes in eating habits
sexual drive changes
excessive anger, hostility or violence
suicidal thinking

I would add that if any of these symptoms are present for two weeks or more, you should contact your doctor or a mental health specialist. One way to find a mental health specialist is to call the National Association for Mental Illness. (Information about this is found on the previous page.)

If you or anyone you know is thinking about suicide, call (in the U.S.) The National Suicide Prevention Lifeline: 1-800-273-8255 or 1-800-273-TALK.

1. One study suggests that 21.8 percent of women in the U.S. have suffered from mental illness (5% severe mental illness) and 14.1% men (3.1% severe). Do those statistics surprise you? Why might women be more likely to suffer from mental illness than men?

2. How does the media portray mental illness? What is the stigma regarding mental illness? If you know anyone who has suffered from mental illness how have they been helped? Have you yourself suffered from mental illness? If so, what has helped you?

3. How have I (Lucille) been helped with my mental illness? Do you think I have fully recovered from mental illness or have I just stabilized? What about yourself or others who are close to you?

I, Lucille, have developed a list of mental health and spiritual practices. These include: medication for depression, manic-depression and sleep disorder, seeing a counselor weekly and a psychiatrist every three months, spending considerable time in nature indoor or out—I have a houseful of plants—eating well, exercising often, always having on hand a project (knitting, photographing flowers or making rugs) developing and maintaining close family and friends relationships, attending and being involved in church, meditating twice a day and praying at least once a day.

1. What mental health or spiritual practices do you have? What might you develop?
2. If you have a friend who suffers from mental illness, how could you help them develop some mental health and spiritual practices?

Part Two

Regarding sexual abuse:

1. Research varies in calculating the statistics of how many people have suffered from sexual abuse. For women, the range is from 1 in 3 to 1 in 5. For men, the range is from 1 in 5 to 1 in 7. Do these statistics fit your own knowledge of sexual abuse?
2. Do you know anyone who has been sexually abused or whom you suspect is currently being abused? If so, do you think it appropriate to speak to that person and offer support in some way? What kind of support could you offer?
3. Have you been sexually abused? If so, where have you gone for support? Where could you go, if you have not done so already? Would you consider reporting this abuse to legal authorities?
4. Is there a person whom you think is a possible abuser? Where would you get support in possibly bringing this into the open, perhaps legally or in-person?

Regarding secrets:

1. One of the most difficult things about sexual abuse is that it often involves keeping secrets. Keeping a secret can be very lonely but to tell can be very frightening. One study has found

that 16% of women never tell these sexual abuse secrets and 34% of men never tell their sexual abuse secrets. Why do you think that women are more likely to tell their secrets than men?

When I was sexually abused at age 15, I told my parents about it. They prayed but never again discussed it with me. I have learned recently that they never discussed it with Edmond, my brother-in-law who abused me, or my sister, Ruth.

2. I kept this secret for 33 years, at which time I told my sister Rachel. I was 48 years old at that time. Ten years later I told my son, my brothers and their wives. Six years after that, Edmond was arrested and I testified that he had abused me 50 years ago. I was 64 years old at that time. Why do you think I kept these secrets for so long?

3. If you are a victim of sexual abuse, are you keeping secrets? What do you fear might happen if you would tell these secrets? Who might you tell about the secrets? What are the first steps you might take in handling the secrets?

4. If you are a friend or family member of a victim, how can you help? Will you go with the victim for appointments? Would you consider make a financial contribution to help pay some of the expenses?

Regarding reporting:

Recently the hashtag #WhyIDidn'tReport is giving us the opportunity to explore the reasons why we have not reported. I am listing some possible reasons:

We were afraid that no one would believe us.

We felt dirty afterwards and did not want to talk about it.

We were afraid that we would be blamed for it. That we were seductive in some way.

We feared that we would not be able to testify in court. It would be too hard emotionally.

We feared that to testify would cause us to relive the trauma.

If the predator was in the family, to tell would upset the family.

If the predator was in the church, to tell would upset the church.

If the predator was at work, we might lose our job.

We did not have the money to pay a lawyer or counselor.

The whole process was totally overwhelming and we could not face it.

Reporting is very, very complicated. It does not involve just the victim and predator. It can also involve families, communities, legal systems—making a police report, hiring lawyers and appearing in court. It usually involves health care systems, such as seeing a therapist or even a psychiatrist. It is, therefore, very understandable that a victim would choose not to report.

1. Do you know anyone who has been abused but has not reported? Do any of the reasons listed above account for that?

2. Have you been abused but not reported? Do any of the reasons listed above account for that?

3. What are some other reasons a victim might not report?

Regarding re-victimization:

1. People who experience child abuse are 1 to 3 times more likely to experience abuse as an adult. (This was clearly the case for me.) Does that statistic surprise you?

2. Do you know someone who has experienced abuse both as a child and as an adult? If so, is there a way you could help them? Have you offered to help them?

3. If you were abused as a child, were you also abused as an adult? How have you dealt with this? If you have not directly attended to this situation, what could you do to help yourself with it?

Regarding triggers and PTSD:

For those of us who have been sexually abused, pain may be re-experienced in many ways. There may be triggers that set off the pain, and this is a form of post-traumatic stress disorder (PTSD).

When Dr. Christine Blasey Ford testified before the Senate Judiciary Committee in the Judge Kavanaugh Supreme Court nomination hearings, she revealed that she wanted her home remodeled to include a second front door so that there would be two ways to exit the front of the house, a need that she believes is related to her own sexual abuse and PTSD. I too have recently experienced this. I feared my apartment was not safe for me. I had seen a door open to my building and I feared that someone could get into my apartment and harm me. I went into a panic mode until my friend Luke came and checked things out carefully and convinced me that there was no way for someone to enter my building in the way I had feared.

At another time I saw an older man pursuing a young woman who was trying to stay away from him. This reminded me of my sexual abuse and caused me considerable discomfort until I was able to calm myself and realize that I was not in danger.

1. If you have been abused in any way, are there triggers that stir up emotional pain for you? How do you handle these situations?

Part Three

Regarding family relationships:

1. It seems that family relationships are always complicated. I always wondered why my parents did not help me when I told them that Edmond had abused me. Do you have any thoughts about why they did not support me? In what way are your family relationships complicated? What have you done to address these issues? What might you try? Have your parents ever disappointed you? How did that change your relationship?

2. As I grew and changed, my religious viewpoints were dissimilar to those of my family members. I essentially handled this by not discussing the differences and simply going my separate way. Do you think that this was a healthy thing to do? If you are in this situation, what could you do?

3. Over the years, most of my family members have been unstintingly supportive and kind. Do you have this kind of support? If not, how could you ask for it? How could you give this kind of support to a family member who might be needing it?

Regarding friendships:

1. I have been truly blessed by having long-term and deep relationships with several friends—among them, Gloria, Luke and Cherry. Do you have at least one such relationship? How do

you foster and maintain that relationship? If you do not have a deep relationship with a friend, how might you develop one?

Part Four

Regarding the spiritual journey:

1. My spiritual journey has taken many twists and turns, although I never have been an agnostic or atheist. Why do you think I always maintained a spiritual foundation, even though my early years were filled with religious fear and rigidity?

2. What has your spiritual journey been like? Has it included times of extreme doubt and/or deep faith? Are you a member of an organized religion?

3. Since my early 30s, meditation has been part of my spiritual path. Do you have any spiritual practices? What has been meaningful to you? If you do not have any favorite spiritual practices, do you think it would be helpful for you to have any? What would this look like for you?

Recently in my spiritual journey, I have had some powerful experiences during which I felt the presence of God. This occurred most powerfully on the retreat during which I felt I was visited by Jesus and after which divine love flowed in and through me to Edmond and Ruth.

4. Have you ever had a powerful religious experience? If so, how do you understand it?

Regarding forgiveness:

Let me first state what I mean by forgiveness. It is: not holding a grudge against someone who has hurt you. Forgiveness does not include forgetfulness. I believe I always will hold on to the fact that Edmond abused me and many others and that he might do this again if given the chance. In other words, I have forgiven him for what he has done but I will never forget that he is an abusive person and always may be.

1. Does the above definition of forgiveness make sense to you? How would you change it?

My journey to forgiveness has been long, with many twists and turns. In fact, I still have moments of ill feelings for my parents for not defending me. For Edmond, I have come to a deep place of forgiveness after which I wrote a forgiveness letter to him and to Ruth.

2. Is there someone in your life whom you have harmed in some way? Are you open to asking that person for forgiveness?
3. Who in your life have you essentially forgiven—and for what? What has your journey to forgiveness been like?
4. Who in your life do you still need to forgive? Are you open to this?

I believe that only in forgiveness can one be truly free.
And that, my dear readers, is my prayer for you.

Related Books

A Guide For Caregivers

by Benjamin Pratt

In one out of three households, someone is a caregiver: women and men who give of body, mind and soul to care for the well being of others. These millions need help, more than financial and medical assistance. They need daily, practical help in reviving their spirits and avoiding burnout. Who are these caregivers? They are folks who have lived this tough life and felt the agonies and the boredom, yet they have extended compassion with a gentle word or a tender touch. As caregivers, they know anger, frustration, joy, laughter, purpose, mortality and immortality.

ISBN: 978-1-93487-927-6

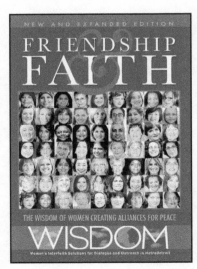

Friendship and Faith
The WISDOM of women creating alliances for peace

The Women of WISDOM

This is a book about making friends, which may be the most important thing you can do to make the world a better place, and transform your own life in the process. Making a new friend often is tricky, as you'll discover in these dozens of real-life stories by women from a wide variety of religious and ethnic backgrounds. But, crossing lines of religion, race and culture is worth the effort, often forming some of life's deepest friendships, these women have found. In Friendship and Faith, you'll discover how we really can change the world one friend at a time.

InterfaithWisdom.com
ISBN: 978-1-94201-193-4

Print and ebooks available on Amazon.com and other retailers.

Related Books

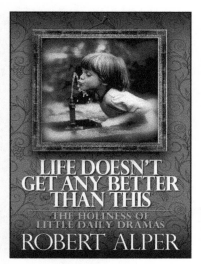

Life Doesn't Get Any Better Than This

by Rabbi Robert Alper

Life Doesn't Get Any Better Than This is a collection of true and moving stories, from tales of fatherhood ('The Glance') to a touching recount of the way small gestures lodge themselves in your heart ('Old Lovers').

"It is hard to choose a single story in this collection and to say: 'This is the best,' or 'this is the one that you really have to read,'" writes Rabbi Jack Riemer, co-founder of the National Rabbinic Network, "Almost all of them pull at my sleeve and say: 'You're not going to talk about me?'"

ISBN: 978-1-93988-087-1

Thanks. I Needed That.

by Rabbi Robert Alper

The Tonight Show, the forests of Vermont, and a tiny Polish village are among the settings for these 32 true stories by Rabbi Bob Alper. This is his latest collection, following an earlier book of stories that a Detroit Free Press reviewer called "a volume of spiritual gems." Bob guides the reader to places as diverse as synagogues in Kentucky and London, a small plane flying over Oklahoma, a refusenik's Moscow apartment, comedy clubs, Vermont towns and forests, and even a convention of rabbis. Bob's unique experiences, from leading large congregations to performing stand-up at Toronto's "Muslimfest," make for a wealth of engaging stories that touch people of all backgrounds with warmth, humor, and wisdom.

ISBN: 978-1-93487-986-3

Print and ebooks available on Amazon.com and other retailers.